STAR FLEET
TECHNICAL
MANUAL

TM: 379260

STAR FLEET HEADQUARTERS
UNITED FEDERATION OF PLANETS

FRANZ JOSEPH
UNITED FEDERATION REPRESENTATIVE
STAR FLEET COMMAND

STAR FLEET COMMAND
STAR FLEET HEADQUARTERS
UNITED FEDERATION OF PLANETS

FRANZ JOSEPH
UNITED FEDERATION REPRESENTATIVE   STARDATE 7512.02

to: Ballantine Books
Planetary Agents, NA, USA, 10022
United Nations/Earth/Sol System

1. A printed Terran version of the Star Fleet Technical Manual was approved by the Federation Council for release to the civilians, and civilian auxiliaries on your planet. We have reviewed copies of this version as printed by you, and wish to assure you and the others that these copies are precisely correct and complete as authorized. We believe some of your civilians are confused because they are unfamiliar with the system and arrangement of Technical Orders, therefore, we offer the following by way of clarification.

2. The print-out version of the Star Fleet Technical Manual, as used by the Star Fleet Academy, is a collection of only those Technical Orders necessary to the indoctrination of new cadets until such time as they have become experienced in the use of the data read-out stations of Mastercom/SFHQ. Further, the Terran version contains even fewer Technical Orders because of the prohibition of the Prime Directive. Neither version is a "book" of "pages" as the questioners seem to think — nor do they contain "all" of the technical information stored in the data banks of Mastercom/SFHQ. Your civilians must understand these technical data banks contain all the knowledge presently known within the United Federation of Planets from all of the Member planets. If it were to be published in "book" form, the sum total would amount to more books than you now have stored in your "libraries." Obviously, this cannot be done. It is equally obvious that you cannot have the galactic knowledge of future centuries given to your planet as a "gift;" you must earn it by your own efforts just as the others have done.

3. In the Terran version, the General Index summarizes the subject area groupings by Technical Order number blocks as a part of the total system of classification. It does not give the total classification system, nor does it indicate whether or not such subject matter is available. The Introduction (T.O:00:00:06) for instance, is not included because it has not been authorized for release at this time. Each Section Index lists the Technical Orders currently approved for each section, and shows which are the correct issue by authentication date (and amendment code — if required). Thus a Section Index shows whether or not a particular Manual contains the correct issues. Those which are listed with an asterisk may become available in a future print-out from Mastercom/SFHQ. Other Technical Order numbers which are missing do not appear by reason of the prohibition of the Prime Directive, or they have not been approved for release at this time.

4. In as gentle and as diplomatic manner as we may, we should like to point out that this confusion is just another example of the many primitive attributes of your planet which prevent its acceptance into the United Federation of Planets at this time in your current calendar. But be patient, the day will come in the future when your planet will have finally overcome these obstacles, and will take its place in the intergalactic community of intelligent life forms.

Live long and prosper.

STAR FLEET
TECHNICAL
MANUAL

FEDERATION CLASSIFIED

THIS MANUAL IS FOR THE SPECIFIC USE OF STAR FLEET
ACADEMY CADETS AND CONTAINS SELECTED MATERIAL
FROM THE DATA BANKS OF THE MASTER COMPUTER. UNDER
THE LAWS OF THE UNITED FEDERATION OF PLANETS AND
ITS MEMBER PLANETS UNAUTHORIZED USE, OR REPRODUC-
TION, IN WHOLE OR IN PART, OF THESE TECHNICAL ORDERS
OR ANY SUBSEQUENTLY ISSUED, WITHOUT THE WRITTEN
PERMISSION OF STAR FLEET OR ITS PLANETARY AGENTS IS
STRICTLY PROHIBITED.

TRAINING COMMAND
STAR FLEET ACADEMY

OFFICIAL VERSION FOR CADETS FROM
UNITED NATIONS, EARTH, SOL SYSTEM

RESEARCHED AND COMPILED BY:
FRANZ JOSEPH*
UNITED FEDERATION REPRESENTATIVE
MILITARY STAFF COMMITTEE
STAR FLEET HEADQUARTERS, 0 MARK 0, R5PC

WITH GRATEFUL APPRECIATION TO THESE CIVILIANS
OF UNITED NATIONS/EARTH/SOL SYSTEM:

ANNE ANDERSON, JUDY LYNN DEL REY, FRED C. DURANT, III,
IRVING FEINBERG, WALTER M. JEFFRIES, ROBERT H. JUSTMAN,
IGOR LABONOFF, LOU MINDLING, GENE RODDENBERRY,
WILLIAM THEISS, BJO TRIMBLE, & STEPHEN E. WHITFIELD

AND ESPECIALLY TO THESE CIVILIANS
AND CIVILIAN AUXILIARIES:

ART CANFIL, DAVID BARBER, SHARON FERRARO, JAMIE
HANRAHAN, DENNIS HUNT, TONI LAY, ROD MARCH, JEFF
MAYNARD, ROBERT MROZ, SANDY SARRIS, KAREN LINDA
SCHNAUBELT, JANICE SCOTT, GREG WEIR, CHARLES WEISS,
HELEN YOUNG, MEMORY ALPHA, SPACE-TIME CONTINUUM,
S.T.A.R. SAN DIEGO, STAR TREK ARCHIVES, & STAR TREK
WELCOMMITTEE

PRINTINGS:
1ST EDITION   STARDATE 7511.01

THE PUBLISHER GRATEFULLY ACKNOWLEDGES THE COOPERATION OF
PARAMOUNT TELEVISION, A DIVISION OF PARAMOUNT PICTURES CORPORATION,
THE PRODUCERS OF THE STAR TREK TELEVISION SERIES, IN GRANTING
PERMISSION TO PUBLISH THIS VOLUME.

PRINTED IN THE UNITED STATES OF AMERICA

BALLANTINE BOOKS
A DIVISION OF RANDOM HOUSE, INC.
201 EAST 50TH STREET, NEW YORK, N.Y. 10022
SIMULTANEOUSLY PUBLISHED BY
BALLANTINE BOOKS, LTD., TORONTO CANADA

*UNITED NATIONS/EARTH IDENTITY:
FRANZ JOSEPH DESIGNS

FOREWORD I

PHOTOCOPY

UNITED STATES MILITARY FORCES
GENERAL STAFF HEADQUARTERS
WASHINGTON, D.C., U.S.A.

memorandum to: Franz Joseph Designs

from: Col. Robert Argon, Director
                Security Control/MFHQ

date: 15 April 1973

subject: MF Security Docket #075140

enclosure: one (1) copy of subject docket

1. Pursuant to your inquiry we are enclosing one (1) copy of subject
    docket without restrictions. The security classification has been
removed, and there is no longer any official interest in the matter.

2. The printed 'message' was: "ALERT.....ALERT.....UNITED FEDERATION
    FLEET HEADQUARTERS MASTER LIBRARY COMPUTER.....TO.....LIBRARY COMPUTER
.....ALL FEDERATION STARSHIPS ON SPECIAL SERVICE.....STARDATE 3113.....
SUBJECT.....TRANSMISSION OF UPDATED TECHNICAL MANUAL MASTER DATA SECTIONS
.....00:00:00.....00:00:__   _._0:02
.....BEGIN TRANSMISSION....."

3. The message and the 'data sheets' which followed were found in the
    memory banks of the master computer at Security Control, Omaha MFB,
and were accidentally discovered in 1970 during a print-out run, while the
computer was being interrogated for another reason. A top security lid
was immediately clamped on the matter while an investigation was launched
to attempt to identify the source of the unusual transmission. Neither
the message or the data could be traced to any known country, or alliance,
in the World. All of the terminology, uniforms, weaponry, and other
material was completely foriegn to the terminology, uniforms, weaponry,
and other material known to be in existence at that time.

4. The investigation was terminated with a final determination that the
    whole affair had been a hoax. That the 'unusual' material had been
inserted into the computer as a prank. And the file was closed, while a
search was initiated to find the person, or persons, responsible for this
breach of Security Control. To date this effort has been fruitless.

FOREWORD II

PHOTOCOPY

OFFICIAL USE ONLY
O MARK O R5PC

STAR FLEET COMMAND
STAR FLEET HEADQUARTERS
UNITED FEDERATION OF PLANETS

SIDRE AEL SARDELAS, DIRECTOR
MILITARY STAFF COMMITTEE   STARDATE 3150.10

to: All Divisions concerned
     Star Fleet Command

1. Pursuant to the matter of the unauthorized transmission of SFAF
material (viz: SFHQ/Mastercom Computer Data) into the Master Computer at
Security Control, Omaha MFB, Earth, Sol System as of stardate 3113, the
Special Review Board examined the following pertinent documentation:

 (a) report of Capt. James T. Kirk, commanding, U.S.S. Enterprise;
 (b) report of Lt. Cmdr. Spock, First Officer, U.S.S. Enterprise;
 (c) report of the investigation by the Special Review Commission;
 (d) report of the historical events sequential review of the data
     banks of Mastercom/SFHQ;

2. The Special Review Board has now concluded its determination. It
finds: (1) that both Capt. James T. Kirk and Lt. Cmdr. Spock cannot be
faulted for the matter since it occurred in the routine computer-to-
computer transmission, which operates independently of the SFAF Communications Systems or human supervision; and: (2) that it occurred as the
result of an unpredicted, and unforeseen gravitational space-warp which
is now known to be a natural phenomenon within the galaxy; and (3) that
it was a purely random matter which occurred without human intervention
and therefore is considered to be a natural accidental occurrence in the
sequential train of historical events.

3. The Special Review Board further finds that in the event the material
now stored in the data banks of the Master Computer at Security Control,
Omaha MFB, should become known in that time period, it would be advisable
to review whatever material is included in that storage to: (a) delete
any technology which is not known to Earth's technology in that time
period, in order to preserve the Prime Directive's doctrine of non-inter-
vention; and: (b) to correct any material which is determined to be "safe"
but which was distorted in the transmission.

4. Therefore, the Planetary Relations Division of Star Fleet Command is
hereby assigned the task of this final determination in the event it should
become necessary, and all Divisions shall support this effort as required.
The Planetary Relations Division shall also prepare a final report upon
the conclusion of any actions they may take, for submission to the Federation Council.

GENERAL INDEX

GENERAL INDEX

Note: (*) indicates Manual Division and Section Title Page

GENERAL SECTION

TM:379260-0
STAR FLEET TECHNICAL ORDER
AUTHENTICATED STARDATE 7407.29

TO:00:00:14

SECTION INDEX

TO. NO:	SUBJECT:	CURRENT	REPLACES
00:00:10	GENERAL SECTION FLYSHEET	7309.14	
» » :12	FOREWORD	*	
» » :14	SECTION INDEX	7407.29	
» :01:00	ARTICLES OF FEDERATION - DECL, CH. I, AR.1, P. 1, 2, & 3	7305.29	
» » :01	A.O.F.-CH. I, AR.1, P. 4, AR.2, P.1,2,3,4, 5,6, & 7, CH.II, AR.3, AR.4, P.1	»	
» » :02	A.O.F.-CH. II, AR. 6, TO CH. IV, AR.11, P. 3	»	
» » :03	A.O.F.-CH. IV, AR. 11, P. 4 TO AR.17, P. 2	»	
» » :04	A.O.F.-CH. IV, AR.17, P. 3 TO CH. V, AR. 23, P.1	»	
» » :05	A.O.F.-CH. V, AR. 23, P. 2 TO AR. 28, P. 1	»	
» » :06	A.O.F.-CH. V, AR. 28, P. 3 TO CH. VI, AR. 35, P. 3	»	
» » :07	A.O.F.-CH. VI, AR. 36, P.1, TO CH. VII, AR. 43	»	
» » :08	A.O.F.-CH. VII, AR. 44 TO AR. 50	»	
» » :09	A.O.F.-CH. VII, AR. 51 TO CH. VIII, AR. 54, P. 1	»	
» » :10	A.O.F.-CH. VIII AP. 54, P. 2 TO CH. IX, AR 60	»	
» » :11	A.O.F.-CH. X, AR. 61 TO AR. 66, P.1	»	
» » :12	A.O.F.-CH. X, AR. 66, P. 2, TO CH. XI, AR. 73	»	
» » :13	A.O.F.-CH. XI, AR. 73 TO CH. XII, AR. 76	»	
» » :14	A.O.F.-CH. XII, AR. 77, P.1 TO AR. 83, P.1	»	
» » :15	A.O.F.-CH. XII, AR. 83, P. 2 TO CH. XIII AR. 87	»	
» » :16	A.O.F.-CH. XIII, AR. 88 TO CH. XIV, AR. 95	»	
» » :17	A.O.F.-CH. XIV, AR. 96 TO CH. XV, AR. 101	»	
» » :18	A.O.F.-CH. XVI, AR. 102 TO CH. XVII, AR. 107	»	
» » :19	ARTICLES OF FEDERATION - CH. XVII, AR. 108 TO - FINAL	7305.29	
00:01:20	STATUTE - INTERPLANETARY SUPREME COURT OF JUSTICE	*	
» » :21	» -CH. I, AR. 5, P. 3 TO AR. 7, P. 6	*	
» » :22	» -CH. I, AR. 7, P. 7 TO AR.11	*	
» » :23	» - CH. I, AR. 12 TO CH. II, AR. 14	*	
» » :24	» -CH. II, AR. 15 TO CH. III, AR.19, P. 3	*	
» » 25	» -CH III, AR. 19, P. 3 TO AR. 23, P.1	*	
» » :26	» -CH. III, AR. 23, P. 2 TO CH. V, AR. 27	*	
» » :27	STATUTE - CH V, AR. 28 TO - FINAL	*	
00:01:30	STATUTE REGULATING INTERPLANETARY COMMERCE	*	
» » :31	» -PART I, SECT. 1, ITEM 12 TO 23	*	
» » :32	» -SECT. 2 TO PART II, SECT. 5, ITEM 01	*	
» » :33	» -SECT. 5, ITEM 02 TO SECT 6, ITEM 04	*	
» » :34	» -SECT. 6, ITEM 05 TO PART III, SECT. 10, ITEM 04	*	
» » :35	» -SECT. 11 TO PART IV, SECT. 16, ITEM 01	*	
» » :36	» -SECT. 16, ITEM 02 TO SECT. 17, ITEM 02	*	
» » :37	» -SECT. 18, ITEM 01 TO 07	*	
» » :38	» -SECT. 18, ITEM 08 TO PART V, SECT. 19, ITEM 05	*	
» » :39	» -SECT. 19, ITEM 06 TO SECT. 21	*	
» » :40	» -SECT. 21, ITEM 01 TO SECT. 22, ITEM 05	*	
» » :41	» -SECT. 23 TO SECT. 27, ITEM 01	*	
» » :42	» -SECT. 27, ITEM 02 TO SECT. 29, ITEM 04	*	
» » :43	» -SECT. 30 TO PART VI, SECT. 33, ITEM 01	*	
» » :44	» -SECT. 33, ITEM 02 TO PART VII, SECT. 36	*	
» » :45	» -SECT. 36, ITEM 01 TO SECT. 38, ITEM 01	*	
» » :46	» -SECT. 38, ITEM 02 TO SECT. 39, ITEM 03	*	
» » :47	» -SECT. 39, ITEM 04 TO SECT. 42	*	
» » :48	» -SECT. 43 TO SECT. 45	*	
» » :49	» -SECT. 46 TO PART VIII, SECT. 47, ITEM 02	*	
» » :50	» -SECT. 47, ITEM 03 TO SECT. 49, ITEM 02	*	

NOTE (*): NO CURRENT PRINT-OUT FROM MASTERCOM DATABANKS/SFHQ

TM:379260-0
STAR FLEET TECHNICAL ORDER
AUTHENTICATED STARDATE 7407.29

SECTION INDEX

TO. NO:	SUBJECT:	CURRENT	REPLACES
00:00:15	SECTION INDEX	7407.29	
00:01:51	STATUTE-SECT. 49, ITEM 03 TO PART IX, SECT. 51, ITEM 05	*	
» » :52	» -SECT. 51, ITEM 06, TO PART X, SECT. 54	*	
» » :53	» -SECT. 55, ITEM 01 TO 05	*	
» » :54	» -SECT 56 TO SECT. 57, ITEM 01	*	
» » :55	» -SECT. 57, ITEM 02 TO SECT. 58, ITEM 04	*	
» » :56	» -SECT. 58, ITEM 05 TO PART XI, SECT. 63	*	
» » :57	STATUTE-SECT 64 TO FINAL	*	
00:01:60	ROMULAN TREATY OF PEACE	7305.30	
» » :62	ORGANIAN TREATY OF PEACE	7305.30	
00:02:00	UNITED FEDERATION OF PLANETS - BANNER	7405.05	
» » :01	» » » » - SEAL	7306.18	
» » :02	UNITED NATIONS, PLANET EARTH, SOL SYSTEM - FLAG	7405.30	
» » :03	» » » » » » - SEAL	7406.15	
» » :04	PLANETARY CONFEDERATION OF 40 ERIDANI - BANNER	7407.13	
» » :05	» » » » » » - SIGNAT	7407.09	
» » :06	UNITED PLANETS OF 61 CYGNI - SHIELD	7407.06	
» » :07	» » » » » - ARMS	7407.07	
» » :08	STAR EMPIRE OF EPSILON INDII - STANDARD	7407.05	
» » :09	» » » » » - SEAL	7407.05	
» » :10	ALPHA CENTAURI CONCORDIUM OF PLANETS - PENNANT	7406.24	
» » :11	» » » » » - ARMS	7406.25	
00:10:10	UNIFORM COLOR CODE - STAR FLEET SPECIFICATION	7407.04	
» :10:00	OFFICIAL TYPE STYLE - EARTH, SOL SYSTEM - SF SPEC.	7405.10	
» » :01	» » » - ALPHA KENTAURUS - » »	7407.05	

NOTE (*): NO CURRENT PRINT-OUT FROM MASTERCOM DATABANKS / SFHQ

ARTICLES OF FEDERATION

WE THE INTELLIGENT LIFE-FORMS OF THE UNITED FEDERATION OF PLANETS DETERMINED

TO SAVE SUCCEEDING GENERATIONS FROM THE SCOURGE OF INTRA-GALACTIC WAR WHICH HAS BROUGHT UNTOLD HORROR AND SUFFERING TO OUR PLANETARY SOCIAL SYSTEMS, AND

TO REAFFIRM FAITH IN THE FUNDAMENTAL INTELLIGENT LIFE-FORM RIGHTS, IN THE DIGNITY AND WORTH OF THE INTELLIGENT LIFE-FORM PERSON, TO THE EQUAL RIGHTS OF MALE AND FEMALE AND OF PLANETARY SOCIAL SYSTEMS LARGE AND SMALL, AND

TO ESTABLISH CONDITIONS UNDER WHICH JUSTICE AND MUTUAL RESPECT FOR THE OBLIGATIONS ARISING FROM TREATIES AND OTHER SOURCES OF INTERPLANETARY LAW CAN BE MAINTAINED, AND

TO PROMOTE SOCIAL PROGRESS AND BETTER STANDARDS OF LIFE IN LARGER FREEDOM,

AND TO THESE ENDS

TO PRACTISE BENEVOLENT TOLERANCE AND LIVE TOGETHER IN PEACE WITH ONE ANOTHER AS GOOD NEIGHBORS, AND

TO UNITE OUR STRENGTH TO MAINTAIN INTRA-GALACTIC PEACE AND SECURITY, AND

TO ENSURE BY THE ACCEPTANCE OF PRINCIPLES AND THE INSTITUTION OF METHODS THAT ARMED FORCE SHALL NOT BE USED EXCEPT IN THE COMMON DEFENSE, AND

TO EMPLOY INTRA-GALACTIC MACHINERY FOR THE PROMOTION OF THE ECONOMIC AND SOCIAL ADVANCEMENT OF ALL INTELLIGENT LIFE-FORMS,

HAVE RESOLVED TO COMBINE OUR EFFORTS TO ACCOMPLISH THESE AIMS.

ACCORDINGLY, THE RESPECTIVE SOCIAL SYSTEMS, THROUGH REPRESENTATIVES ASSEMBLED ON THE PLANET BABEL, WHO HAVE EXHIBITED THEIR FULL POWERS TO BE IN GOOD AND DUE FORM, HAVE AGREED TO THESE ARTICLES OF FEDERATION OF THE UNITED FEDERATION OF PLANETS, AND DO HEREBY ESTABLISH AN INTER-PLANETARY ORGANIZATION TO BE KNOWN AS THE UNITED FEDERATION OF PLANETS.

CHAPTER I
PURPOSES AND PRINCIPLES

ARTICLE 1

THE PURPOSES OF THE UNITED FEDERATION OF PLANETS ARE:

1. TO MAINTAIN INTERPLANETARY PEACE AND SECURITY WITHIN THE TREATY EXPLORA-TION TERRITORY, AND TO THAT END: TO TAKE EFFECTIVE COLLECTIVE MEASURES FOR THE PREVENTION OF THREATS TO THE PEACE, THE SUPPRESSION OF ACTS OF AGGRES-SION, AND TO BRING ABOUT BY PEACEFUL MEANS, AND EMPLOYING THE PRINCIPLES OF JUSTICE AND INTRA-GALACTIC LAW, ADJUSTMENT OR SETTLEMENT OF INTERPLANETARY DISPUTES WHICH MIGHT LEAD TO A BREACH OF THE PEACE;

2. TO DEVELOP FRIENDLY RELATIONS AMONG PLANETS BASED ON RESPECT FOR THE PRINCIPLES OF EQUAL RIGHTS AND SELF-DETERMINATION OF INTELLIGENT LIFE-FORMS, AND TO OTHER APPROPRIATE MEASURES TO STRENGTHEN UNIVERSAL PEACE;

3. TO ACHIEVE INTERPLANETARY COOPERATION IN SOLVING INTRA-GALACTIC PROBLEMS OF ECONOMIC, SOCIAL, CULTURAL, OR HUMANITARIAN CHARACTER; IN PROMOTING AND ENCOURAGING RESPECT FOR INTELLIGENT LIFE-FORM RIGHTS; AND FOR FUNDAMENTAL FREEDOMS FOR ALL WITHOUT DISTINCTION AS TO CULTURE, SEX, LIFE-FORM, OR RELIGOUS BELIEF; AND

ARTICLES OF FEDERATION

4. TO BE A CENTER FOR CONCILIENCE OF THE ACTIONS OF ALL SOCIAL SYSTEMS IN THE ATTAINMENT OF THESE COMMON ENDS.

ARTICLE 2

THE FEDERATION AND ITS MEMBERS, IN PURSUIT OF THE PURPOSES STATED, SHALL ACT IN ACCORDANCE WITH THE FOLLOWING PRINCIPLES:

1. THE FEDERATION IS BASED ON THE SOVERIEGN EQUALITY OF ALL ITS MEMBERS;

2. IN ORDER TO ENSURE TO ALL OF THEM THE RIGHTS AND BENEFITS RESULTING FROM MEMBERSHIP, ALL MEMBERS SHALL FULFILL IN GOOD FAITH THE OBLIGATIONS ASSUMED BY THEM IN ACCORDANCE WITH THESE ARTICLES OF FEDERATION;

3. ALL MEMBERS SHALL SETTLE THEIR INTERPLANETARY DISPUTES BY PEACEFUL MEANS IN SUCH MANNER THAT INTRA-GALACTIC PEACE, SECURITY, AND JUSTICE, ARE NOT ENDANGERED;

4. IN ALL INTERPLANETARY RELATIONS, ALL MEMBERS SHALL REFRAIN FROM THE THREAT, OR USE, OF FORCE AGAINST THE TERRITORIAL INTEGRITY OR POLITICAL INDEPENDENCE OF ANY PLANETARY SOCIAL SYSTEM, OR IN ANY MANNER INCONSISTENT WITH THE PURPOSES OF THE UNITED FEDERATION;

5. ALL MEMBERS SHALL GIVE THE UNITED FEDERATION EVERY ASSISTANCE IN ANY ACTION TAKEN IN ACCORDANCE WITH THESE ARTICLES OF FEDERATION, AND SHALL RE-FRAIN FROM ASSISTING ANY PLANETARY SOCIAL SYSTEM AGAINST WHICH THE FEDERATION IS TAKING PREVENTIVE OR ENFORCEMENT ACTION;

6. THE UNITED FEDERATION SHALL ENSURE THAT PLANETARY SOCIAL SYSTEMS WHICH ARE NOT MEMBERS OF THE FEDERATION ACT IN ACCORDANCE WITH THESE PRINCIPLES AS NECESSARY FOR THE MAINTENANCE OF INTRA-GALACTIC PEACE AND SECURITY;

7. NOTHING WITHIN THESE ARTICLES OF FEDERATION SHALL AUTHORIZE THE FEDERA-TION TO INTERVENE IN MATTERS WHICH ARE ESSENTIALLY THE DOMESTIC JURISDIC-TION OF ANY PLANETARY SOCIAL SYSTEM, OR SHALL REQUIRE THE MEMBERS TO SUBMIT SUCH MATTERS TO SETTLEMENT UNDER THESE ARTICLES OF FEDERATION; BUT THIS PRINCIPLE SHALL NOT PREJUDICE THE APPLICATION OF ENFORCEMENT MEASURES UNDER CHAPTER VII.

CHAPTER II
MEMBERSHIP

ARTICLE 3

THE ORIGINAL MEMBERS OF THE UNITED FEDERATION OF PLANETS SHALL BE THOSE PLANETARY SOCIAL SYSTEMS WHICH, HAVING PARTICIPATED IN THE INTERPLANETARY CONFERENCE ON INTERPLANETARY FEDERATION AT BABEL, OR HAVING PREVIOUSLY SIGNED THE DECLARATION OF THE UNITED FEDERATION OF PLANETS OF STARDATE 0963, SIGN THESE ARTICLES OF FEDERATION AND RATIFY THEM IN ACCORDANCE WITH ARTICLE 110.

ARTICLE 4

1. MEMBERSHIP IN THE UNITED FEDERATION IS OPEN TO ANY OTHER PEACEFUL PLANET-ARY SOCIAL SYSTEMS WHICH ACCEPT THE OBLIGATIONS CONTAINED IN THESE ARTICLES OF FEDERATION AND, IN THE JUDGEMENT OF THE FEDERATION, ARE CAPABLE AND WILL-ING TO CARRY OUT THESE OBLIGATIONS;

2. THE ADMISSION OF ANY SUCH PLANETARY SOCIAL SYSTEM TO MEMBERSHIP IN THE UNITED FEDERATION OF PLANETS IS CONTINGENT UPON THE DECISION OF THE SUPREME ASSEMBLY UPON RECOMMENDATION OF THE FEDERATION COUNCIL.

ARTICLE 5

THE SUPREME ASSEMBLY MAY SUSPEND THE RIGHTS AND PRIVILEGES OF MEMBERSHIP OF ANY MEMBER OF THE UNITED FEDERATION AGAINST WHICH THE FEDERATION COUNCIL HAS TAKEN PREVENTIVE OR ENFORCEMENT ACTION. THE FEDERATION COUNCIL MAY RESTORE THESE RIGHTS AND PRIVILEGES OF MEMBERSHIP AT ITS DISCRETION;

ARTICLES OF FEDERATION

ARTICLE 6

ANY MEMBER OF THE UNITED FEDERATION WHICH HAS PERSISTENTLY VIOLATED THE PURPOSES AND PRINCIPLES CONTAINED IN THESE ARTICLES OF FEDERATION MAY BE EXPELLED FROM THE FEDERATION BY THE SUPREME ASSEMBLY UPON THE RECOMMENDATION OF THE FEDERATION COUNCIL.

CHAPTER III
AGENCIES

ARTICLE 7

1. THERE ARE ESTABLISHED AS THE PRINCIPAL AGENCIES OF THE UNITED FEDERATION OF PLANETS: A SUPREME ASSEMBLY, A FEDERATION COUNCIL, AN ECONOMIC AND SOCIAL COUNCIL, A TRUSTEESHIP COUNCIL, AN INTERPLANETARY SUPREME COURT OF JUSTICE, A STAR FLEET COMBINED PEACE-KEEPING FORCE, AND A SECRETARIAT;

2. SUCH SUBSIDIARY AGENCIES AS MAY BE DEEMED NECESSARY FROM TIME TO TIME MAY BE ESTABLISHED IN ACCORDANCE WITH THESE ARTICLES OF FEDERATION;

ARTICLE 8

THE UNITED FEDERATION SHALL PLACE NO RESTRICTION ON THE ELIGIBILITY OF MALE AND FEMALE LIFE-FORMS OF ANY MEMBER PLANETARY SOCIAL SYSTEM TO PARTICI-PATE IN ANY CAPACITY UNDER CONDITIONS OF EQUALITY IN ITS PRINCIPAL AND SUB-SIDIARY AGENCIES.

CHAPTER IV
THE SUPREME ASSEMBLY

ARTICLE 9
COMPOSITION

THE SUPREME ASSEMBLY SHALL CONSIST OF ALL THE MEMBERS OF THE UNITED FEDERATION OF PLANETS. EACH MEMBER SHALL BE ENTITLED TO HAVE NOT MORE THAN FIVE (5) REPRESENTATIVES IN THIS BODY;

FUNCTIONS AND POWERS
ARTICLE 10

THE SUPREME ASSEMBLY MAY DISCUSS ANY QUESTIONS ON ANY MATTERS WITHIN THE SCOPE OF THESE ARTICLES OF FEDERATION OR RELATING TO THE POWERS AND FUNCTIONS OF ANY AGENCIES PROVIDED FOR IN THESE ARTICLES OF FEDERATION AND, EXCEPT AS PROVIDED IN ARTICLE 12, MAY MAKE RECOMMENDATIONS TO THE MEMBERS AND THE FEDERATION COUNCIL OR BOTH ON ANY SUCH QUESTIONS OR MATTERS;

ARTICLE 11

1. THE SUPREME ASSEMBLY MAY CONSIDER THE GENERAL PRINCIPLES OF COOPERATION IN MAINTAINING INTERPLANETARY PEACE AND SECURITY, INCLUDING DISARMAMENT AND THE REGULATION OF ARMAMENTS, AND MAY MAKE RECOMMENDATIONS WITH REGARD TO SUCH PRINCIPLES TO THE MEMBERS OR THE FEDERATION COUNCIL OR TO BOTH;

2. THE SUPREME ASSEMBLY MAY DISCUSS ANY QUESTIONS RELATIVE TO THE MAINTEN-ANCE OF INTRA-GALACTIC PEACE AND SECURITY PUT TO IT BY ANY MEMBER OR THE FEDERATION COUNCIL, OR A NON-MEMBER PLANETARY SOCIAL SYSTEM IN ACCORDANCE WITH ARTICLE 25 PARAGRAPH 2 AND, EXCEPT AS PROVIDED IN ARTICLE 12, MAY MAKE RECOMMENDATIONS WITH REGARD TO ANY SUCH QUESTIONS TO THE MEMBERS, THE FEDERATION COUNCIL, OR THE PLEADING PLANETARY SOCIAL SYSTEM, OR TO ALL OF THEM. ANY SUCH QUESTION ON WHICH ACTION IS NECESSARY SHALL BE REFERRED TO THE FEDERATION COUNCIL BY THE SUPREME ASSEMBLY EITHER BEFORE OR AFTER DISCUSSION;

3. THE SUPREME ASSEMBLY MAY CALL SITUATIONS WHICH ARE LIKELY TO ENDANGER THE INTERPLANETARY AND INTRA-GALACTIC PEACE AND SECURITY TO THE ATTENTION OF THE FEDERATION COUNCIL;

ARTICLES OF FEDERATION

4. THE POWERS OF THE SUPREME ASSEMBLY AS SET FORTH IN THIS ARTICLE SHALL NOT LIMIT THE SCOPE OF ARTICLE 10;

ARTICLE 12

1. WHERE THE FEDERATION COUNCIL IS EXECUTING THE FUNCTIONS ASSIGNED TO IT UNDER THESE ARTICLES OF FEDERATION WITH RESPECT TO ANY DISPUTE OR SITUATION, THE SUPREME ASSEMBLY SHALL MAKE NO RECOMMENDATION WITH REGARD TO THAT DISPUTE OR SITUATION UNLESS SO REQUESTED BY THE FEDERATION COUNCIL;

2. THE SUPREME-SECRETARIAT, WITH THE CONSENT OF THE FEDERATION COUNCIL, SHALL NOTIFY THE SUPREME ASSEMBLY AT EACH SESSION OF ANY MATTERS RELATING TO THE MAINTENANCE OF INTERPLANETARY PEACE AND SECURITY WHICH ARE UNDER DISCUSSION IN THE FEDERATION COUNCIL, AND SHALL NOTIFY THE SUPREME ASSEMBLY, OR THE MEMBERS IF THE SUPREME ASSEMBLY IS NOT IN SESSION, IMMEDIATELY WHEN THE FEDERATION COUNCIL COMPLETES ITS DELIBERATIONS ON ANY SUCH MATTERS;

ARTICLE 13

1. THE SUPREME ASSEMBLY SHALL INITIATE STUDIES AND MAKE RECOMMENDATIONS FOR THE PURPOSE OF:

A) PROMOTING INTERPLANETARY COOPERATION IN POLITICAL FIELDS AND ENCOURAGING THE PROGRESSIVE DEVELOPMENT OF INTERPLANETARY LAW AND ITS CODIFICATION;

B) PROMOTING INTERPLANETARY COOPERATION IN THE ECONOMIC, SOCIAL, CULTURAL, EDUCATIONAL, AND HEALTH FIELDS, AND ASSISTING IN THE REALIZATION OF INTELLIGENT LIFE-FORM RIGHTS AND FUNDAMENTAL FREEDOMS FOR ALL WITHOUT DISTINCTION AS TO CULTURE, SEX, LANGUAGE, OR RELIGION;

2. THE FURTHER RESPONSIBILITIES, FUNCTIONS, AND POWERS OF THE SUPREME ASSEMBLY WITH RESPECT TO MATTERS MENTIONED IN PARAGRAPH 1(B) ABOVE ARE SET FORTH IN CHAPTERS IX AND X;

ARTICLE 14

SUBJECT TO THE PROVISIONS OF ARTICLE 12, THE SUPREME ASSEMBLY MAY RECOMMEND MEASURES FOR THE PEACEFUL ADJUSTMENT OF ANY SITUATION, REGARDLESS OF ORIGIN, WHICH IT DEEMS LIKELY TO IMPAIR THE GENERAL WELFARE OR FRIENDLY RELATIONS AMONG THE PLANETS, INCLUDING SITUATIONS RESULTING FROM VIOLATIONS OF THE PROVISIONS OF THESE ARTICLES OF FEDERATION SETTING FORTH THE PURPOSES AND PRINCIPLES OF THE UNITED FEDERATION OF PLANETS;

ARTICLE 15

1. THE SUPREME ASSEMBLY SHALL RECEIVE AND CONSIDER REGULAR AND SPECIAL REPORTS FROM THE FEDERATION COUNCIL; WHICH REPORTS SHALL INCLUDE AN ACCOUNT OF THE MEASURES THAT THE FEDERATION COUNCIL HAS DECIDED UPON OR TAKEN TO MAINTAIN INTERPLANETARY PEACE AND SECURITY;

2. THE SUPREME ASSEMBLY SHALL RECEIVE AND CONSIDER REPORTS FROM THE OTHER AGENCIES OF THE UNITED FEDERATION ON AGREED UPON REGULAR PERIODS OR REPORTING;

ARTICLE 16

THE SUPREME ASSEMBLY SHALL PERFORM SUCH FUNCTIONS OF INTRA-GALACTIC TRUSTEESHIP AS ARE ASSIGNED TO IT UNDER CHAPTERS XII AND XIII, INCLUDING THE APPROVAL OF THE TRUSTEESHIP AGREEMENTS FOR AREAS WHICH ARE NOT DESIGNATED AS STRATEGIC;

ARTICLE 17

1. THE SUPREME ASSEMBLY SHALL CONSIDER AND APPROVE THE BUDGET OF THE UNITED FEDERATION OF PLANETS;

2. THE EXPENSES OF THE UNITED FEDERATION OF PLANETS SHALL BE BORNE BY THE MEMBERS AS APPORTIONED BY THE SUPREME ASSEMBLY;

ARTICLES OF FEDERATION

3.   THE SUPREME ASSEMBLY SHALL CONSIDER AND APPROVE ANY FINANCIAL AND BUDGE-
TARY ARRANGEMENTS WITH SPECIALIZED AGENCIES REFERRED TO IN ARTICLE 57 AND
SHALL EXAMINE THE ADMINISTRATIVE BUDGETS OF SUCH SPECIALIZED AGENCIES WITH A
VIEW TO MAKING RECOMMENDATIONS TO THE AGENCIES CONCERNED;

4.   ALL BUDGETS OF, AND EXPENSES OF THE UNITED FEDERATION SHALL BE MADE AND
PAID IN THE COMMON INTERPLANETARY CREDIT.   THE COMMON INTERPLANETARY CREDIT
SHALL BE THE OFFICIAL MEDIUM OF EXCHANGE WITHIN THE UNITED FEDERATION TREATY
EXPLORATION TERRITORY;

VOTING
ARTICLE 18

1.   EACH MEMBER OF THE SUPREME ASSEMBLY SHALL HAVE ONE VOTE;

2.   DECISIONS OF THE SUPREME ASSEMBLY ON IMPORTANT QUESTIONS SHALL BE MADE
ON A TWO-THIRDS (2/3) MAJORITY VOTE OF THE MEMBERS PRESENT AND VOTING.   THESE
QUESTIONS SHALL INCLUDE: RECOMMENDATIONS WITH RESPECT TO THE MAINTENANCE OF
INTERPLANETARY PEACE AND SECURITY; THE ELECTION OF NON-PERMANENT MEMBERS TO
THE FEDERATION COUNCIL; THE ELECTION OF MEMBERS OF THE TRUSTEESHIP COUNCIL IN
ACCORDANCE WITH PARAGRAPH 1(C) OF ARTICLE 86; THE ADMISSION OF NEW MEMBERS
TO THE FEDERATION; THE SUSPENSION OF THE RIGHTS AND PRIVILEGES OF MEMBER-
SHIP; THE EXPULSION OF MEMBERS; QUESTIONS RELATING TO THE OPERATION OF THE
TRUSTEESHIP SYSTEM; AND BUDGETARY QUESTIONS;

3.   DECISIONS ON OTHER QUESTIONS, INCLUDING THE DETERMINATION OF ADDITIONAL
CATEGORIES OF QUESTIONS TO BE DECIDED BY A TWO-THIRDS (2/3) MAJORITY, SHALL
BE MADE BY A MAJORITY VOTE OF THE MEMBERS PRESENT AND VOTING;

ARTICLE 19

A MEMBER OF THE UNITED FEDERATION WHICH IS IN ARREARS IN THE PAYMENT OF
ITS FINANCIAL OBLIGATIONS TO THE FEDERATION SHALL HAVE NO VOTE IN THE
SUPREME ASSEMBLY IF THE AMOUNT IT IS IN ARREARS EQUALS OR EXCEEDS THE AMOUNT
OF THE CONTRIBUTIONS DUE FROM IT FOR THE PRECEDING TWO ACCOUNTING PERIODS.
THE SUPREME ASSEMBLY MAY, NEVERTHELESS, PERMIT SUCH A MEMBER TO VOTE IF IT IS
SATISFIED THAT THE FAILURE TO PAY IS DUE TO CONDITIONS BEYOND THE CONTROL OF
THE MEMBER.

PROCEDURE
ARTICLE 20

THE SUPREME ASSEMBLY SHALL MEET IN REGULAR PERIODIC SESSIONS AND IN SUCH
SPECIAL SESSIONS AS OCCASION MAY REQUIRE.   SPECIAL SESSIONS SHALL BE CON-
VOKED BY THE SUPREME-SECRETARIAT AT THE REQUEST OF THE FEDERATION COUNCIL OR
OF A MAJORITY OF THE MEMBERS OF THE UNITED FEDERATION;

ARTICLE 21

THE SUPREME ASSEMBLY SHALL ADOPT ITS OWN RULES OF PROCEDURE.   IT SHALL
ELECT ITS PRESIDENT FOR EACH SESSION;

ARTICLE 22

THE SUPREME ASSEMBLY MAY ESTABLISH SUCH SUBSIDIARY AGENCIES AS IT DEEMS
NECESSARY FOR THE PERFORMANCE OF ITS FUNCTIONS.

CHAPTER V
THE FEDERATION COUNCIL

ARTICLE 23
COMPOSITION

1.   THE FEDERATION COUNCIL SHALL CONSIST OF ELEVEN (11) MEMBERS OF THE UNI-
TED FEDERATION.   THE UNITED NATIONS OF THE PLANET EARTH, THE PLANETARY CON-
FEDERATION OF 40 ERIDANI, THE UNITED PLANETS OF 61 CYGNI, THE STAR EMPIRE
OF EPSILON INDII, AND THE ALPHA CENTAURI CONCORDIUM OF PLANETS SHALL BE
PERMANENT MEMBERS OF THE FEDERATION COUNCIL.   THE SUPREME ASSEMBLY SHALL

ARTICLES OF FEDERATION

ELECT SIX (6) OTHER MEMBERS OF THE UNITED FEDERATION TO BE NON-PERMANENT MEM-
BERS OF THE FEDERATION COUNCIL, DUE REGARD BEING ESPECIALLY PAID, IN THE
FIRST INSTANCE, TO THE CONTRIBUTION OF THE MEMBERS OF THE UNITED FEDERATION
TO THE MAINTENANCE OF INTERPLANETARY PEACE AND SECURITY AND TO THE OTHER
PURPOSES OF THE FEDERATION, AND ALSO TO EQUITABLE GEO-GALACTICAL DISTRIBU-
TION;

2.   THE NON-PERMANENT MEMBERS OF THE FEDERATION COUNCIL SHALL BE ELECTED FOR
A TERM OF TWO (2) SESSION PERIODS.   IN THE FIRST ELECTION OF NON-PERMANENT
MEMBERS, HOWEVER, THREE (3) SHALL BE ELECTED FOR A TERM OF ONE (1) SESSION
PERIOD.   A RETIRING MEMBER SHALL NOT BE ELIGIBLE FOR IMMEDIATE RE-ELECTION;

FUNCTIONS AND POWERS
ARTICLE 24

1.   IN ORDER TO ASSURE PROMPT AND EFFECTIVE ACTION BY THE UNITED FEDERATION
OF PLANETS, ITS MEMBERS CONFER ON THE FEDERATION COUNCIL PRIMARY RESPONSI-
BILITY FOR THE MAINTENANCE OF INTERPLANETARY PEACE AND SECURITY, AND AGREE
THAT IN CARRYING OUT ITS DUTIES UNDER THIS RESPONSIBILITY THE FEDERATION
COUNCIL ACTS ON THEIR BEHALF;

2.   IN DISCHARGING THESE DUTIES THE FEDERATION COUNCIL SHALL ACT IN ACCORD-
ANCE WITH THE PURPOSES AND PRINCIPLES OF THE UNITED FEDERATION.   THE SPECI-
FIC POWERS GRANTED TO THE FEDERATION COUNCIL FOR THE DISCHARGE OF THESE
DUTIES ARE LAID DOWN IN CHAPTERS VI, VII, VIII, AND XII;

3.   THE FEDERATION COUNCIL SHALL SUBMIT REGULAR AND, WHEN NECESSARY, SPECIAL
REPORTS TO THE SUPREME ASSEMBLY FOR ITS CONSIDERATION;

ARTICLE 25

THE MEMBERS OF THE UNITED FEDERATION AGREE TO ACCEPT AND CARRY OUT THE
DECISIONS OF THE FEDERATION COUNCIL IN ACCORDANCE WITH THESE ARTICLES OF
FEDERATION;

ARTICLE 26

IN ORDER TO PROMOTE THE ESTABLISHMENT AND MAINTENANCE OF INTERPLANETARY
PEACE AND SECURITY WITH THE LEAST DIVERSION OF THE FEDERATION'S LIFE-FORMS,
AND ECONOMIC RESOURCES FOR ARMAMENTS, THE FEDERATION COUNCIL SHALL BE
RESPONSIBLE FOR FORMULATING, WITH THE ASSISTANCE OF STAR FLEET HEADQUARTERS
STAFF REFERRED TO IN ARTICLE 47, PLANS TO BE SUBMITTED TO THE MEMBERS OF THE
UNITED FEDERATION FOR THE ESTABLISHMENT OF A SYSTEM FOR THE REGULATION OF
ARMAMENTS;

ARTICLE 27
VOTING

1.   EACH MEMBER OF THE FEDERATION COUNCIL SHALL HAVE ONE VOTE;

2.   DECISIONS OF THE FEDERATION COUNCIL ON PROCEDURAL MATTERS SHALL BE MADE
BY AN AFFIRMATIVE VOTE OF SEVEN (7) MEMBERS;

3.   DECISIONS OF THE FEDERATION COUNCIL ON ALL OTHER MATTERS SHALL BE MADE
ON AFFIRMATIVE VOTE OF SEVEN (7) MEMBERS INCLUDING THE CONCURRING VOTES OF
THE PERMANENT MEMBERS, PROVIDED THAT, IN DECISIONS UNDER CHAPTER VI, AND
UNDER PARAGRAPH 3 OF ARTICLE 52, A PARTY TO THE DISPUTE SHALL REFRAIN FROM
VOTING;

PROCEDURE
ARTICLE 28

1.   THE FEDERATION COUNCIL SHALL BE SO ORGANIZED AS TO BE ABLE TO FUNCTION
CONTINUOUSLY.   EACH MEMBER OF THE FEDERATION COUNCIL SHALL, FOR THIS PUR-
POSE, BE REPRESENTED AT ALL TIMES AT THE SEAT OF THE FEDERATION;

2.   THE FEDERATION COUNCIL SHALL HOLD PERIODIC MEETINGS AT WHICH EACH OF ITS
MEMBERS MAY, IF IT SO DESIRES, BE REPRESENTED BY A MEMBER OF ITS GOVERNMENT

ARTICLES OF FEDERATION

OR BY SOME OTHER SPECIALLY DESIGNATED REPRESENTATIVE;

3.   THE FEDERATION COUNCIL MAY HOLD MEETINGS AT SUCH PLACES OTHER THAN THE SEAT OF THE FEDERATION AS IN ITS JUDGEMENT WILL FACILITATE ITS WORK;

ARTICLE 29

THE FEDERATION COUNCIL MAY ESTABLISH SUCH SUBSIDIARY AGENCIES AS IT DEEMS NECESSARY FOR THE PERFORMANCE OF ITS FUNCTIONS;

ARTICLE 30

THE FEDERATION COUNCIL SHALL ADOPT ITS OWN RULES OF PROCEDURE, INCLUDING THE METHOD OF SELECTING ITS GOVERNOR;

ARTICLE 31

ANY MEMBER OF THE UNITED FEDERATION WHICH IS NOT A MEMBER OF THE FEDERATION COUNCIL MAY PARTICIPATE, WITHOUT VOTE, IN THE DISCUSSION OF ANY QUESTION BROUGHT BEFORE THE FEDERATION COUNCIL WHENEVER THE LATTER CONSIDERS THAT THE INTERESTS OF THE MEMBER ARE SPECIFICALLY AFFECTED;

ARTICLE 32

ANY MEMBER OF THE UNITED FEDERATION WHICH IS NOT A MEMBER OF THE FEDERATION COUNCIL OR ANY PLANETARY SOCIAL SYSTEM WHICH IS NOT A MEMBER OF THE UNITED FEDERATION OF PLANETS, IF IT IS A PARTY TO A DISPUTE UNDER CONSIDERATION BY THE FEDERATION COUNCIL, SHALL BE INVITED TO PARTICIPATE, WITHOUT VOTE, IN THE DISCUSSION RELATING TO THE DISPUTE.   THE FEDERATION COUNCIL SHALL LAY DOWN THE CONDITIONS AS IT DEEMS JUST FOR THE PARTICIPATION OF A PLANETARY SOCIAL SYSTEM WHICH IS NOT A MEMBER OF THE UNITED FEDERATION OF PLANETS.

CHAPTER VI
PACIFIC SETTLEMENT OF DISPUTES

ARTICLE 33

1.   THE PARTIES TO ANY DISPUTE, THE CONTINUANCE OF WHICH IS LIKELY TO ENDANGER THE MAINTENANCE OF INTERPLANETARY PEACE AND SECURITY, SHALL, FIRST OF ALL, SEEK A SOLUTION BY NEGOTIATION, ENQUIRY, MEDIATION, CONCILLIATION, ARBITRATION, JUDICIAL SETTLEMENT, RESORT TO REGIONAL AGENCIES OR ARRANGEMENTS, OR OTHER PEACEFUL MEANS OF THEIR OWN CHOICE;

2.   THE FEDERATION COUNCIL SHALL, WHEN IT DEEMS NECESSARY, CALL UPON THE PARTIES TO SETTLE THEIR DISPUTE BY SUCH MEANS;

ARTICLE 34

THE FEDERATION COUNCIL MAY INVESTIGATE ANY DISPUTE, OR ANY SITUATION THAT MIGHT LEAD TO INTERPLANETARY FRICTION OR GIVE RISE TO A DISPUTE, IN ORDER TO DETERMINE WHETHER THE CONTINUANCE OF THE DISPUTE OR SITUATION IS LIKELY TO ENDANGER THE MAINTENANCE OF INTERPLANETARY PEACE AND SECURITY;

ARTICLE 35

1.   ANY MEMBER OF THE UNITED FEDERATION MAY BRING ANY DISPUTE, OR ANY SITUATION OF THE NATURE REFERRED TO IN ARTICLE 34, TO THE ATTENTION OF THE FEDERATION COUNCIL OR THE SUPREME ASSEMBLY;

2.   A PLANETARY SOCIAL SYSTEM WHICH IS NOT A MEMBER OF THE UNITED FEDERATION OF PLANETS MAY BRING TO THE ATTENTION OF THE FEDERATION COUNCIL OR THE SUPREME ASSEMBLY ANY DISPUTE TO WHICH IT IS A PARTY IF IT ACCEPTS IN ADVANCE, FOR THE PURPOSES OF THE DISPUTE, THE OBLIGATION OF PACIFIC SETTLEMENT PROVIDED IN THESE ARTICLES OF FEDERATION;

3.   THE PROCEEDINGS OF THE SUPREME ASSEMBLY IN RESPECT TO MATTERS BROUGHT TO ITS ATTENTION UNDER THIS ARTICLE WILL BE SUBJECT TO THE PROVISIONS OF ARTICLES 11 AND 12;

ARTICLE 36   ARTICLES OF FEDERATION

1.   THE FEDERATION COUNCIL MAY, AT ANY STAGE OF A DISPUTE OF THE NATURE REFERRED TO IN ARTICLE 33 OR OF A SITUATION OF LIKE NATURE, RECOMMEND PRO-CEDURES OR APPROPRIATE METHODS OF ADJUSTMENT;

2.   THE FEDERATION COUNCIL SHALL TAKE INTO CONSIDERATION ANY PROCEDURES FOR THE SETTLEMENT OF THE DISPUTE WHICH HAVE ALREADY BEEN ADOPTED BY THE PARTIES;

3.   IN MAKING RECOMMENDATIONS UNDER THE ARTICLE THE FEDERATION COUNCIL SHOULD ALSO TAKE INTO CONSIDERATION THAT LEGAL DISPUTES SHOULD AS A GENERAL RULE BE REFERRED TO THE INTERPLANETARY SUPREME COURT OF JUSTICE IN ACCORDANCE WITH THE PROVISIONS OF THE STATUTE OF THE COURT;

ARTICLE 37

1.   SHOULD THE PARTIES TO A DISPUTE AS REFERRED TO IN ARTICLE 33 FAIL TO SETTLE IT BY MEANS INDICATED IN THAT ARTICLE, THEY SHALL REFER IT TO THE FEDERATION COUNCIL;

2.   IF THE FEDERATION COUNCIL DEEMS THAT THE CONTINUANCE OF THE DISPUTE IS IN FACT LIKELY TO ENDANGER THE MAINTENANCE OF INTERPLANETARY PEACE AND SECURITY, IT SHALL DECIDE WHETHER TO TAKE ACTION UNDER ARTICLE 36 OR TO RECOMMEND SUCH TERMS AS IT MAY CONSIDER APPROPRIATE;

ARTICLE 38

WITHOUT PREJUDICE TO THE PROVISIONS OF ARTICLES 33 TO 37, THE FEDERATION COUNCIL MAY, IF ALL THE PARTIES TO ANY DISPUTE SO REQUEST, MAKE RECOMMENDA-TIONS TO THE PARTIES WITH A VIEW TO A PACIFIC SETTLEMENT OF THE DISPUTE.

CHAPTER VII
ACTION WITH RESPECT TO THREATS TO THE PEACE,
BREACHES OF THE PEACE, AND ACTS OF AGGRESSION

ARTICLE 39

THE FEDERATION COUNCIL SHALL DETERMINE THE EXISTENCE OF ANY THREAT TO THE PEACE, BREACH OF THE PEACE, OR ACT OF AGRESSION AND SHALL MAKE RECOMMENDATIONS TO MAINTAIN OR RESTORE INTERPLANETARY PEACE AND SECURITY;

ARTICLE 40

IN ORDER TO PREVENT AGGRAVATION OF THE SITUATION, THE FEDERATION COUNCIL MAY CALL UPON THE PARTIES CONCERNED TO COMPLY WITH SUCH PROVISIONAL MEASURES AS IT DEEMS NECESSARY OR DESIRABLE. SUCH PROVISIONAL MEASURES SHALL BE WITH-OUT PREJUDICE TO THE RIGHTS, CLAIMS, OR POSITION OF THE PARTIES CONCERNED. THE FEDERATION COUNCIL SHALL TAKE INTO ACCOUNT ANY FAILURE TO COMPLY WITH SUCH PROVISIONAL MEASURES;

ARTICLE 41

THE FEDERATION COUNCIL MAY DECIDE WHAT MEASRUES SHORT OF THE USE OF ARMED FORCE ARE TO BE EMPLOYED TO GIVE EFFECT TO ITS DECISIONS, AND MAY CALL UPON THE MEMBERS OF THE UNITED FEDERATION TO APPLY SUCH MEASURES. THESE MAY INCLUDE PARTIAL OR COMPLETE INTERRUPTION OF ECONOMIC RELATIONS, INTER-PLANET RADIO AND SPACE TRAVEL, AND SEVERANCE OF DIPLOMATIC RELATIONS;

ARTICLE 42

SHOULD THE FEDERATION COUNCIL CONSIDER THAT MEASURES UNDER ARTICLE 41 WOULD BE INADEQUATE OR HAVE PROVED TO BE INADEQUATE, IT MAY TAKE SUCH ACTION BY ARMED FORCE AS NECESSARY TO MAINTAIN OR RESTORE INTERPLANETARY PEACE AND SECURITY. SUCH ACTION MAY INCLUDE DEMONSTRATIONS, BLOCKADES, AND OTHER OPERATIONS BY STAR FLEET COMBINED PEACE-KEEPING FORCES;

ARTICLE 43

ALL MEMBERS OF THE UNITED FEDERATION IN OBLIGATION TO THE MAINTENANCE OF INTERPLANETARY PEACE AND SECURITY, AGREE TO MAKE AVAILABLE TO STAR FLEET, ON

ARTICLES OF FEDERATION

CALL OF THE FEDERATION COUNCIL, ARMED FORCES, ASSISTANCE, AND FACILITIES, INCLUDING RIGHTS OF PASSAGE, NECESSARY FOR THE MAINTENANCE OF INTERPLANETARY PEACE AND SECURITY;

ARTICLE 44

WHEN THE FEDERATION COUNCIL HAS DECIDED TO USE FORCE IT SHALL, BEFORE CALLING UPON A MEMBER NOT REPRESENTED ON IT TO PROVIDE ARMED FORCES IN FUL-FILLMENT OF OBLIGATIONS ASSUMED UNDER ARTICLE 43, INVITE THAT MEMBER TO PARTICIPATE IN THE DECISIONS OF THE FEDERATION COUNCIL RELATING TO THE EMPLOYMENT OF CONTINGENTS OF THE MEMBER'S ARMED FORCES;

ARTICLE 45

IN ORDER TO ENABLE THE UNITED FEDERATION TO TAKE URGENT MILITARY MEAS-URES, ALL MEMBERS SO CAPABLE, SHALL ASSIGN CONTINGENTS OF THEIR ARMED FORCES TO STAR FLEET TO BE EMPLOYED AS A SINGLE PEACE-KEEPING FORCE OF THE UNITED FEDERATION OF PLANETS. ALL CONTINGENTS SO ASSIGNED, AND FOR THE DURATION OF THEIR ASSIGNMENT, SHALL HOLD FULL FAITH AND LOYALTY TO THE UNITED FEDERATION OF PLANETS AND THE PROTECTION OF THE PURPOSES AND PRINCIPLES OF THESE ARTI-CLES OF FEDERATION;

ARTICLE 46

PLANS FOR THE APPLICATION OF STAR FLEET ARMED FORCES SHALL BE MADE BY THE FEDERATION COUNCIL WITH THE ASSISTANCE OF THE MILITARY STAFF COMMITTEE OF STAR FLEET HEADQUARTERS;

ARTICLE 47

1.   THERE SHALL BE ESTABLISHED WITHIN STAR FLEET A MILITARY STAFF COMMITTEE TO ADVISE AND ASSIST THE FEDERATION COUNCIL ON ALL MATTERS RELATING TO THE UNITED FEDERATION'S MILITARY REQUIREMENTS FOR MAINTAINING INTERPLANETARY PEACE AND SECURITY;

2.   THE MILITARY STAFF COMMITTEE SHALL CONSIST OF THE CHIEFS OF STAFF OF THE PERMANENT MEMBERS OF THE FEDERATION COUNCIL, OR THEIR REPRESENTATIVES. ANY MEMBER OF THE UNITED FEDERATION MAY BE INVITED TO PROVIDE REPRESENTATION ON THE MILITARY STAFF COMMITTEE WHERE ITS RESPONSIBILITIES REQUIRES THE PARTICI-PATION OF THAT MEMBER IN ITS WORK;

3.   THE MILITARY STAFF COMMITTEE, WITH THE AUTHORIZATION OF THE FEDERATION COUNCIL, SHALL ESTABLISH A STAR FLEET AS THE ARMED, PEACE-KEEPING, FORCES OF THE UNITED FEDERATION OF PLANETS. IT SHALL BE RESPONSIBLE FOR THE ESTABLISH-MENT AND MAINTENANCE OF ALL FACILITIES OF STAR FLEET, INCLUDING ARMED SHIPS, STARBASES, AND TRAINING FACILITIES;

4.   THE MILITARY STAFF COMMITTEE SHALL BE RESPONSIBILE UNDER THE FEDERATION COUNCIL FOR THE STRATEGIC DIRECTION OF STAR FLEET ARMED FORCES, AND THE OTHER ARMED FORCES OF THE MEMBERS WHEN REQUIRED FOR THE MAINTENANCE OF INTER-PLANETARY PEACE AND SECURITY;

ARTICLE 48

THE ACTION REQUIRED TO CARRY OUT DECISIONS OF THE FEDERATION COUNCIL FOR THE MAINTENANCE OF INTERPLANETARY PEACE AND SECURITY SHALL BE TAKEN BY STAR FLEET, USING SUCH CONTINGENTS AS APPROPRIATE TO THE SPECIFIC ACTION;

ARTICLE 49

THE MEMBERS OF THE UNITED FEDERATION SHALL JOIN IN AFFORDING MUTUAL ASSISTANCE IN CARRYING OUT THE MEASURES DECIDED UPON BY THE FEDERATION COUNCIL AND IN ASSISTING STAR FLEET IN THE PERFORMANCE OF ITS DUTIES AND OBLIGATIONS;

ARTICLE 50

IF PREVENTIVE OR ENFORCEMENT MEASURES AGAINST ANY PLANET ARE TAKEN BY THE FEDERATION COUNCIL, ANY OTHER PLANET, WHETHER A MEMBER OF THE UNITED FEDERA-

ARTICLES OF FEDERATION

TION OR NOT, WHICH FINDS ITSELF CONFRONTED WITH SPECIAL ECONOMIC PROBLEMS ARISING FROM THE CARRYING OUT OF THESE MEASURES SHALL HAVE THE RIGHT TO CONSULT WITH THE FEDERATION COUNCIL WITH REGARD TO THE SOLUTION OF ITS PROBLEMS;

ARTICLE 51

NOTHING IN THESE ARTICLES OF FEDERATION SHALL IMPAIR THE INHERENT RIGHT OF INDIVIDUAL OR COLLECTIVE SELF-DEFENSE AGAINST ARMED ATTACKS OCCURRING TO MEMBERS OF THE UNITED FEDERATION, UNTIL THE FEDERATION COUNCIL HAS TAKEN MEASURES NECESSARY TO MAINTAIN INTERPLANETARY PEACE AND SECURITY, AND STAR FLEET FORCES CAN BE BROUGHT INTO ACTION. SUCH ACTIONS TAKEN BY MEMBERS OF THE UNITED FEDERATION IN THEIR SELF-DEFENSE SHALL BE IMMEDIATELY REPORTED TO THE FEDERATION COUNCIL.

CHAPTER VIII
STAR FLEET

ARTICLE 52

1. THERE IS ESTABLISHED A STAR FLEET AS THE ARMED PEACE-KEEPING FORCES OF THE UNITED FEDERATION OF PLANETS. IT SHALL INITIALLY BE COMPRISED OF CONTINGENTS ASSIGNED TO IT BY MEMBERS OF THE UNITED FEDERATION UNDER ARTICLE 43 UNTIL SUCH TIME AS FACILITIES, RECRUITMENT, AND TRAINING OBVIATES THE NECESSITY OF DRAWING UPON THE ARMAMENT OF ANY MEMBER, EXCEPT AS PROVIDED IN ARTICLE 49;

2. THE OPERATIONS AND ACTIONS OF STAR FLEET SHALL AT ALL TIMES BE UNDER THE DIRECT COGNIZANCE OF THE FEDERATION COUNCIL AND THE MILITARY STAFF COMMITTEE WHICH SHALL ALSO PREPARE AND APPROVE THE BUDGET FOR STAR FLEET OPERATIONS;

3. INITIAL EXPENDITURE IS AUTHORIZED UNDER THESE ARTICLES OF FEDERATION FOR THE ESTABLISHMENT OF A STAR FLEET HEADQUARTERS AND TWO STARBASES TO BE EQUITABLY LOCATED WITHIN THE BOUNDARY OF THE UNITED FEDERATION OF PLANETS AND OUTSIDE OF ANY POSSIBLE CONFLICT WITH THE TERRITORIAL BOUNDARIES OF ANY MEMBER OF THE UNITED FEDERATION. THE FEDERATION COUNCIL SHALL REVIEW AND APPROVE SUCH OTHER EXPANSIONS OF STARBASES AND OTHER FACILITIES AS SHALL SEEM APPROPRIATE FROM TIME TO TIME IN THE MAINTENANCE OF INTERPLANETARY PEACE AND SECURITY;

4. INITIAL EXPENDITURE IS ALSO GRANTED UNDER THESE ARITCLES OF FEDERATION FOR THE ESTABLISHMENT OF A STAR FLEET ACADEMY FOR THE PURPOSE OF TRAINING OFFICERS AND PERSONNEL FOR STAR FLEET DUTY. THE STANDARDS FOR TRAINING SUCH OFFICERS AND PERSONNEL SHALL BE DETERMINED BY THE MILITARY STAFF COMMITTEE AND APPROVED BY THE FEDERATION COUNCIL;

ARTICLE 53

1. INITIAL EXPENDITURE IS GRANTED UNDER THESE ARTICLES OF FEDERATION FOR THE DESIGN, PROCUREMENT, AND OPERATION OF FOURTEEN (14) HEAVY CRUISER TYPE OF STARSHIPS TO PROVIDE THE NUCLEUS OF STAR FLEET'S PEACE-KEEPING ARMED FORCES. THESE CRUISERS SHALL BE CAPABLE OF EXTENDED DURATION PATROL OF INTRA-GALACTIC RANGE, WITH WEAPONRY APPROPRIATE TO SUCH CLASS OF STARSHIPS. THEY SHALL BE PROVIDED WITH FIRE-POWER SUPERIOR TO THAT NOW EMPLOYED BY ANY MEMBER OF THE UNITED FEDERATION, AND APPROPRIATE TO THE TASKS EXPECTED OF THEM;

2. EXPENDITURE IS ALSO GRANTED UNDER THESE ARTICLES OF FEDERATION FOR THE PROCUREMENT OR CONSTRUCTION OF SUCH LESSER CLASSES OF SPACE FORCES AS SHALL BE REQUIRED TO SUPPORT STAR FLEET OPERATIONS AND THE HEAVY CRUISER CLASS OF STARSHIPS. THESE MAY BE, BUT NOT NECESSARILY LIMITED TO, TYPES SUCH AS SCOUTS, DESTROYERS, TRANSPORTS, RE-SUPPLY, SHUTTLECRAFT, AND SURVEY SHIPS;

ARTICLE 54

1. THE TRAINING OF BASE PERSONNEL AND SHIP COMPLEMENTS SHALL INCLUDE ALL FIELDS OF SCIENCE AND TECHNOLOGY AS WELL AS THE MILITARY ARTS IN STAR FLEET. IT IS THE INTENT OF THESE ARTICLES OF FEDERATION THAT STAR FLEET SHALL BE

ARTICLES OF FEDERATION

USED TO CONDUCT MISSIONS OF SCIENTIFIC EXPLORATION AND INVESTIGATION WITHIN THE TREATY EXPLORATION TERRITORY WHENEVER ITS SERVICES ARE NOT REQUIRED IN THE MAINTENANCE OF INTERPLANETARY PEACE AND SECURITY;

2.   STAR FLEET HEADQUARTERS AND THE FEDERATION COUNCIL SHALL BE AT ALL TIMES KEPT INFORMED OF THE ACTIVITIES UNDERTAKEN, OR CONTEMPLATED, FOR THE SCIENTIFIC EXPLORATION AND INVESTIGATION OF THE TREATY EXPLORATION TERRITORY.   ANY SHIP SO EMPLOYED SHALL BE DETACHED FROM MILITARY FLEET DUTY AND RE-ASSIGNED AS A NON-MILITARY SCIENTIFIC UNIT OF THE UNITED FEDERATION.

CHAPTER IX
INTERPLANETARY ECONOMIC
AND SOCIAL COOPERATION

ARTICLE 55

WITH A VIEW TO CREATING CONDITIONS OF STABILITY AND WELL-BEING WHICH ARE NECESSARY FOR PEACEFUL RELATIONS AMONG PLANETARY SOCIAL SYSTEMS BASED ON RESPECT FOR THE PRINCIPLES OF EQUAL RIGHTS AND SELF-DETERMINATION OF ALL INTELLIGENT LIFE-FORMS, THE UNITED FEDERATION OF PLANETS SHALL PROMOTE:

A)   HIGHER STANDARDS OF LIVING, FULL EMPLOYMENT, AND CONDITIONS OF ECONOMIC AND SOCIAL PROGRESS AND DEVELOPMENT;

B)   SOLUTION OF INTERPLANETARY ECONOMIC, SOCIAL, HEALTH, AND RELATED PROBLEMS; AND INTERPLANETARY CULTURAL AND EDUCATIONAL COOPERATION; AND

C)   UNIVERSAL RESPECT FOR, AND OBSERVANCE OF, INTELLIGENT LIFE-FORM RIGHTS AND FUNDAMENTAL FREEDOMS FOR ALL WITHOUT DISTINCTION AS TO CULTURE, SEX, LANGUAGE, OR RELIGION;

ARTICLE 56

ALL MEMBERS PLEDGE THEMSELVES TO TAKE JOINT AND SEPARATE ACTION IN COOPERATION WITH THE UNITED FEDERATION FOR THE ACHIEVEMENT OF THE PURPOSES AND GOALS SET FORTH IN ARTICLE 55;

ARTICLE 57

1.   THE VARIOUS SPECIALIZED AGENCIES, ESTABLISHED BY INTERPLANETARY AGREEMENT AND HAVING WIDE INTERPLANETARY RESPONSIBILITIES AS DEFINED IN THEIR BASIC INSTRUMENTS IN ECONOMIC, SOCIAL, CULTURAL, EDUCATIONAL, HEALTH, AND RELATED FIELDS, SHALL BE BROUGHT INTO RELATIONSHIP WITH THE UNITED FEDERATION IN ACCORDANCE WITH ARTICLE 63;

2.   SUCH AGENCIES THUS BROUGHT INTO RELATIONSHIP WITH THE UNITED FEDERATION ARE HEREAFTER REFERRED TO AS SPECIALIZED AGENCIES;

ARTICLE 58

THE UNITED FEDERATION SHALL MAKE RECOMMENDATIONS FOR THE COORDINATION OF THE POLICIES AND ACTIVITIES OF THE SPECIALIZED AGENCIES;

ARTICLE 59

THE UNITED FEDERATION SHALL, WHERE APPROPRIATE, INITIATE NEGOTIATIONS AMONG ITS MEMBERS CONCERNED FOR THE CREATION OF ANY NEW SPECIALIZED AGENCIES REQUIRED FOR THE ACCOMPLISHMENT OF THE PURPOSES SET FORTH IN ARTICLE 55;

ARTICLE 60

RESPONSIBILITY FOR THE DISCHARGE OF THE FUNCTIONS OF THE UNITED FEDERATION AS SET FORTH IN THIS CHAPTER SHALL BE VESTED IN THE SUPREME ASSEMBLY AND, UNDER THE AUTHORITY OF THE SUPOREME ASSEMBLY, IN THE ECONOMIC AND SOCIAL COUNCIL WHICH SHALL HAVE FOR THIS PURPOSE THE POWERS SET FORTH IN CHAPTER X.

CHAPTER X
THE ECONOMIC AND SOCIAL COUNCIL

ARTICLES OF FEDERATION

COMPOSITION
ARTICLE 61

1. THE ECONOMIC AND SOCIAL COUNCIL SHALL CONSIST OF EIGHTEEN (18) MEMBERS OF THE UNITED FEDERATION AS ELECTED BY THE SUPREME ASSEMBLY;

2. SUBJECT TO THE PROVISIONS OF PARAGRAPH 3, SIX (6) MEMBERS OF THE ECONOMIC AND SOCIAL COUNCIL SHALL BE ELECTED EACH SESSION PERIOD FOR A TERM OF THREE (3) SESSION PERIODS. A RETIRING MEMBER SHALL BE ELIGIBLE FOR IMMEDIATE RE-ELECTION;

3. AT THE FIRST ELECTION, EIGHTEEN (18) MEMBERS OF THE ECONOMIC AND SOCIAL COUNCIL SHALL BE CHOSEN, THE TERM OF OFFICE OF SIX (6) MEMBERS SO CHOSEN WILL EXPIRE AT THE END OF ONE (1) SESSION PERIOD, AND THE TERMS OF SIX (6) OTHER MEMBERS AT THE END OF TWO (2) SESSION PERIODS IN ACCORDANCE WITH ARRANGEMENTS MADE BY THE SUPREME ASSEMBLY;

4. EACH MEMBER OF THE ECONOMIC AND SOCIAL COUNCIL SHALL HAVE ONE (1) REPRE-SENTATIVE;

FUNCTIONS AND POWERS
ARTICLE 62

1. THE ECONOMIC AND SOCIAL COUNCIL MAY MAKE OR INITIATE STUDIES AND REPORTS WITH RESPECT TO INTERPLANETARY ECONOMIC, SOCIAL, CULTURAL, EDUCATIONAL, HEALTH, AND RELATED MATTERS AND MAY MAKE RECOMMENDATIONS WITH RESPECT TO ANY SUCH MATTERS TO THE SUPREME ASSEMBLY, TO THE MEMBERS OF THE UNITED FEDERATION, AND TO SPECIALIZED AGENCIES CONCERNED;

2. IT MAY MAKE RECOMMENDATIONS FOR THE PURPOSE OF PROMOTING RESPECT FOR, AND OBSERVANCE OF, INTELLIGENT LIFE-FORM RIGHTS AND FUNDAMENTAL FREEDOMS FOR ALL;

3. IT MAY PREPARE DRAFT INSTRUMENTS WITH THE RULES PRESCRIBED BY THE UNITED FEDERATION;

4. IT MAY PREPARE DRAFT INSTRUMENTS FOR ADMISSION TO THE SUPREME ASSEMBLY, WITH RESPECT TO MATTERS FALLING WITHIN ITS COMPETENCE;

5. IT MAY CALL, IN ACCORDANCE WITH THE RULES PRESCRIBED BY THE UNITED FEDERA-TION, INTERPLANETARY CONFERENCES ON MATTERS FALLING WITHIN ITS COMPETENCE;

ARTICLE 63

1. THE ECONOMIC AND SOCIAL COUNCIL MAY ENTER INTO AGREEMENTS WITH ANY OF ITS AGENCIES REFERRED TO IN ARTICLE 57, DEFINING THE TERMS ON WHICH THE AGENCY CONCERNED SHALL BE BROUGHT INTO RELATIONSHIP WITH THE UNITED FEDERATION. SUCH AGREEMENTS SHALL BE SUBJECT TO APPROVAL BY THE SUPREME ASSEMBLY;

2. IT MAY COORDINATE THE ACITIVITIES OF THE SPECIALIZED AGENCIES THROUGH CON-SULTATION WITH AND RECOMMENDATIONS TO SUCH AGENCIES AND THROUGH RECOMMENDA-TIONS TO THE SUPREME ASSEMBLY AND TO THE MEMBERS OF THE UNITED FEDERATION;

ARTICLE 64

THE ECONOMIC AND SOCIAL COUNCIL MAY TAKE APPROPRIATE STEPS TO OBTAIN REPORTS FROM THE SPECIALIZED AGENCIES. IT MAY MAKE ARRANGEMENTS WITH THE MEMBERS OF THE UNITED FEDERATION AND WITH THE SPECIALIZED AGENCIES TO OBTAIN REPORTS ON THE STEPS TAKEN TO GIVE EFFECT TO ITS OWN RECOMMENDATIONS AND TO RECOMMENDATIONS ON MATTER FALLING WITHIN ITS COMPETENCE BY THE SUPREME ASSEMBLY;

ARTICLE 65

THE ECONOMIC AND SOCIAL COUNCIL MAY FURNISH INFORMATION TO THE FEDERATION COUNCIL AND SHALL ASSIST THE FEDERATION COUNCIL UPON ITS REQUEST;

ARTICLE 66

1. THE ECONOMIC AND SOCIAL COUNCIL SHALL PERFORM SUCH FUNCTIONS AS FALL

ARTICLES OF FEDERATION

WITHIN ITS COMPETENCE IN CONNECTION WITH THE CARRYING OUT OF THE RECOMMENDA-
TIONS OF THE SUPREME ASSEMBLY;

2. IT MAY, WITH THE APPROVAL OF THE SUPREME ASSEMBLY, PERFORM SERVICES AT
THE REQUEST OF MEMBERS OF THE UNITED FEDERATION AND AT THE REQUEST OF SPECIAL-
IZED AGENCIES;

3. IT SHALL PERFORM SUCH OTHER FUNCTIONS AS ARE SPECIFIED ELSEWHERE IN THESE
ARTICLES OF FEDERATION OR AS MAY BE ASSIGNED TO IT BY THE SUPREME ASSEMBLY;

VOTING
ARTICLE 67

1. EACH MEMBER OF THE ECONOMIC AND SOCIAL COUNCIL SHALL HAVE ONE VOTE;

2. DECISIONS OF THE ECONOMIC AND SOCIAL COUNCIL SHALL BE MADE BY A MAJORITY
OF THE MEMBERS PRESENT AND VOTING;

PROCEDURES
ARTICLE 68

    THE ECONOMIC AND SOCIAL COUNCIL SHALL SET UP COMMISSIONS IN ECONOMIC AND
SOCIAL FIELDS AND FOR THE PROMOTION OF INTELLIGENT LIFE-FORM RIGHTS, AND SUCH
OTHER COMMISSIONS AS MAY BE REQUIRED FOR THE PERFORMANCE OF ITS FUNCTIONS;

ARTICLE 69

    THE ECONOMIC AND SOCIAL COUNCIL SHALL INVITE ANY MEMBER OF THE UNITED
FEDERATION TO PARTICIPATE, WITHOUT VOTE, IN ITS DELIBERATIONS ON ANY MATTER
OF PARTICULAR CONCERN TO THAT MEMBER;

ARTICLE 70

    THE ECONOMIC AND SOCIAL COUNCIL MAY MAKE ARRANGEMENTS FOR REPRESENTATIVES
OF THE SPECIALIZED AGENCIES TO PARTICIPATE, WITHOUT VOTE, IN ITS DELIBERATIONS
AND IN THOSE COMMISSIONS ESTABLISHED BY IT, AND FOR ITS REPRESENTATIVES TO
PARTICIPATE IN THE DELIBERATIONS OF THE SPECIALIZED AGENCIES;

ARTICLE 71

    THE ECONOMIC AND SOCIAL COUNCIL MAY MAKE SUITABLE ARRANGEMENTS FOR CON-
SULTATION WITH NON-GOVERNMENTAL INTRA-PLANET ORGANIZATIONS WHICH ARE CONCERN-
ED WITH MATTERS WITHIN ITS COMPETENCE. SUCH ARRANGEMENTS MAY BE MADE WITH
INTERPLANETARY ORGANIZATIONS AND, WHERE APPROPRIATE, WITH PLANETARY ORGANIZA-
TIONS AFTER CONSULTATION WITH MEMBERS OF THE UNITED FEDERATION CONCERNED;

ARTICLE 72

1. THE ECONOMIC AND SOCIAL COUNCIL SHALL ADOPT ITS OWN RULES OF PROCEDURE,
INCLUDING THE METHOD OF SELECTING ITS DIRECTOR;

2. THE ECONOMIC AND SOCIAL COUNCIL SHALL MEET AS REQUIRED IN ACCORDANCE WITH
ITS RULES, WHICH SHALL INCLUDE PROVISION FOR THE CONVENING OF MEETINGS ON THE
REQUEST OF A MAJORITY OF ITS MEMBERS.

CHAPTER XI
DECLARATION REGARDING NON-
SELF-GOVERNING REGIONS

ARTICLE 73

    MEMBERS OF THE UNITED FEDERATION WHICH HAVE ASSUMED RESPONSIBILITIES FOR
THE ADMINISTRATION OF REGIONS WHOSE INTELLIGENT LIFE-FORMS HAVE NOT YET
ATTAINED A FULL MEASURE OF SELF-GOVERNMENT RECOGNIZE THE PRINCIPLE THAT THE
INTERESTS OF THE INHABITANTS OF THESE REGIONS ARE PARAMOUNT, AND ACCEPT AS A
SACRED TRUST THE OBLIGATION TO PROMOTE TO THE UTMOST, WITHIN THE SYSTEM OF
INTERPLANETARY PEACE AND SECURITY ESTABLISHED BY THESE ARTICLES OF FEDERATION,
THE WELL-BEING OF THE INHABITANTS OF THESE REGIONS, AND, TO THIS END:

    A) TO ENSURE, WITH DUE RESPECT FOR THE CULTURES OF THE INTELLIGENT LIFE-

ARTICLES OF FEDERATION

FORMS CONCERNED, THEIR POLITICAL, ECONOMIC, SOCIAL, AND EDUCATIONAL ADVANCEMENT, THEIR JUST TREATMENT, AND THEIR PROTECTION AGAINST ABUSES;

B) TO DEVELOP SELF-GOVERNMENT, TO TAKE DUE ACCOUNT OF THE POLITICAL ASPIRATIONS OF THE INTELLIGENT LIFE-FORMS, AND TO ASSIST THEM IN THE PROGRESSIVE DEVELOPMENT OF THEIR FREE POLITICAL INSTITUTIONS, ACCORDING TO THE PARTICULAR CIRCUMSTANCES OF EACH REGION AND ITS INTELLIGENT LIFE-FORMS AND THEIR VARYING STAGES OF ADVANCEMENT;

C) TO FURTHER INTERPLANETARY PEACE AND SECURITY;

D) TO PROMOTE CONSTRUCTIVE MEASURES OF DEVELOPMENT, TO ENCOURAGE RE-SEARCH, AND TO COOPERATE WITH ONE-ANOTHER AND, WHEN AND WHERE APPROPRIATE, WITH SPECIALIZED INTERPLANETARY BODIES WITH A VIEW TO THE PRACTICAL ACHIEVEMENT OF THE SOCIAL, ECONOMIC, AND SCIENTIFIC PURPOSES SET FORTH IN THIS ARTICLE; AND

E) TO TRANSMIT REGULARLY TO THE SUPREME-SECRETARIAT FOR INFORMATION PURPOSES, SUBJECT TO SUCH LIMITATIONS AS SECURITY AND STATUTORY CONSIDERATIONS MAY REQUIRE, STATISTICAL AND OTHER INFORMATION OF A TECHNICAL NATURE RELATING TO ECONOMIC, SOCIAL, AND EDUCATIONAL CONDITIONS IN THE REGIONS FOR WHICH THEY ARE RESPECTIVELY RESPONSI-BLE OTHER THAN THOSE REGIONS TO WHICH CHAPTER XII AND XIII APPLY;

ARTICLE 74

MEMBERS OF THE UNITED FEDERATION ALSO AGREE THAT THEIR POLICY IN RESPECT OF THE REGIONS TO WHICH THIS CHAPTER APPLIES, NO LESS THAN IN RESPECT OF THEIR METROPLOITAN AREAS, MUST BE BASED ON THE GENERAL PRINCIPLE OF GOOD-NEIGHBORLINESS, DUE ACCOUNT BEING TAKEN OF THE INTERESTS AND WELL-BEING OF THE REST OF THE FEDERATION TERRITORY IN SOCIAL, ECONOMIC, AND COMMERICIAL MATTERS.

CHAPTER XII
INTERPLANETARY TRUSTEESHIP SYSTEM

ARTICLE 75

THE UNITED FEDERATION SHALL ESTABLISH UNDER ITS AUTHORITY AN INTERPLANET-ARY TRUSTEESHIP SYSTEM FOR THE ADMINISTRATION AND SUPERVISION OF SUCH REGIONS AS MAY BE PLACED THEREUNDER BY SUBSEQUENT INIDIVIDUAL AGREEMENTS. THESE REGIONS ARE HEREINAFTER REFERRED TO AS TRUST REGIONS;

ARTICLE 76

THE BASIC OBJECTIVES OF THE TRUSTEESHIP SYSTEM, IN ACCORDANCE WITH THE PURPOSES AND PRINCIPLES OF THE UNITED FEDERATION AS LAID DOWN IN THESE ARTICLES OF FEDERATION, SHALL BE:

A) TO FURTHER INTERPLANETARY PEACE AND SECURITY;

B) TO PROMOTE THE POLITICAL, ECONOMIC, SOCIAL, AND EDUCATIONAL ADVANCE-MENT OF THE INHABITANTS OF THE TRUST REGIONS, AND THEIR PROGRESSIVE DEVELOPMENT TOWARDS SELF-GOVERNMENT OR INDEPENDENCE AS MAY BE APPRO-PRIATE TO THE PARTICULAR CIRCUMSTANCES OF EACH REGION AND ITS INTELLI-GENT LIFE-FORMS CONCERNED, AND AS MAY BE PROVIDED BY THE TERMS OF THE TRUSTEESHIP AGREEMENT;

C) TO ENCOURAGE RESPECT FOR INTELLIGENT LIFE-FORM RIGHTS AND FOR FUNDA-MENTAL FREEDOMS FOR ALL WITHOUT DISTINCTION AS TO CULTURE, SEX, LANGUAGE, OR RELIGION, AND TO ENCOURAGE RECOGNITION OF THE INTER-DEPENDENCE OF THE INTELLIGENT LIFE-FORMS OF THE GALAXY; AND

D) TO ENSURE EQUAL TREATMENT IN SOCIAL, ECONOMIC, AND COMMERCIAL MATTERS FOR ALL MEMBERS OF THE UNITED FEDERATION AND THEIR NATIONALS, AND ALSO

ARTICLES OF FEDERATION

EQUAL TREATMENT FOR THE LATTER IN THE ADMINISTRATION OF JUSTICE, WITH-
OUT PREJUDICE TO THE ADJUSTMENT OF THE FOREGOING OBJECTIVES AND SUB-
JECT TO THE PROVISIONS OF ARTICLE 80;

ARTICLE 77

1.   THE TRUSTEESHIP SYSTEM SHALL APPLY TO SUCH REGIONS IN THE FOLLOWING CATE-
GORIES AS MAY BE PLACED THEREUNDER BY MEANS OF TRUSTEESHIP AGREEMENTS:

   A)   REGIONS NOW HELD UNDER MANDATE;

   B)   REGIONS WHICH MAY BE DETACHED FROM ALIEN SOCIAL SYSTEMS AS A RESULT OF
        INTERPLANETARY WAR; AND

   C)   REGIONS VOLUNTARILY PLACED UNDER THE TRUSTEESHIP SYSTEM BY SOCIAL
        SYSTEMS RESPONSIBLE FOR THEIR ADMINISTRATION;

2.   IT WILL BE A MATTER FOR SUBSEQUENT AGREEMENT AS TO WHICH REGIONS IN THE
FOREGOING CATEGORIES WILL BE BROUGHT UNDER THE TRUSTEESHIP SYSTEM AND UPON
WHAT TERMS;

ARTICLE 78

   THE TRUSTEESHIP SYSTEM SHALL NOT APPLY TO REGIONS WHICH HAVE BECOME MEM-
BERS OF THE UNITED FEDERATION OF PLANETS, RELATIONSHIP AMONG WHICH SHALL BE
BASED ON THE RESPECT FOR THE PRINCIPLE OF SOVERIEGN EQUALITY;

ARTICLE 79

   THE TERMS OF TRUSTEESHIP FOR EACH REGION TO BE PLACED UNDER THE TRUSTEE-
SHIP SYSTEM, INCLUDING ANY ALTERATION OR AMENDMENT, SHALL BE AGREED UPON BY
THE SOCIAL SYSTEMS DIRECTLY CONCERNED, INCLUDING THE MANDATORY POWER IN THE
CASE OF REGIONS HELD UNDER MANDATE BY A MEMBER OF THE UNITED FEDERATION, AND
SHALL BE APPROVED AS PROVIDED FOR IN ARTICLES 83 AND 85;

ARTICLE 80

1.   EXCEPT AS MAY BE AGREED UPON IN INDIVIDUAL TRUSTEESHIP AGREEMENTS, MADE
UNDER ARTICLES 77, 79, AND 81, PLACING EACH REGION UNDER THE TRUSTEESHIP SYS-
TEM, AND UNTIL SUCH AGREEMENTS HAVE BEEN CONCLUDED, NOTHING IN THIS CHAPTER
SHALL BE CONSTRUED IN OR OF ITSELF TO ALTER IN ANY MANNER THE RIGHTS WHATSO-
EVER OF ANY SOCIAL SYSTEMS OR ANY INTELLIGENT LIFE-FORMS OR THE TERMS OF
EXISTING AGREEMENTS TO WHICH MEMBERS OF THE UNITED FEDERATION MAY RESPECTIVE-
LY BE PARTIES;

2.   PARAGRAPH 1 OF THIS ARTICLE SHALL NOT BE INTERPRETED AS GIVING GROUNDS
FOR DELAY OR POSTPONEMENT OF THE NEGOTIATION AND CONCLUSION OF AGREEMENTS FOR
PLACING MANDATED AND OTHER REGIONS UNDER THE TRUSTEESHIP SYSTEM AS PROVIDED
FOR IN ARTICLE 77;

ARTICLE 81

   THE TRUSTEESHIP AGREEMENT SHALL IN EACH CASE INCLUDE THE TERMS UNDER WHICH
THE TRUST REGION WILL BE ADMINISTERED AND DESIGNATE THE AUTHORITY WHICH WILL
BE EXERCISING THE ADMINISTRATION OF THE TRUST REGION.   SUCH AUTHORITY HEREIN-
AFTER CALLED THE ADMINISTERING AUTHORITY, MAY BE ONE OR MORE SOCIAL SYSTEMS
OF THE UNITED FEDERATION ITSELF;

ARTICLE 82

   THERE MAY BE DESIGNATED, IN THE TRUSTEESHIP AGREEMENT, A STRATEGIC AREA
OR AREAS WHICH MAY INCLUDE PART OR ALL OF THE TRUST REGION TO WHICH THE AGREE-
MENT APPLIES, WITHOUT PREJUDICE TO ANY SPECIAL AGREEMENT OR AGREEMENTS MADE
UNDER ARTICLE 43;

ARTICLE 83

1.   ALL FUNCTIONS OF THE UNITED FEDERATION RELATING TO STRATEGIC AREAS, IN-

ARTICLES OF FEDERATION

CLUDING THE APPROVAL OF THE TERMS OF THE TRUSTEESHIP AGREEMENTS AND OF THEIR SUBSEQUENT ALTERATION OR AMENDMENT, SHALL BE EXERCISED BY THE FEDERATION COUNCIL;

2. THE BASIC PRINCIPLES SET FORTH IN ARTICLE 76 SHALL APPLY TO THE INTELLIGENT LIFE-FORMS OF EACH STRATEGIC AREA;

3. THE FEDERATION COUNCIL SHALL, SUBJECT TO THE PROVISIONS OF THE TRUSTEESHIP AGREEMENTS AND WITHOUT PREJUDICE TO SECURITY CONSIDERATIONS, AVAIL ITSELF OF THE ASSISTANCE OF THE TRUSTEESHIP COUNCIL TO PERFORM THOSE FUNCTIONS OF THE UNITED FEDERATION UNDER THE TRUSTEESHIP SYSTEM RELATING TO POLITICAL, ECONOMIC, SOCIAL, AND EDUCATIONAL MATTERS IN THE STRATEGIC AREAS;

ARTICLE 84

IT SHALL BE THE DUTY OF THE ADMINISTERING AUTHORITY TO ENSURE THAT THE TRUST REGION SHALL PLAY ITS PART IN THE MAINTENANCE OF INTERPLANETARY PEACE AND SECURITY. TO THIS END THE ADMINISTERING AUTHORITY MAY MAKE USE OF VOLUNTEER FORCES, FACILITIES, AND ASSISTANCE FROM THE TRUST REGION IN CARRYING OUT THE OBLIGATIONS TOWARDS THE FEDERATION COUNCIL UNDERTAKEN IN THIS REGARD BY THE ADMINISTERING AUTHORITY, AS WELL AS FOR THE LOCAL DEFENSE AND THE MAINTENANCE OF LAW AND ORDER WITHIN THE TRUST REGION;

ARTICLE 85

1. THE FUNCTIONS OF THE UNITED FEDERATION WITH REGARD TO TRUSTEESHIP AGREEMENTS FOR ALL REGIONS NOT DESIGNATED AS STRATEGIC, INCLUDING THE APPROVAL OF THE TERMS OF THE TRUSTEESHIP AGREEMENTS AND THEIR ALTERATION OR AMENDMENT, SHALL BE EXERCISED BY THE SUPREME ASSEMBLY;

2. THE TRUSTEESHIP COUNCIL, OPERATING UNDER THE AUTHORITY OF THE SUPREME ASSEMBLY, SHALL ASSIST THE SUPREME ASSEMBLY IN CARRYING OUT THESE FUNCTIONS.

CHAPTER XIII
THE TRUSTEESHIP COUNCIL

COMPOSITION
ARTICLE 86

1. THE TRUSTEESHIP COUNCIL SHALL CONSIST OF THE FOLLOWING MEMBERS OF THE UNITED FEDERATION:

  A) THOSE MEMBERS ADMINISTERING TRUST REGIONS;

  B) SUCH OF THOSE MEMBERS MENTIONED BY NAME IN ARTICLE 23 AS ARE NOT ADMINISTERING TRUST REGIONS; AND

  C) AS MANY OTHER MEMBERS ELECTED FOR THREE (3) SESSION PERIODS BY THE SUPREME ASSEMBLY AS MAY BE NECESSARY TO ENSURE THAT THE TOTAL NUMBER OF MEMBERS OF THE TRUSTEESHIP COUNCIL IS EQUALLY DIVIDED BETWEEN THOSE MEMBERS OF THE UNITED FEDERATION WHICH ADMINISTER TRUST REGIONS AND THOSE WHICH DO NOT;

2. EACH MEMBER OF THE TRUSTEESHIP COUNCIL SHALL DESIGNATE ONE (1) SPECIALLY QUALIFIED INTELLIGENT LIFE-FORM TO REPRESENT IT THEREIN;

FUNCTIONS AND POWERS
ARTICLE 87

THE SUPREME ASSEMBLY AND, UNDER ITS AUTHORITY, THE TRUSTEESHIP COUNCIL, IN CARRYING OUT THEIR FUNCTIONS, MAY:

  A) CONSIDER REPORTS SUBMITTED BY THE ADMINISTERING AUTHORITY;

  B) ACCEPT PETITIONS AND EXAMINE THEM IN CONSULTATION WITH THE ADMINISTERING AUTHORITY;

  C) PROVIDE FOR PERIODIC VISITS TO THE RESPECTIVE TRUST REGIONS AT TIMES AGREED UPON WITH THE ADMINISTERING AUTHORITY; AND

ARTICLES OF FEDERATION

D) TAKE THESE AND OTHER ACTIONS IN CONFORMITY WITH THE TERMS OF THE TRUSTEESHIP AGREEMENTS;

ARTICLE 88

THE TRUSTEESHIP COUNCIL SHALL FORMULATE A QUESTIONAIRE ON THE POLITICAL, ECONOMIC, SOCIAL, AND EDUCATIONAL ADVANCEMENT OF THE INHABITANTS OF EACH TRUST REGION, AND THE ADMINISTERING AUTHORITY FOR EACH TRUST REGION WITHIN THE COMPETENCE OF THE SUPREME ASSEMBLY SHALL MAKE A PERIODIC REPORT TO THE SUPREME ASSEMBLY UPON THE BASIS OF SUCH QUESTIONAIRE;

VOTING
ARTICLE 89

1. EACH MEMBER OF THE TRUSTEESHIP COUNCIL SHALL HAVE ONE VOTE;

2. DECISIONS OF THE TRUSTEESHIP COUNCIL SHALL BE MADE BY A MAJORITY OF THE MEMBERS PRESENT AND VOTING;

PROCEDURE
ARTICLE 90

1. THE TRUSTEESHIP COUNCIL SHALL ADOPT ITS OWN RULES OF PROCEDURE, INCLUD-ING THE METHOD OF SELECTING ITS DIRECTOR;

2. THE TRUSTEESHIP COUNCIL SHALL MEET AS REQUIRED IN ACCORDANCE WITH ITS RULES WHICH SHALL INCLUDE PROVISION FOR THE CONVENING OF MEETINGS ON THE REQUEST OF A MAJORITY OF ITS MEMBERS;

ARTICLE 91

THE TRUSTEESHIP COUNCIL SHALL, WHEN APPROPRIATE, AVAIL ITSELF OF THE ASSISTANCE OF THE ECONOMIC AND SOCIAL COUNCIL AND OF THE SPECIALIZED AGENCIES IN REGARD TO MATTERS WITH WHICH THEY ARE RESPECTIVELY CONCERNED.

CHAPTER XIV
.THE INTERPLANETARY SUPREME
COURT OF JUSTICE

ARTICLE 92

THE INTERPLANETARY SUPREME COURT OF JUSTICE SHALL BE THE PRINCIPAL JUDICIAL INSTRUMENT OF THE UNITED FEDERATION OF PLANETS. IT SHALL FUNCTION IN ACCORDANCE WITH THE APPENDED STATUTE, WHICH IS BASED UPON THE STATUTE OF THE TRIBUNALS OF ALPHA III, AND FORMS AN INTEGRAL PART OF THESE ARTICLES OF FEDERATION;

ARTICLE 93

1. ALL MEMBERS OF THE UNITED FEDERATION ARE 'IPSO FACTO' PARTIES TO THE STATUTE OF THE INTERPLANETARY SUPREME COURT OF JUSTICE;

2. A SOCIAL SYSTEM WHICH IS NOT A MEMBER OF THE UNITED FEDERATION MAY BECOME A PARTY TO THE STATUTE OF THE INTERPLANETARY SUPREME COURT OF JUSTICE ON CONDITIONS TO BE DETERMINED IN EACH CASE BY THE SUPREME ASSEMBLY UPON THE RECOMMENDATION OF THE FEDERATION COUNCIL;

ARTICLE 94

1. EACH MEMBER OF THE UNITED FEDERATION UNDERTAKES TO COMPLY WITH THE DECI-SION OF THE INTERPLANETARY SUPREME COURT OF JUSTICE IN ANY CASE TO WHICH IT IS A PARTY;

2. IF ANY PARTY TO A CASE FAILS TO PERFORM THE OBLIGATIONS INCUMBENT UPON IT UNDER A JUDGEMENT RENDERED BY THE COURT, THE OTHER PARTY MAY HAVE RECOURSE TO THE FEDERATION COUNCIL, WHICH MAY, IF IT DEEMS NECESSARY, MAKE RECOMMENDATIONS OR DECIDE UPON MEASURES TO BE TAKEN TO GIVE EFFECT TO THE JUDGEMENT;

ARTICLE 95

NOTHING IN THESE ARTICLES OF FEDERATION SHALL PREVENT MEMBERS OF THE

ARTICLES OF FEDERATION

UNITED FEDERATION OF PLANETS FROM ENTRUSTING THE SOLUTION OF THEIR DIFFER-
ENCES TO OTHER TRIBUNALS BY VIRTUE OF AGREEMENTS ALREADY IN EXISTENCE OR
WHICH MAY BE CONCLUDED IN THE FUTURE;

ARTICLE 96

1.   THE SUPREME ASSEMBLY OR THE FEDERATION COUNCIL MAY REQUEST THE INTERPLANET-
ARY SUPREME COURT OF JUSTICE TO GIVE AN ADVISORY OPINION ON ANY LEGAL QUESTION;

2.   OTHER BODIES OF THE UNITED FEDERATION AND THE SPECIALIZED AGENCIES, WHICH
MAY AT ANY TIME BE SO AUTHORIZED BY THE SUPREME ASSEMBLY, MAY ALSO REQUEST
ADVISORY OPINIONS OF THE COURT ON LEGAL QUESTIONS ARISING WITHIN THE SCOPE OF
THEIR ACTIVITIES.

CHAPTER XV
THE SUPREME-SECRETARIAT

ARTICLE 97

     THE SECRETARIAT SHALL BE COMPRISED OF A SUPREME-SECRETARIAT AND SUCH STAFF
AS THE UNITED FEDERATION MAY REQUIRE.   THE SUPREME-SECRETRAIAT SHALL BE
APPOINTED BY THE SUPREME ASSEMBLY UPON THE RECOMMENDATION OF THE FEDERATION
COUNCIL, AND SHALL BE THE CHIEF ADMINISTRATIVE OFFICER OF THE UNITED FEDERATION;

ARTICLE 98

     THE SUPREME-SECRETARIAT SHALL ACT IN THAT CAPACITY IN ALL MEETINGS OF THE
SUPREME ASSEMBLY, OF THE FEDERATION COUNCIL, OF THE ECONOMIC AND SOCIAL
COUNCIL, AND OF THE TRUSTEESHIP COUNCIL, AND SHALL PERFORM SUCH OTHER FUNCTIONS
AS ARE ENTRUSTED TO THE SECRETARIAT BY THESE BODIES.   THE SUPREME-SECRETARIAT
SHALL MAKE A PERIODIC REPORT TO THE SUPREME ASSEMBLY ON THE WORK OF THE
UNITED FEDERATION OF PLANETS;

ARTICLE 99

     THE SUPREME-SECRETARIAT MAY BRING TO THE ATTENTION OF THE FEDERATION
COUNCIL ANY MATTER WHICH IN HIS OPINION MAY THREATEN THE MAINTENANCE OF INTER-
PLANETARY PEACE AND SECURITY;

ARTICLE 100

1.   IN THE PERFORMANCE OF THEIR DUTIES THE SUPREME-SECRETARIAT AND THE STAFF
SHALL NOT SEEK OR RECEIVE INSTRUCTIONS FROM ANY GOVERNMENT OR FROM ANY OTHER
AUTHORITY EXTERNAL TO THE UNITED FEDERATION OF PLANETS.   THEY SHALL REFRAIN
FROM ANY ACTION WHICH MIGHT REFLECT ON THEIR POSITIONS AS INTERPLANETARY
OFFICIALS RESPONSIBLE ONLY TO THE UNITED FEDERATION;

2.   EACH MEMBER OF THE UNITED FEDERATION UNDERTAKES TO RESPECT THE EXCLUSIVE-
LY INTERPLANETARY CHARACTER OF THE RESPONSIBILITIES OF THE SUPREME-SECRETARIAT
AND THE STAFF AND SHALL NOT SEEK TO INFLUENCE THEM IN THE DISCHARGE OF THEIR
RESPONSIBILITIES;

ARTICLE 101

1.   THE STAFF SHALL BE APPOINTED BY THE SUPREME-SECRETARIAT UNDER REGULATIONS
ESTABLISHED BY THE SUPREME ASSEMBLY;

2.   APPROPRIATE STAFFS SHALL BE PERMANENTLY ASSIGNED TO THE ECONOMIC AND
SOCIAL COUNCIL, THE TRUSTEESHIP COUNCIL, AND, AS REQUIRED, TO OTHER BODIES OF
THE UNITED FEDERATION.   THESE STAFFS SHALL FORM A PART OF THE SECRETARIAT;

3.   THE PARAMOUNT CONSIDERATION IN THE EMPLOYMENT OF THE STAFF AND IN THE
DETERMINATION OF THE CONDITIONS OF SERVICE SHALL BE THE NECESSITY OF SECURING
THE HIGHEST STANDARDS OF EFFICIENCY, COMPETENCE, AND INTEGRITY.   DUE REGARD
SHALL BE PAID TO THE IMPORTANCE OF RECRUITING THE STAFF ON AS WIDE A GEO-
GALACTICAL BASIS AS POSSIBLE.

CHAPTER XVI
MISCELANEOUS PROVISIONS

ARTICLES OF FEDERATION

ARTICLE 102

1. EVERY TREATY AND EVERY INTERPLANETARY AGREEMENT ENTERED INTO BY ANY MEMBER OF THE UNITED FEDERATION AFTER THESE ARTICLES OF FEDERATION COME INTO FORCE SHALL AS SOON AS POSSIBLE BE REGISTERED WITH THE SUPREME-SECRETARIAT AND PUBLISHED BY HIM;

2. NO PARTY TO ANY SUCH TREATY OR INTERPLANETARY AGREEMENT WHICH HAS NOT BEEN REGISTERED IN ACCORDANCE WITH THE PROVISIONS OF PARAGRAPH 1 OF THIS ARTICLE MAY INVOKE THAT TREATY OR AGREEMENT BEFORE ANY BODY OF THE UNITED FEDERATION;

ARTICLE 103

IN THE EVENT OF A CONFLICT BETWEEN THE OBLIGATIONS OF THE MEMBERS OF THE UNITED FEDERATION UNDER THESE ARTICLES OF FEDERATION AND THEIR OBLIGATIONS UNDER ANY OTHER INTERPLANETARY AGREEMENT, THEIR OBLIGATIONS UNDER THESE ARTI-CLES OF FEDERATION SHALL PREVAIL;

ARTICLE 104

THE UNITED FEDERATION SHALL ENJOY IN THE TERRITORY OF EACH OF ITS MEMBERS SUCH LEGAL CAPACITY AS MAY BE NECESSARY FOR THE EXERCISE OF ITS FUNCTIONS AND THE FULFILLMENT OF ITS PURPOSES;

ARTICLE 105

1. THE UNITED FEDERATION SHALL ENJOY IN THE TERRITORY OF EACH OF ITS MEMBERS SUCH PRIVILEGES AND IMMUNITIES AS ARE NECESSARY FOR THE FULFILLMENT OF ITS PURPOSES;

2. REPRESENTATIVES OF THE MEMBERS OF THE UNITED FEDERATION AND OFFICIALS OF THE ORGANIZATION SHALL SIMILARLY ENJOY SUCH PRIVILEGES AND IMMUNITIES AS ARE NECESSARY FOR THE INDEPENDENT EXERCISE OF THEIR FUNCTIONS IN CONNECTION WITH THE ORGANIZATION;

3. THE SUPREME ASSEMBLY MAY MAKE RECOMMENDATIONS WITH A VIEW TO DETERMINING THE DETAILS OF THE APPLICATION OF PARAGRAPHS 1 AND 2 OF THIS ARTICLE OR MAY PROPOSE CONVENTIONS TO THE MEMBERS OF THE UNITED FEDERATION FOR THIS PURPOSE.

CHAPTER XVII
TRANSITORY SECURITY ARRANGEMENTS

ARTICLE 106

1. PENDING THE COMING INTO FULL FORCE OF SUCH SPECIAL AGREEMENTS REFERRED TO IN ARTICLE 43 AS IN THE OPINION OF THE FEDERATION COUNCIL ENABLE IT TO BEGIN THE EXERCISE OF ITS RESPONSIBILITIES UNDER ARTICLE 42, THE PARTIES TO THE DECLARATION OF THE UNITED FEDERATION SHALL CONSULT WITH ONE ANOTHER AND THE OTHER MEMBERS OF THE UNITED FEDERATION WITH A VIEW TO SUCH JOINT ACTION ON BEHALF OF THE ORGANIZATION AS MAY BE NECESSARY FOR THE PURPOSE OF MAINTAINING INTERPLANETARY PEACE AND SECURITY;

2. NOTHING IN THESE ARTICLES OF FEDERATION SHALL INVALIDATE OR PRECLUDE ACTION IN RELATION TO ANY SOCIAL SYSTEM WHICH HAS BEEN AN ADVERSARY OF ANY SIGNATORY TO THESE ARTICLES OF FEDERATION, TAKEN OR AUTHORIZED AS A RESULT OF THAT WAR BY THE GOVERNMENTS HAVING RESPONSIBILITY FOR SUCH ACTION;

ARTICLE 107

AMENDMENTS TO THESE ARTICLES OF FEDERATION SHALL COME INTO FORCE FOR ALL MEMBERS OF THE UNITED FEDERATION WHEN THEY HAVE BEEN ADOPTED BY A TWO-THIRDS (2/3) VOTE OF THE MEMBERS OF THE SUPREME ASSEMBLY AND RATIFIED IN ACCORDANCE WITH THEIR RESPECTIVE STATUTORY PROCESSES BY TWO-THIRDS (2/3) OF THE MEMBERS OF THE UNITED FEDERATION, INCLUDING ALL THE PERMANENT MEMBERS OF THE FEDERA-TION COUNCIL;

ARTICLES OF FEDERATION

ARTICLE 108

1.   A GENERAL CONFERENCE OF THE MEMBERS OF THE UNITED FEDERATION FOR THE PUR-
POSE OF REVIEWING THESE ARTICLES OF FEDERATION MAY BE HELD AT A DATE AND
PLACE TO BE FIXED BY A TWO-THIRDS (2/3) VOTE OF THE MEMBERS OF THE SUPREME
ASSEMBLY AND BY A VOTE OF ANY SEVEN (7) MEMBERS OF THE FEDERATION COUNCIL.
EACH MEMBER OF THE UNITED FEDERATION SHALL HAVE ONE (1) VOTE IN THE CONFERENCE;

2.   ANY ALTERATIONS OF THESE ARTICLES OF FEDERATION RECOMMENDED BY A TWO-
THIRDS (2/3) VOTE OF THE CONFERENCE SHALL TAKE EFFECT WHEN RATIFIED IN ACCORD-
ANCE WITH THEIR RESPECTIVE STATUTORY PROCESSES BY TWO-THIRDS (2/3) OF THE
MEMBERS OF THE UNITED FEDERATION INCLUDING ALL THE PERMANENT MEMBERS OF THE
FEDERATION COUNCIL;

3.   IF SUCH CONFERENCE HAS NOT BEEN HELD BEFORE THE TENTH REGULAR SESSION OF
THE SUPREME ASSEMBLY FOLLOWING THE COMING INTO FORCE OF THESE ARTICLES OF
FEDERATION, THE PROPOSAL TO CALL SUCH A CONFERENCE SHALL BE PLACED ON THE
AGENDA OF THAT SESSION OF THE SUPREME ASSEMBLY, AND THE CONFERENCE SHALL BE
HELD IF SO DECIDED BY A MAJORITY VOTE OF THE MEMBERS OF THE SUPREME ASSEMBLY
AND BY A VOTE OF ANY SEVEN (7) MEMBERS OF THE FEDERATION COUNCIL.

CHAPTER XVIII
RATIFICATION AND SIGNATURE

ARTICLE 109

1.   THESE ARTICLES OF FEDERATION SHALL BE RATIFIED BY THE SIGNATORY GOVERN-
MENTS IN ACCORDANCE WITH THEIR RESPECTIVE STATUTORY PROCESSES;

2.   THE RATIFICATIONS SHALL BE DEPOSITED WITH THE GOVERNMENT OF THE UNITED
NATIONS OF THE PLANET EARTH, WHICH SHALL NOTIFY ALL OF THE SIGNATORY GOVERN-
MENTS OF EACH DEPOSIT AS WELL AS THE SUPREME-SECRETARIAT OF THE ORGANIZATION
WHEN HE HAS BEEN APPOINTED;

3.   THESE ARTICLES OF FEDERATION SHALL COME INTO FULL FORCE UPON THE DEPOSIT
OF THE RATIFICATIONS BY THE UNITED NATIONS OF THE PLANET EARTH, THE PLANETARY
CONFEDERATION OF 40 ERIDANI, THE UNITED PLANETS OF 61 CYGNI, THE STAR EMPIRE
OF EPSILON INDII, THE ALPHA CENTAURI CONCORDIUM OF PLANETS, AND BY A MAJORITY
OF THE OTHER SIGNATORY SOCIAL SYSTEMS. A PROTOCOL OF THE RATIFICATIONS
DEPOSITED SHALL THEREUPON BY DRAWN UP BY THE GOVERNMENT OF THE UNITED NATIONS
WHICH SHALL COMMUNICATE COPIES THEREOF TO ALL OF THE SIGNATORY GOVERNMENTS;

4.   THE GOVERNMENTS SIGNATORY TO THESE ARTICLES OF FEDERATION WHICH RATIFY
IT AFTER IT HAS COME INTO FORCE WILL BECOME ORIGINAL MEMBERS OF THE UNITED
FEDERATION ON THE DATE OF THE DEPOSIT OF THEIR RESPECTIVE RATIFICATIONS;

ARTICLE 110

THESE ARTICLES OF FEDERATION, OF WHICH THE VARIOUS LANGUAGE TEXTS ARE
EQUALLY AUTHENTIC, UPON THE COMING INTO FULL FORCE OF THE UNITED FEDERATION
OF PLANETS, SHALL BE TRANSFERRED BY THE UNITED NATIONS TO THE ORGANIZATION
FOR PERMANENT DEPOSIT IN ITS ARCHIVES. DULY CERTIFIED COPIES THEREOF SHALL
BE TRANSMITTED BY THE SUPREME-SECRETARIAT TO THE GOVERNMENTS OF ALL THE
SIGNATORY SOCIAL SYSTEMS.

IN FAITH WHEREOF THE REPRESENTATIVES OF THE GOVERNMENTS OF THE UNITED FEDERA-
TION OF PLANETS HAVE SIGNED THESE ARTICLES OF FEDERATION.

DONE AT THE PLANET BABEL STARDATE 0965

(FOLLOWED BY THE SIGNATURE SHEETS OF THE
 ORIGINAL SIGNATORY GOVERNMENTS)

TREATY OF PEACE

BETWEEN THE ROMULAN STAR EMPIRE
AND THE UNITED FEDERATION OF PLANETS

NEGOTIATED BY SUBSPACE COMMUNICATION STARDATE 1200.5

PART I — THE TERMS AND CONDITIONS HAVING BEEN NEGOTIATED AND AGREED TO BE IDENTICALLY UNDERSTOOD, THE ROMULAN STAR EMPIRE AND THE UNITED FEDERATION OF PLANETS MUTUALLY PLEDGE TO EACH OTHER THEIR SOLEMN WORD TO IMMEDIATELY CEASE HOSTILITIES BETWEEN THE TWO PARTIES EFFECTIVE STARDATE 1200.5;

PART II — BETWEEN THE ADJACENT TERRITORIAL BOUNDARIES OF THE TWO PARTIES THERE IS ESTABLISHED A NEUTRAL ZONE, SEVEN HUNDRED AND FIFTY PARSECS IN WIDTH IN THE GALACTIC LONGITUDINAL PLANE, AND EXTENDING TO THE OUTER BOUNDARY OF THE GALAXY IN THE VERTICAL PLANE;

PART III — ALL PERSONS AND FACILITIES OF ANY MANNER WHATSOEVER IDENTIFIABLE WITH EITHER PARTY SHALL BE IMMEDIATELY REMOVED FROM THIS ZONE. EFFECTIVE STARDATE 1210, NO PERSONS OR FACILITIES OF ANY MANNER WHATSOEVER IDENTIFIABLE WITH EITHER PARTY SHALL THEREAFTER BY INTRUDED INTO THIS ZONE. THE ROMULAN STAR EMPIRE AND THE UNITED FEDERATION OF PLANETS MUTUALLY PLEDGE TO EACH OTHER TO FAITHFULLY MAINTAIN THE NEUTRALITY OF THIS ZONE THEREAFTER;

PART IV — ANY INTRUSION WHATSOEVER BY ANY PERSON OR FACILITY IDENTIFIABLE WITH EITHER PARTY INTO THIS NEUTRAL ZONE SHALL BE CONSIDERED TO BE A HOSTILE ACTION AND BREACH OF THIS PEACE. IN SUCH EVENT AN IMMEDIATE STATE OF WAR SHALL BE DECLARED TO EXIST BETWEEN THE ROMULAN STAR EMPIRE AND THE UNITED FEDERATION OF PLANETS; EXCEPT ONLY WHERE:

PART V — SUCH INTRUSION BY ANY PERSON OR FACILITY IDENTIFIABLE WITH EITHER PARTY CAN BE UNDENIABLY DEMONSTRATED TO BE THE ACCIDENTAL RESULT OF CONDITIONS BEYOND THE CONTROL OF THAT PERSON OR THAT FACILITY AND DID, IN FACT, OCCUR WITHOUT HOSTILE INTENT;

PART VI — TO THIS END, AND FOR PURPOSES OF MUTUAL MAINTENANCE OF THIS TREATY OF PEACE AND THIS NEUTRAL ZONE, THE ROMULAN STAR EMPIRE AND THE UNITED FEDERATION OF PLANETS AGREE TO KEEP OPEN AND MAINTAIN A CONSTANT SURVEILLANCE OF, SUBSPACE COMMUNICATION FREQUENCY K;

PART VII — I, PRAETOR KARZAN, HAVING READ THE TERMS OF THIS TREATY VERBATIM OVER SUBSPACE COMMUNICATION FREQUENCY K, AND BEING IDENTIFIABLE BY VOICEPRINT OF THIS TRANSMISSION, DO HEREBY CERTIFY THAT I AM PRAETOR OF THE ROMULAN STAR EMPIRE WITH FULL POWERS TO EXECUTE THIS TREATY ON BEHALF OF THE EMPIRE;

PART VIII — I, CRISTOFUR THORPE, HAVING READ THE TERMS OF THIS TREATY VERBATIM OVER SUBSPACE COMMUNICATION FREQUENCY K, AND BEING IDENTIFIABLE BY VOICEPRINT OF THIS TRANSMISSION, DO HEREBY CERTIFY THAT I AM GOVERNOR OF THE FEDERATION COUNCIL OF THE UNITED FEDERATION OF PLANETS WITH FULL POWERS TO EXECUTE THIS TREATY ON BEHALF OF THIS GOVERNMENT.

TREATY OF PEACE
IMPOSED BY ORGANIA STARDATE 3199.5

CONDITION 1:

THIS TREATY OF PEACE IS SIMULTANEOUSLY IMPOSED UPON THE KLINGON
EMPIRE AND THE UNITED FEDERATION OF PLANETS. UNLESS YOUR GOVERN-
MENTS AND COMBATANTS IN GALACTIC SPACE AGREE TO AN IMMEDIATE
CESSATION OF HOSTILITIES, YOUR ARMED FORCES WHEREVER THEY MAY BE
WILL BE IMMEDIATELY DISABLED;

CONDITION 2:

HENCEFORTH FROM THIS TIME, WITHIN A ZONE SEVEN HUNDRED AND FIFTY
PARSECS IN WIDTH BETWEEN THE ADJACENT TERRITORIAL BOUNDARIES OF
BOTH PARTIES, NO ARMED HOSTILITIES MAY TAKE PLACE BETWEEN THE
KLINGON EMPIRE AND THE UNITED FEDERATION OF PLANETS;

CONDITION 3:

AT ANY TIME, SHOULD A PERSON OR UNIT OF EITHER PARTY ATTEMPT TO
ACT OR USE WEAPONRY IN A HOSTILE MANNER AGAINST THE PERSON OR A
UNIT OF THE OTHER PARTY WITHIN THIS ZONE, THAT PERSON OR UNIT,
AND THAT WEAPONRY, SHALL BE RENDERED IMMEDIATELY HARMLESS;

CONDITION 4:

THE TIME WILL COME IN THE FUTURE WHEN THE KLINGON EMPIRE AND THE
UNITED FEDERATION OF PLANETS WILL BECOME ALLIES AND GOOD FRIENDS,
WORKING TOGETHER IN PEACE AND HARMONY FOR THE BETTERMENT OF BOTH.
UNTIL THAT TIME, NEITHER PARTY MAY DENY TO THE OTHER PEACEFUL
ACCESS TO ITS PLANETARY BASES WITHIN THE NEUTRAL ZONE FOR SHORE
LEAVE, REST, AND REHABILITATION;

CONDITION 5:

BOTH PARTIES WILL RESPECT THE TERRITORIAL INTEGRITY OF ORGANIA AND
WILL MAKE NO FURTHER ATTEMPT TO INTRUDE INTO OUR PLANET'S TERRI-
TORY OR AFFAIRS. WHEN THE TIME ARRIVES IN THE FUTURE FOR US TO
JOIN WITH BOTH PARTIES IN THE PEACEFUL DEVELOPMENT OF INTRA-
GALACTIC RELATIONS, WE WILL MAKE KNOWN TO YOU OUR INTENTIONS;

CONDITION 6:

WE ARE AWARE THAT, WITHIN THE NEUTRAL ZONE, THERE ARE MANY PLANETARY
SUB-CULTURES IN VARIOUS LEVELS OF EVOLUTIONARY DEVELOPMENT WHICH
COULD BENEFIT FROM THE ADVANCED CULTURES OF THE KLINGON EMPIRE AND
THE UNITED FEDERATION OF PLANETS. TO THIS END, ORGANIA WILL PERMIT
SUCH PEACEFUL DEVELOPMENT AND, IN EACH SPECIFIC CASE, WILL AWARD
SUCH RIGHTS TO THE PARTY WHICH DEMONSTRATES IT CAN MOST EFFICIENTLY
DEVELOP THE PLANET TO THE BENEFIT OF ITS SOCIAL SYSTEMS.

FOR **ORGANIA**:
AYELBORNE
CLAYMARE
TREFAYNE

UNITED FEDERATION
OF PLANETS - M-O GALAXY

BANNER

B/W AS SHOWN
OFFICIAL COLORS:

☐ RED   N° SF10UC
■ SILVER N° SF01UC

UNITED FEDERATION
OF PLANETS - M·O GALAXY

SEAL

B/W AS SHOWN
OFFICIAL COLORS:

☐	BLUE N⁰SF20UC
■	SILVER N⁰. SF0IUC

UNITED NATIONS
PLANET EARTH - SOL SYSTEM

FLAG

OFFICIAL GARRISON PROPORTIONS

OFFICIAL PARADE PROPORTIONS

B/W AS SHOWN
OFFICIAL COLORS:

☐	SKY BLUE № SF16UC
■	SILVER № SF01UC

UNITED NATIONS
PLANET EARTH - SOL SYSTEM

SEAL

B/W AS SHOWN

OFFICIAL COLORS:

 SKY BLUE N°SF16UC

SILVER N°SF01UC

PLANETARY CONFEDERATION
OF 40 ERIDANI

BANNER

B/W AS SHOWN
OFFICIAL COLORS:

SKY BLUE	N°SF16UC	RED	N°SF10UC
ORANGE	N°SF11UC	INDIGO	N°SF19UC

PLANETARY CONFEDERATION
OF 40 ERIDANI

SIGNAT

BLACK & WHITE AS SHOWN
OFFICIAL COLORS:

	SKY BLUE	N°SF16UC
	ORANGE	N°SF11UC
	RED	N°SF10UC
	INDIGO	N°SF19UC

UNITED PLANETS
OF 61 CYGNI

SHIELD*

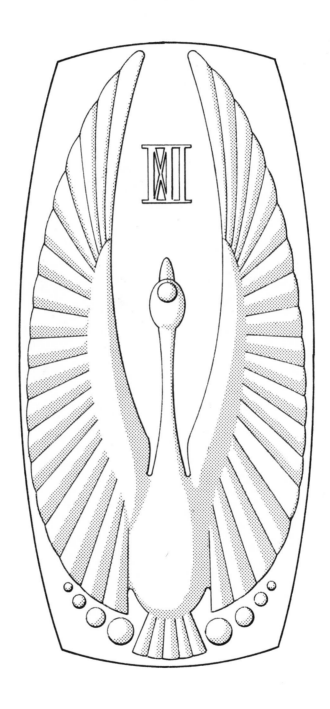

B/W AS SHOWN
OFFICIAL COLORS:
[░░░░] COPPER N° SF05UC

*EQUIVALENT OF A FLAG, RAISED TOOLING
ON DOUBLE CONVEX CYGNUSIUM SHIELD

UNITED PLANETS
OF 61 CYGNI

ARMS

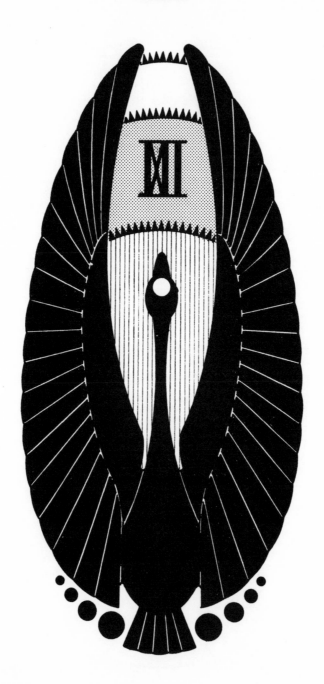

B/W AS SHOWN
OFFICIAL COLORS:

▢	YELLOW Nº SF12UC
▨	ORANGE Nº SF11UC
▥	RED Nº SF10UC
▰	COPPER Nº SF05UC

STAR EMPIRE
OF EPSILON INDII

STANDARD

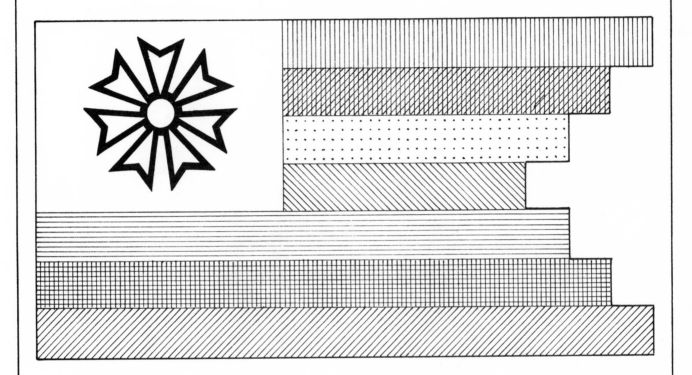

B/W AS SHOWN
OFFICIAL COLORS:

	WHITE	No SF06UC
	RED	No SF10UC
	ORANGE	No SF11UC
	YELLOW	No SF12UC
	GREEN	No SF15UC
	GOLD	No SF03UC
	BLUE	No SF18UC
	INDIGO	No SF19UC
	VIOLET	No SF21UC

STAR EMPIRE
OF EPSILON INDII

SEAL

B/W AS SHOWN
OFFICIAL COLORS:

WHITE	№ SF 06 UC	
RED	№ SF 10 UC	BLUE № SF 18 UC
ORANGE	№ SF 11 UC	INDIGO № SF 19 UC
YELLOW	№ SF 12 UC	VIOLET № SF 21 UC
GREEN	№ SF 15 UC	GOLD № SF 03 UC

ALPHA CENTAURI
CONCORDIUM OF PLANETS

PENNANT

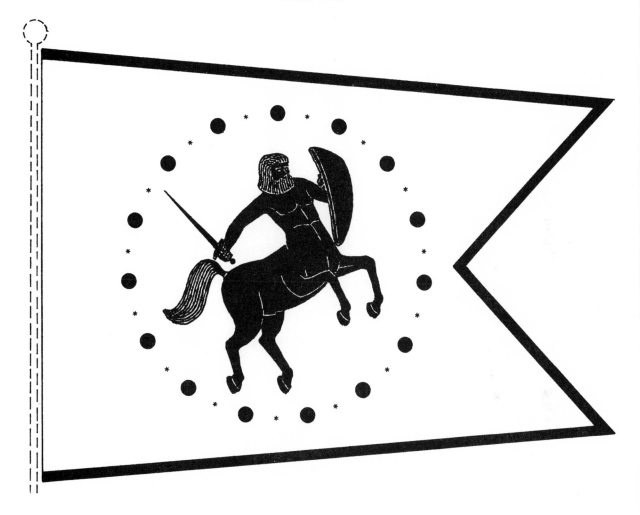

B/W AS SHOWN
OFFICIAL COLORS:

☐	PURPLE NºSF26UC
■	GOLD NºSF03UC

ALPHA CENTAURI
CONCORDIUM OF PLANETS

ARMS

B/W AS SHOWN
OFFICIAL COLORS:

	PURPLE	N°SF26UC
	YELLOW	N°SF12UC
	ORANGE	N°SF11UC
	RED	N°SF10UC
	GOLD	N°SF03UC

OFFICIAL TYPE STYLE
STAR FLEET SPECIFICATION

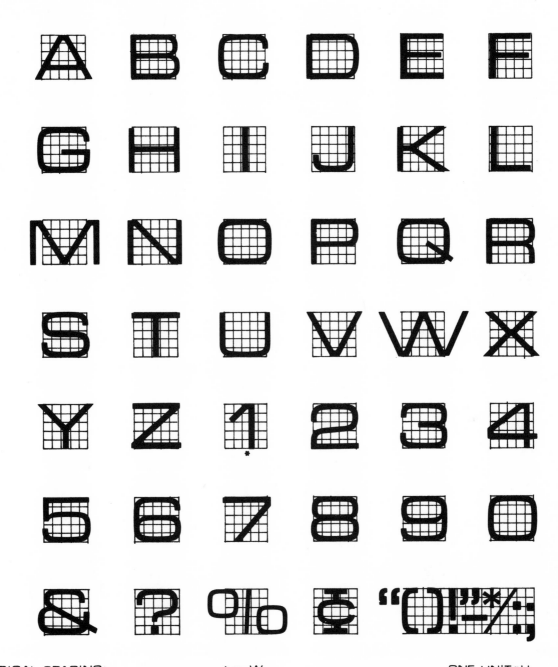

TYPICAL SPACING:

COMMON UNITED NATIONS LANGUAGE FORM.   EARTH FONT NAME: **Microgramma Ext.**
*DO NOT USE "1" IN FLEET OPERATIONS, INSTRUMENTATION, OR SHIP DESIGNATIONS.

OFFICIAL TYPE STYLE
STAR FLEET SPECIFICATION

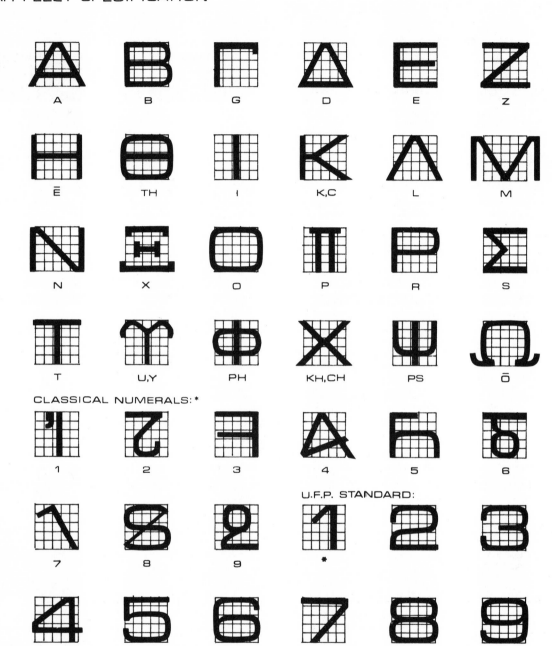

A	B	G	D	E	Z
Ē	TH	I	K,C	L	M
N	X	O	P	R	S
T	U,Y	PH	KH,CH	PS	Ō

CLASSICAL NUMERALS:*

1	2	3	4	5	6

U.F.P. STANDARD:

			1	2	3
7	8	9	*		

4	5	6	7	8	9

TYPICAL SPACING: →|←2W   ONE UNIT~H

ΥΣΣ. ΑΙΡΗ N.K.K-905
ΑΣΤΗΡ ΠΛΕΙΝ ΓΑΛΑΖΙΑ

.66 H~MINIMUM   PREFERRED

COMMON ALPHA KENTAURUS LANGUAGE FORM. TYPE FONT: **Microgramma Ext.**
*DO NOT USE IN FLEET OPERATIONS, INSTRUMENTATION, OR SHIP DESIGNATIONS.

STAR FLEET TECHNICAL ORDER

UNIFORM COLOR CODE
STAR FLEET SPECIFICATION

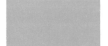
01 SILVER

02 ANTIMONY

03 GOLD

04 BRONZE

05 COPPER

06 WHITE

07 IVORY

08 SAND

09 BLOOD

10 RED

11 ORANGE

12 YELLOW

13 TENNE

14 OLIVE

15 GREEN

16 SKY BLUE

17 ULTRAMARINE

18 BLUE

19 INDIGO

20 MIDNIGHT

21 VIOLET

22 CORN

23 TAN

24 BROWN

25 NUDE

26 PURPLE

27 OXIDE

28 TAUPE

29 PLATINUM

30 GRAY

31 BLUEGRAY

32 BLACK

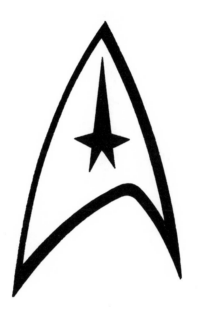

COMMAND SECTION

	SECTION INDEX		
TO. NO:	SUBJECT	CURRENT	REPLACES
01:00:00	COMMAND SECTION FLYSHEET	7305.30	
» » :02	FOREWORD	*	
» » :04	SECTION INDEX	7309.10	
» :01:00	STAR FLEET ARMED FORCES - ORGANIZATION	7407.27	
» » :01	SFAF - ORG - MIL. STAFF COMM./STAR FLEET COMMAND	7407.29	
» » :02	» » - FLEET OPERATIONS	7407.31	
» » :03	» » - LOGISTICS/INSPECTOR GENERAL	7408.01	
» » :04	» » - PERSONNEL/JUDGE ADVOCATE GENERAL	*	
» » :05	» » - SURGEON GENERAL/SCIENCES	*	
» » :06	» » - ENGINEERING/COMPTROLLER GENERAL	*	
» » :07	» » - TECHNOLOGY/COMMUNICATIONS	*	
» » :08	» » - NAV. GEN./PLANETARY REL./GALAXY EXP.	*	
» » :09	» » - TACTICIAN/COSMOLOGIST/ALIENOLOGIST	*	
» :01:20	THE STAR FLEET ACADEMY	7408.05	
» :01:30	STAR FLEET HEADQUARTERS - EXTERNAL ARRANGEMENT	7305.31	
» » :31	SFHQ - TYPICAL CROSS-SECTION	» »	
» » :32	» - TYP. SECTION THRU DOCK	» »	
» » :33	» - TYP. LONG. SECTION	» »	
» » :34	» - GROUND PLAN - BAYS 1 & 2	» »	
» » :35	» - » » - BAYS 3 & 4	» »	
» » :36	» - » » - BAYS 5 & 6	7305.31	
» :03:00	STAR FLEET INSIGNIA AND RANK	7304.28	
» » :10	DUTY UNIFORM - MALE - ALL SFAF	7304.26	
» » :11	N/C TUNIC PATTERN	7308.05	
» » :12	DUTY UNIFORM - FEMALE - OFFICERS SFAF	7304.26	
» » :13	N/C TUNIC AND PANTY PATTERN	7308.05	
» » :14	DUTY UNIFORM - FEMALE - ENSIGNS SFAF	7304.26	
» » :15	N/C TUNIC AND PANTY PATTERN	7308.05	
» » :16	DUTY UNIFORM - FEMALE - MEDICAL SFAF	7304.26	
» » :17	N/C TUNIC AND PANTY PATTERN	7308.05	
» » :16	DUTY UNIFORM - ACADEMY CADET - MALE	*	
» » :19	N/C TUNIC PATTERN	*	
» » :20	DUTY UNIFORM - ACADEMY CADET - FEMALE	*	
» » :21	N/C TUNIC AND PANTY PATTERN	*	
» :04:00	FLEET SHIP CLASSIFICATIONS - SFAF - CLASS I STARSHIPS	7306.03	
» » :10	CLASS I HEAVY CRUISER - MK-IX	7304.15	
» » :11	AUTHORIZED CONSTRUCTION	7306.16	
» » :12	CLASS I DESTROYER - MK-VIII	7306.03	
» » :13	AUTH. CONST.	7306.09	
» » :14	CLASS I SCOUT - MK-VII	7306.03	
» » :15	AUTH. CONST.	7306.19	
» » :16	CLASS I TRANSPORT/TUG - MK-VI	7306.03	
» » :17	AUTH. CONST.	7306.14	
» » :18	CLASS I TRANSPORT CONTAINERS - MK-V AND MK-III	7306.03	
» » :19	» » » » - MK-II AND MK-I	» »	
» » :20	» » » » - MK-IV STARLINER	» »	
» » :21	» » » » - MK-IV DECK PLANS	7306.03	
	NOTE (*): NO CURRENT PRINT-OUT FROM MASTERCOM DATABANKS/SFHQ		

SECTION INDEX

TO. NO:	SUBJECT	CURRENT	REPLACES
01:00:05	SECTION INDEX	7309.10	
» :04:22	CLASS I TRANSP. CONT. - MK-IV DECK PLANS	7306.03	
» » :24	CLASS I DREADNOUGHT - MK-X	7306.09	
» » :25	AUTH. CONST.	7306.15	
» » :80	SHUTTLECRAFT - 7 PERS. - MK-12B - EXTERNAL ARR.	7502.20	
» » :81	» » » » » - INTERNAL ARR.	7502.20	
» :05:82	TYP. SINGLE STATEROOM - PRIMARY HULL - CLASS I SS	7312.21	
» » :83	» DOUBLE » - » » - » » »	7312.21	
» :06:10	MAIN BRIDGE - PRIMARY HULL - CLASS I SS - DECK I PLAN	7409.07	
» » :11	» » » » » » » - ELEVATIONS	7409.09	
» » :12	COMMAND MODULE - MAIN BRIDGE - PLAN & PROFILE	7408.26	
» » :13	» » - » » - ELEVATIONS	7408.26	
» » :14	MAIN BRIDGE - PRI. HULL - HELMSMAN'S STATION	7409.02	
» » :15	» » - » » - NAVIGATOR'S »	7409.02	
» » :16	» » - » » - COMMAND CON	7409.04	
» » :17	» » - » » - ASTROGATOR	7409.05	
» :07:20	SECURITY SECTION - PRIMARY HULL - CLASS I SS	7312.21	
» :08:00	DEFENSE & WEAPONS STATION - MAIN BRIDGE	*	
» » :01	CONTROLS CONSOLE	*	
» » :50	HAND PHASER - TYPE I - GENERAL ARRANGEMENT	7304.16	
» » :52	HAND PHASER - TYPE II - GEN. ARR.	7304.30	
» » :53	» » » » - DETAILS	7304.30	
» » :58	OFFENSIVE / DEFENSIVE RAY GUN - GEN. ARR.	7503.22	

NOTE (*): NO CURRENT PRINT-OUT FROM MASTERCOM DATABANKS/SFHQ

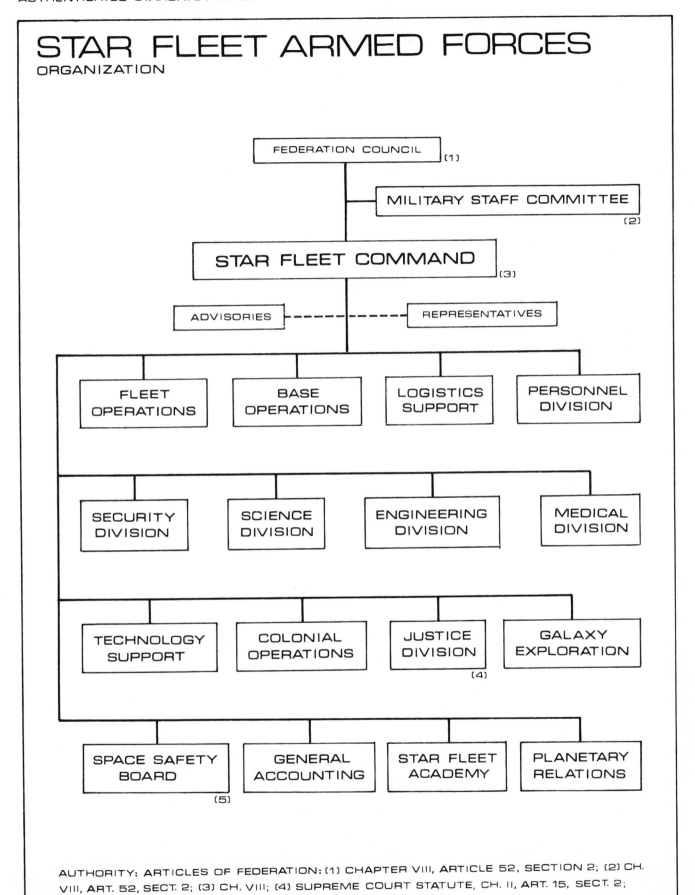

STAR FLEET ARMED FORCES
ORGANIZATION

FEDERATION COUNCIL (1)

MILITARY STAFF COMMITTEE (2)

STAR FLEET COMMAND (3)

ADVISORIES — — — REPRESENTATIVES

FLEET OPERATIONS

BASE OPERATIONS

LOGISTICS SUPPORT

PERSONNEL DIVISION

SECURITY DIVISION

SCIENCE DIVISION

ENGINEERING DIVISION

MEDICAL DIVISION

TECHNOLOGY SUPPORT

COLONIAL OPERATIONS

JUSTICE DIVISION (4)

GALAXY EXPLORATION

SPACE SAFETY BOARD (5)

GENERAL ACCOUNTING

STAR FLEET ACADEMY

PLANETARY RELATIONS

AUTHORITY: ARTICLES OF FEDERATION: (1) CHAPTER VIII, ARTICLE 52, SECTION 2; (2) CH. VIII, ART. 52, SECT. 2; (3) CH. VIII; (4) SUPREME COURT STATUTE, CH. II, ART. 15, SECT. 2; (5) INTERPLANETARY COMMERCE STATUTE, PART VIII, SECT. 47, ITEM 01.

STAR FLEET ARMED FORCES
ORGANIZATION

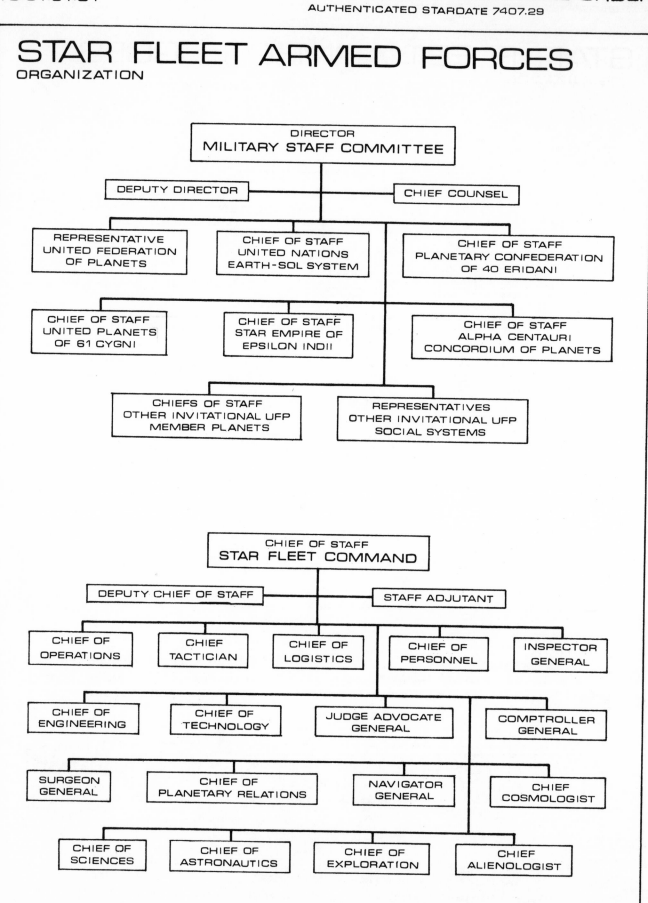

STAR FLEET ARMED FORCES
ORGANIZATION

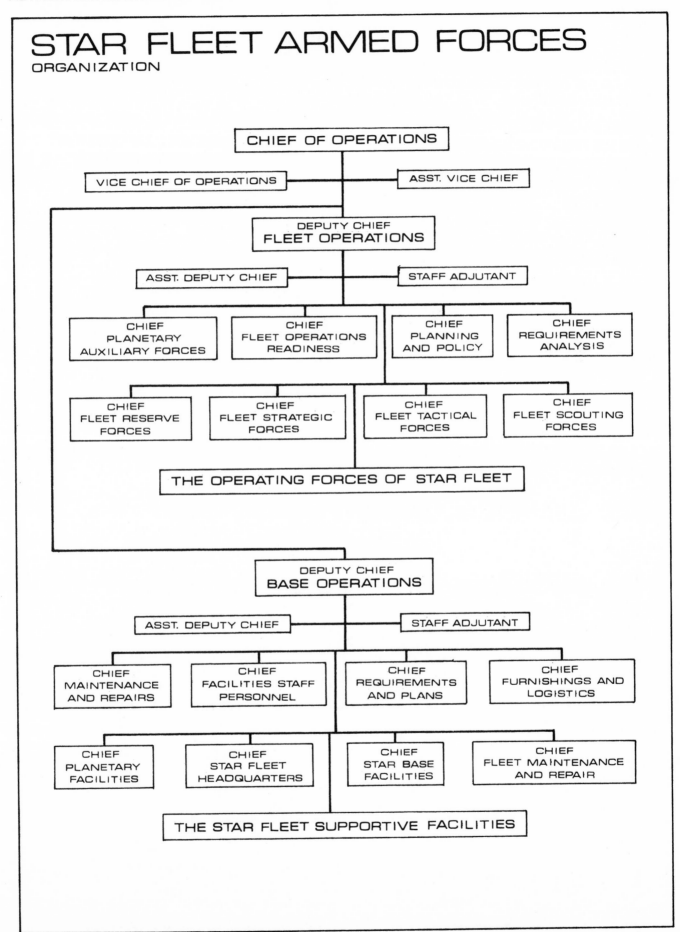

STAR FLEET ARMED FORCES
ORGANIZATION

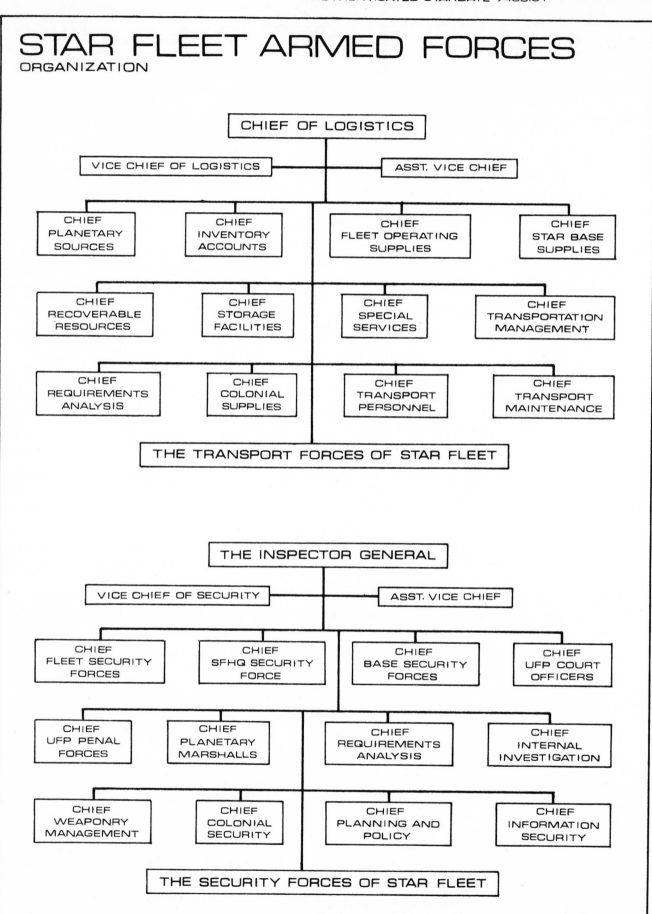

CHIEF OF LOGISTICS

VICE CHIEF OF LOGISTICS — ASST. VICE CHIEF

CHIEF PLANETARY SOURCES | CHIEF INVENTORY ACCOUNTS | CHIEF FLEET OPERATING SUPPLIES | CHIEF STAR BASE SUPPLIES

CHIEF RECOVERABLE RESOURCES | CHIEF STORAGE FACILITIES | CHIEF SPECIAL SERVICES | CHIEF TRANSPORTATION MANAGEMENT

CHIEF REQUIREMENTS ANALYSIS | CHIEF COLONIAL SUPPLIES | CHIEF TRANSPORT PERSONNEL | CHIEF TRANSPORT MAINTENANCE

THE TRANSPORT FORCES OF STAR FLEET

THE INSPECTOR GENERAL

VICE CHIEF OF SECURITY — ASST. VICE CHIEF

CHIEF FLEET SECURITY FORCES | CHIEF SFHQ SECURITY FORCE | CHIEF BASE SECURITY FORCES | CHIEF UFP COURT OFFICERS

CHIEF UFP PENAL FORCES | CHIEF PLANETARY MARSHALLS | CHIEF REQUIREMENTS ANALYSIS | CHIEF INTERNAL INVESTIGATION

CHIEF WEAPONRY MANAGEMENT | CHIEF COLONIAL SECURITY | CHIEF PLANNING AND POLICY | CHIEF INFORMATION SECURITY

THE SECURITY FORCES OF STAR FLEET

THE STAR FLEET ACADEMY
ORGANIZATION

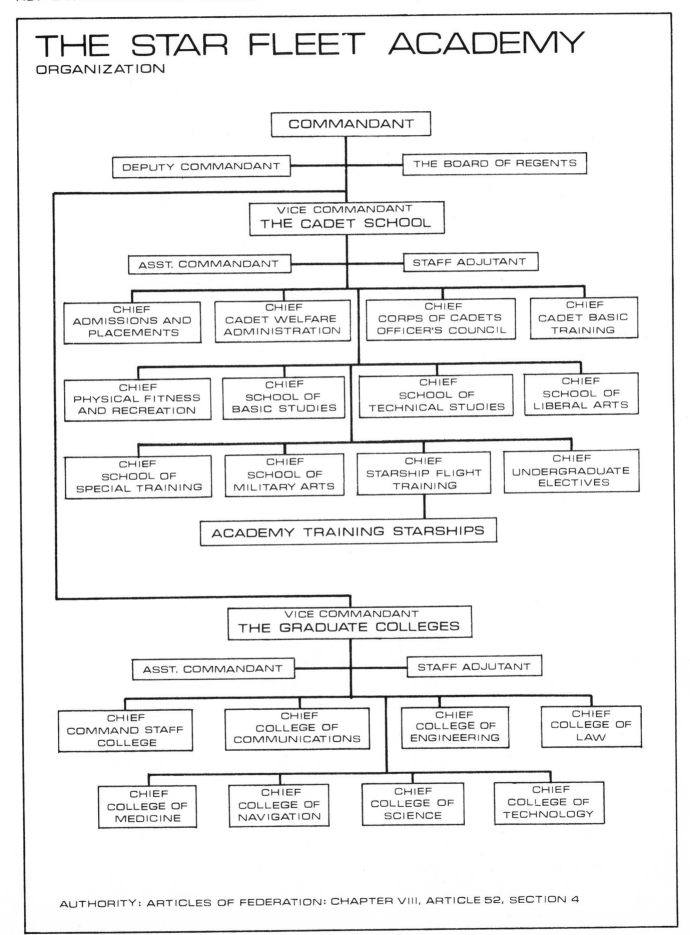

AUTHORITY: ARTICLES OF FEDERATION: CHAPTER VIII, ARTICLE 52, SECTION 4

FLEET HEADQUARTERS
GENERAL ARRANGEMENT

PLAN VIEW

CENTRAL BODY

UNITED FEDERATION OF PLANETS

STAR FLEET HEADQUARTERS

B1 B2 B3 B4 B5 B6

A

A
(TO:01:01:31)

DEFLECTOR SHIELD

STARSHIP DOCK AND BERTHS (6)

A
(TO:01:01:32)

ELEVATION VIEW

BEACON (N/S)

HIGH RESOLUTION/RANGE DETECTOR/SCANNER (N/S)

0 1 2 3 4 5
METERS x 100

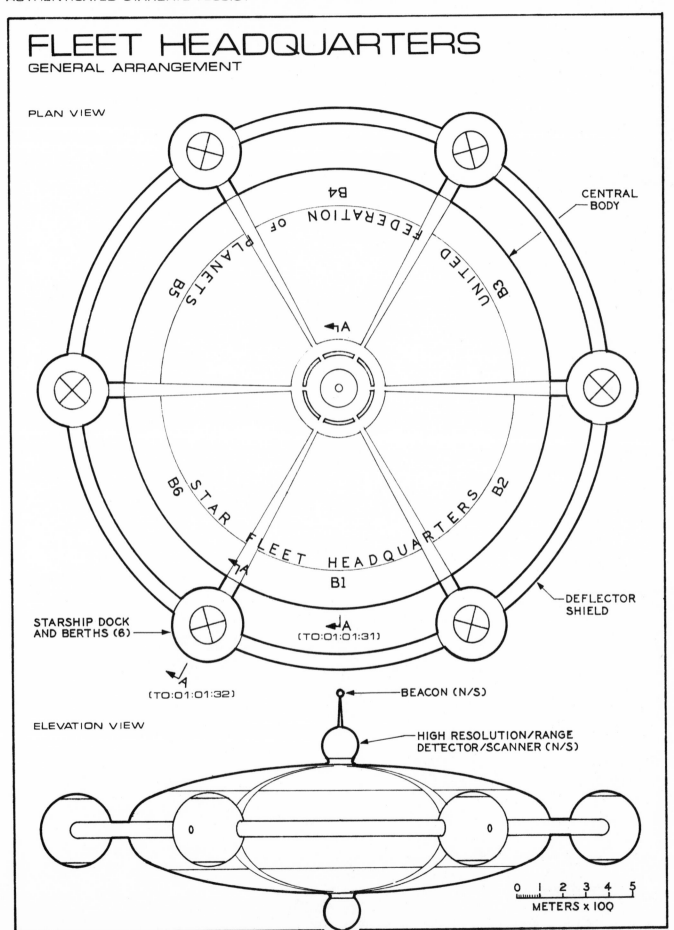

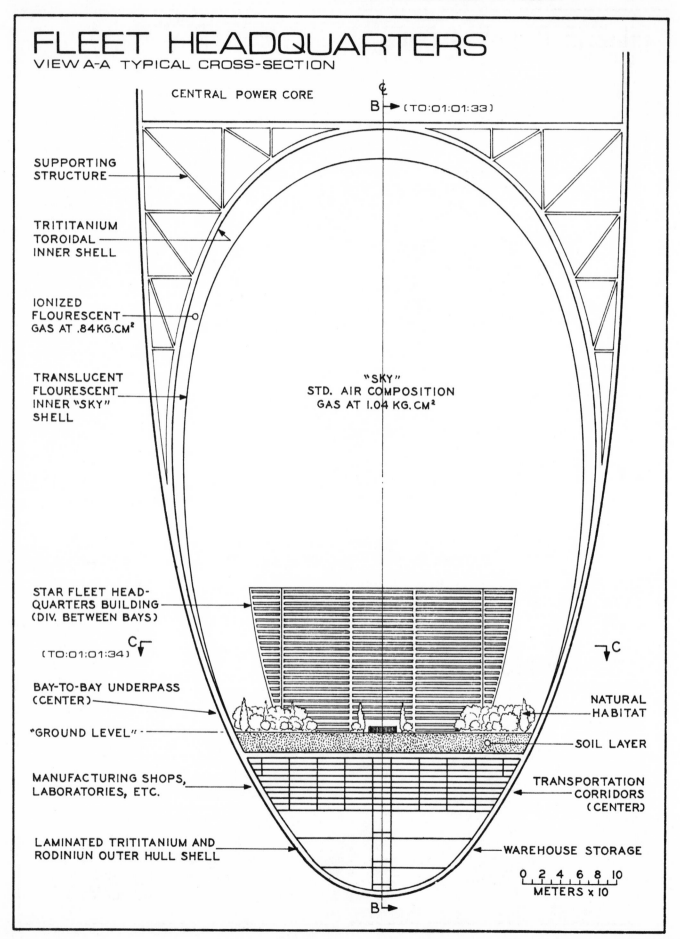

FLEET HEADQUARTERS
VIEW A-A TYPICAL CROSS-SECTION

CENTRAL POWER CORE

¢
B → (TO:01:01:33)

SUPPORTING STRUCTURE

TRITITANIUM TOROIDAL INNER SHELL

IONIZED FLOURESCENT GAS AT .84 KG.CM²

TRANSLUCENT FLOURESCENT INNER "SKY" SHELL

"SKY"
STD. AIR COMPOSITION
GAS AT 1.04 KG. CM²

STAR FLEET HEAD-QUARTERS BUILDING (DIV. BETWEEN BAYS)

C
(TO:01:01:34)

C

BAY-TO-BAY UNDERPASS (CENTER)

NATURAL HABITAT

"GROUND LEVEL"

SOIL LAYER

MANUFACTURING SHOPS, LABORATORIES, ETC.

TRANSPORTATION CORRIDORS (CENTER)

LAMINATED TRITITANIUM AND RODINIUN OUTER HULL SHELL

WAREHOUSE STORAGE

0 2 4 6 8 10
METERS x 10

B →

FLEET HEADQUARTERS
VIEW A-A TYPICAL DOCK CROSS-SECTION

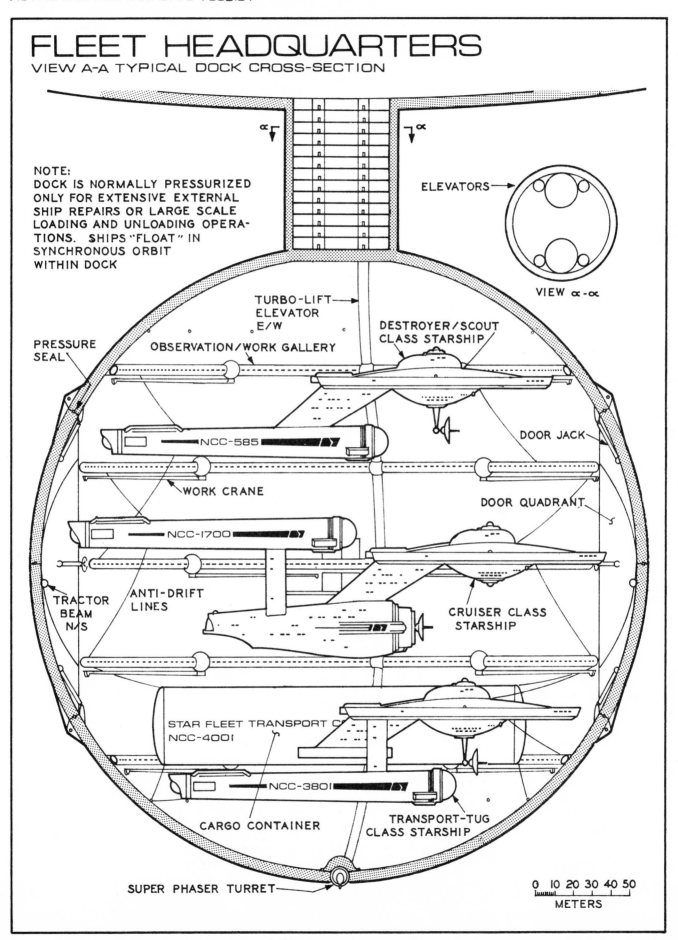

NOTE:
DOCK IS NORMALLY PRESSURIZED
ONLY FOR EXTENSIVE EXTERNAL
SHIP REPAIRS OR LARGE SCALE
LOADING AND UNLOADING OPERA-
TIONS. SHIPS "FLOAT" IN
SYNCHRONOUS ORBIT
WITHIN DOCK

ELEVATORS

VIEW ∝-∝

TURBO-LIFT
ELEVATOR
E/W

DESTROYER/SCOUT
CLASS STARSHIP

PRESSURE
SEAL

OBSERVATION/WORK GALLERY

NCC-585

DOOR JACK

WORK CRANE

DOOR QUADRANT

NCC-1700

TRACTOR
BEAM
N/S

ANTI-DRIFT
LINES

CRUISER CLASS
STARSHIP

STAR FLEET TRANSPORT C
NCC-4001

NCC-3801

CARGO CONTAINER

TRANSPORT-TUG
CLASS STARSHIP

SUPER PHASER TURRET

0 10 20 30 40 50

METERS

FLEET HEADQUARTERS
VIEW B-B TYPICAL EQUITORIAL SECTION

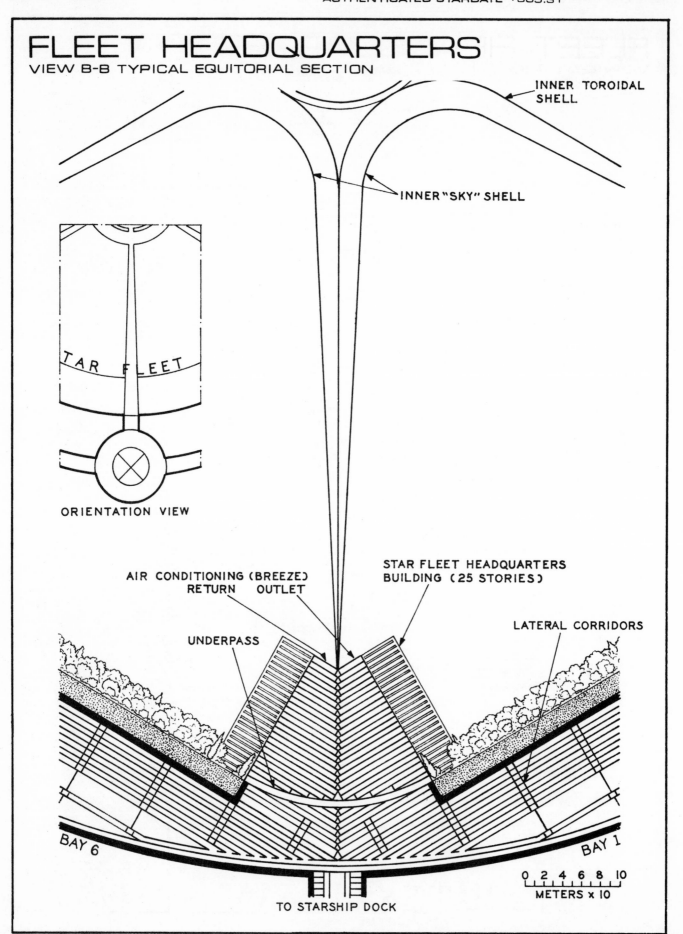

INNER TOROIDAL SHELL

INNER "SKY" SHELL

STAR FLEET

ORIENTATION VIEW

AIR CONDITIONING (BREEZE) RETURN OUTLET

STAR FLEET HEADQUARTERS BUILDING (25 STORIES)

LATERAL CORRIDORS

UNDERPASS

BAY 6

BAY 1

0 2 4 6 8 10
METERS x 10

TO STARSHIP DOCK

FLEET HEADQUARTERS
VIEW C-C GROUND LEVEL PLANS

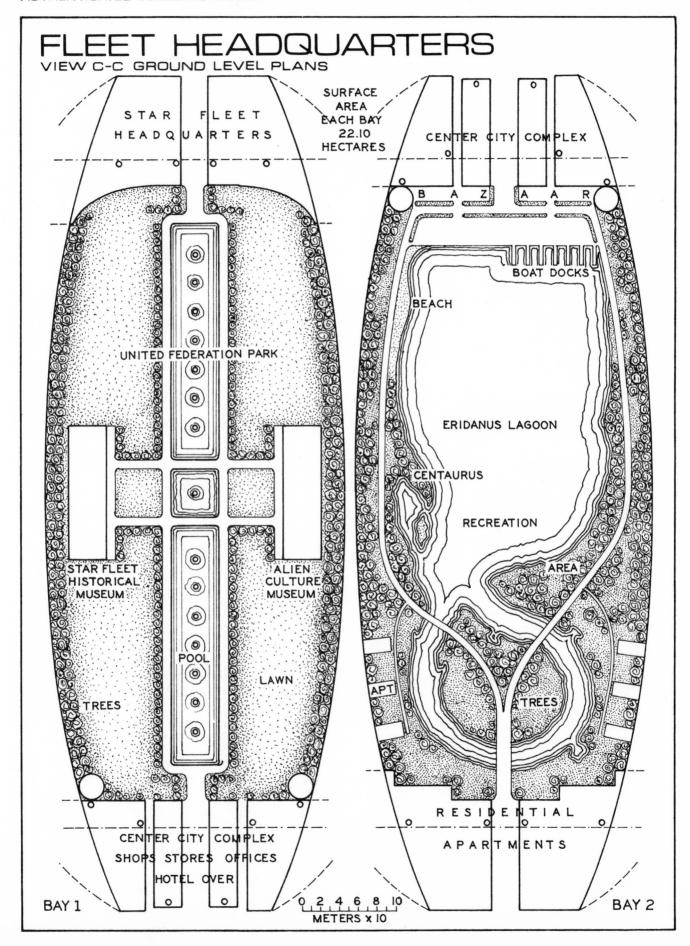

STAR FLEET HEADQUARTERS

SURFACE AREA EACH BAY 22.10 HECTARES

CENTER CITY COMPLEX

B A Z A A R

UNITED FEDERATION PARK

BOAT DOCKS

BEACH

ERIDANUS LAGOON

CENTAURUS

RECREATION

AREA

STAR FLEET HISTORICAL MUSEUM

ALIEN CULTURE MUSEUM

POOL

LAWN

TREES

APT

TREES

CENTER CITY COMPLEX

SHOPS STORES OFFICES

HOTEL OVER

R E S I D E N T I A L

A P A R T M E N T S

BAY 1

0 2 4 6 8 10
METERS x 10

BAY 2

FLEET HEADQUARTERS
VIEW C-C GROUND LEVEL PLANS

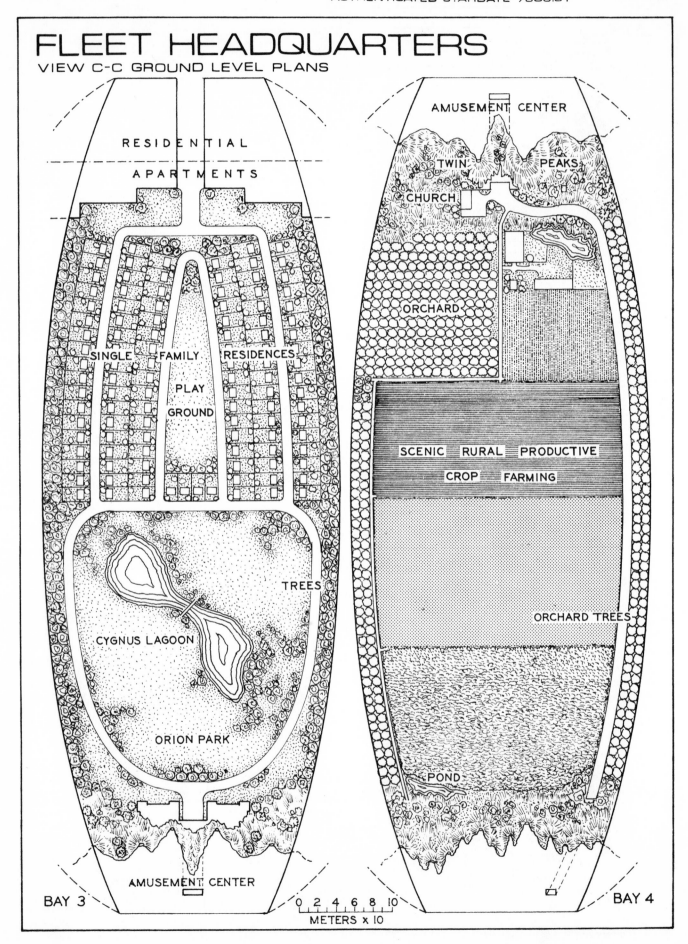

RESIDENTIAL

APARTMENTS

AMUSEMENT CENTER

TWIN   PEAKS

CHURCH

ORCHARD

SINGLE   FAMILY   RESIDENCES

PLAY

GROUND

SCENIC   RURAL   PRODUCTIVE

CROP   FARMING

TREES

ORCHARD TREES

CYGNUS LAGOON

ORION PARK

POND

AMUSEMENT CENTER

BAY 3

BAY 4

0 2 4 6 8 10
METERS x 10

FLEET HEADQUARTERS
VIEW C-C GROUND LEVEL PLANS

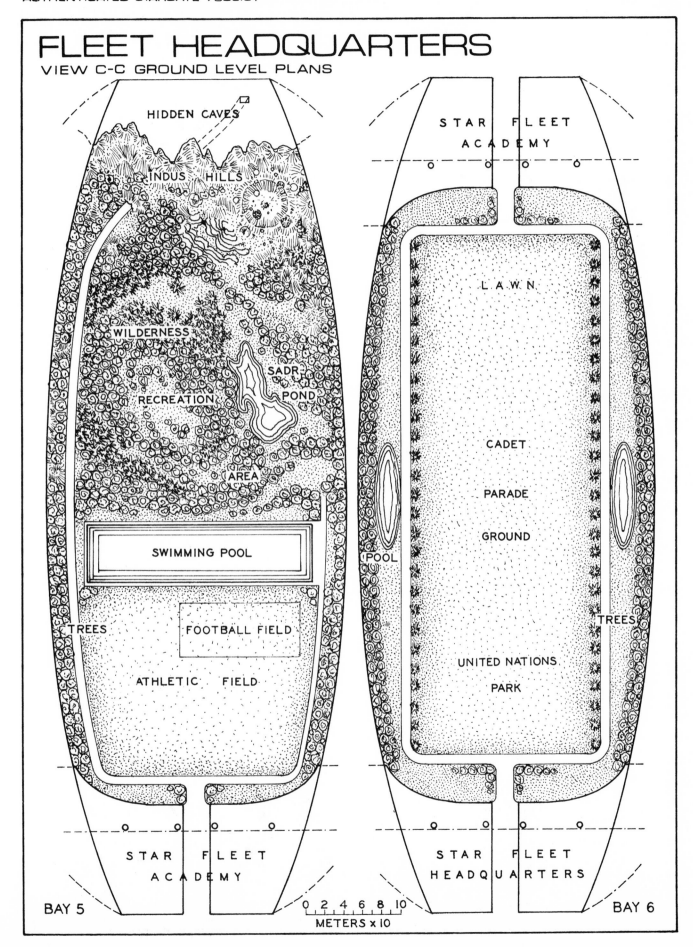

HIDDEN CAVES

INDUS HILLS

WILDERNESS

SADR
POND

RECREATION

AREA

SWIMMING POOL

TREES

FOOTBALL FIELD

ATHLETIC FIELD

STAR FLEET
ACADEMY

BAY 5

STAR FLEET
ACADEMY

LAWN

POOL

CADET

PARADE

GROUND

TREES

UNITED NATIONS

PARK

STAR FLEET
HEADQUARTERS

BAY 6

0 2 4 6 8 10
METERS x 10

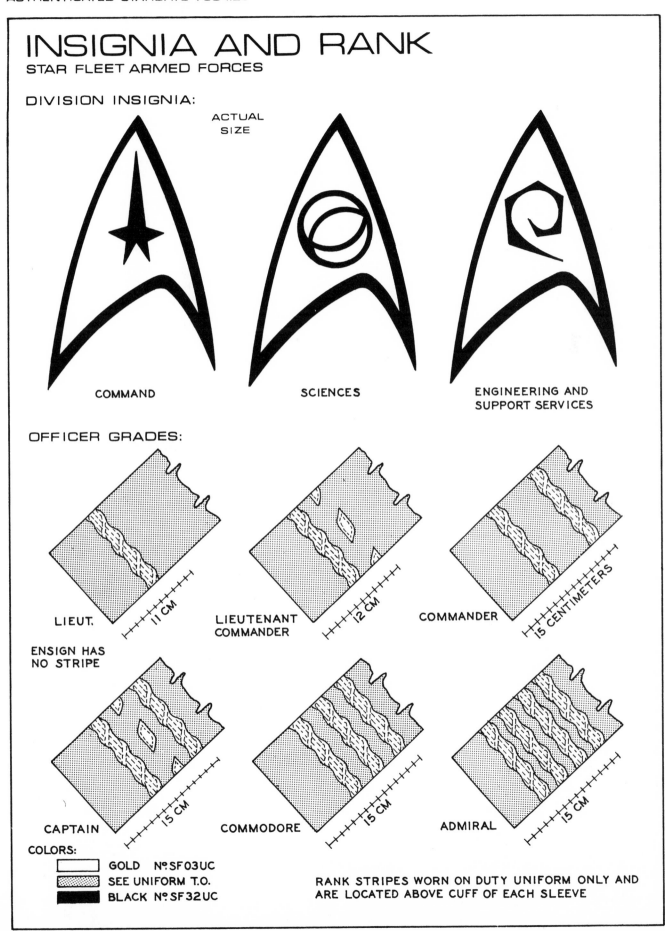

INSIGNIA AND RANK
STAR FLEET ARMED FORCES

DIVISION INSIGNIA:

ACTUAL SIZE

COMMAND

SCIENCES

ENGINEERING AND SUPPORT SERVICES

OFFICER GRADES:

LIEUT.　11 CM

LIEUTENANT COMMANDER　12 CM

COMMANDER　15 CENTIMETERS

ENSIGN HAS NO STRIPE

CAPTAIN　15 CM

COMMODORE　15 CM

ADMIRAL　15 CM

COLORS:

　□　GOLD　NºSF03UC
　▒　SEE UNIFORM T.O.
　■　BLACK　NºSF32UC

RANK STRIPES WORN ON DUTY UNIFORM ONLY AND ARE LOCATED ABOVE CUFF OF EACH SLEEVE

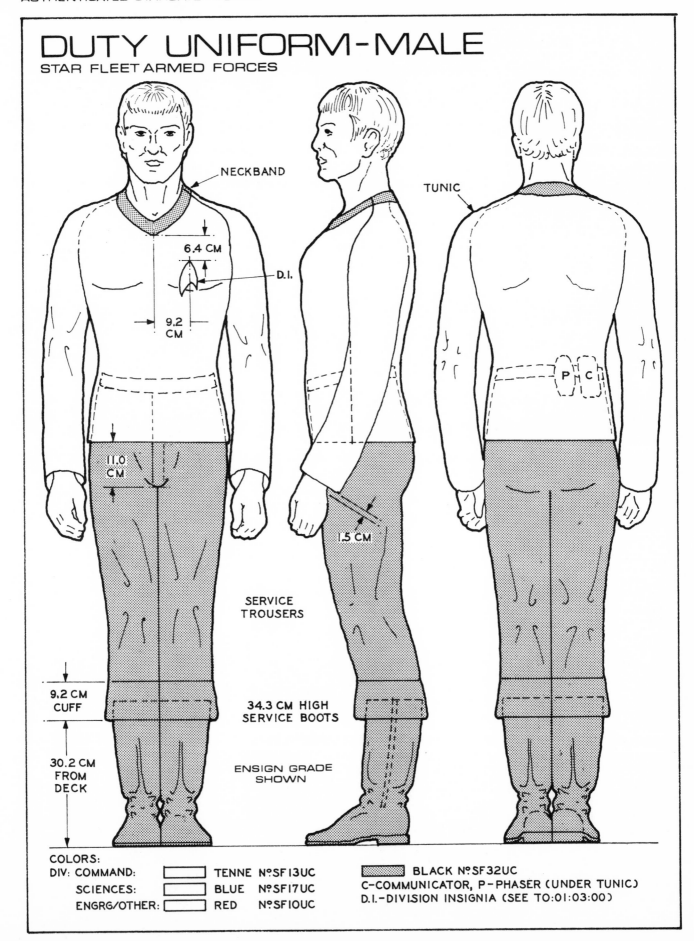

DUTY UNIFORM-MALE
STAR FLEET ARMED FORCES

NECKBAND

6.4 CM

D.I.

9.2 CM

TUNIC

11.0 CM

1.5 CM

P   C

SERVICE TROUSERS

9.2 CM CUFF

34.3 CM HIGH SERVICE BOOTS

30.2 CM FROM DECK

ENSIGN GRADE SHOWN

COLORS:

DIV: COMMAND: TENNE   Nº SF13UC

SCIENCES: BLUE   Nº SF17UC

ENGRG/OTHER: RED   Nº SF10UC

BLACK Nº SF32UC

C-COMMUNICATOR, P-PHASER (UNDER TUNIC)

D.I.-DIVISION INSIGNIA (SEE TO:01:03:00)

UNIFORM PATTERN
MALE - NON-COMPUTERIZED FABRICATION

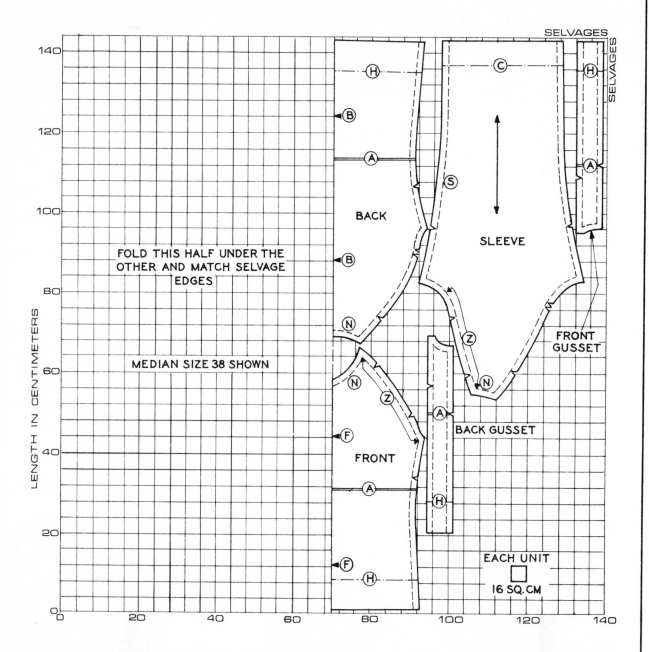

RATIO UNIT UP OR DOWN FOR LARGER OR SMALLER SIZES. CUT TWO TOGETHER OF EACH GUSSET AND SLEEVE PATTERN. MAKE COLLAR FROM 13 x 44 CM BLACK RIBBING. PATTERN FOR USE WITH REGULATION STRETCH FABRICS ONLY. TROUSERS ARE REGULATION PATTERN WITHOUT POCKETS OR BELT – USE FITTED WAISTBAND. A – LENGTHEN OR SHORTEN PATTERN HERE. B, F – PLACE CENTERLINE ON FOLD OF FABRIC. C – CUFF FOR LONG ARM LENGTH. H – APPROXIMATE HEM LINE. N – NECK LINE. S – SEAM WIDTH ---- 1.60 CM. Z – INVISIBLE ZIPPER IN SEAM W/ TALON UP – IT MUST INCLUDE COLLAR. ADJUST PATTERN AT SEAMS FOR SMOOTH FIT.

DUTY UNIFORM-FEMALE
STAR FLEET ARMED FORCES

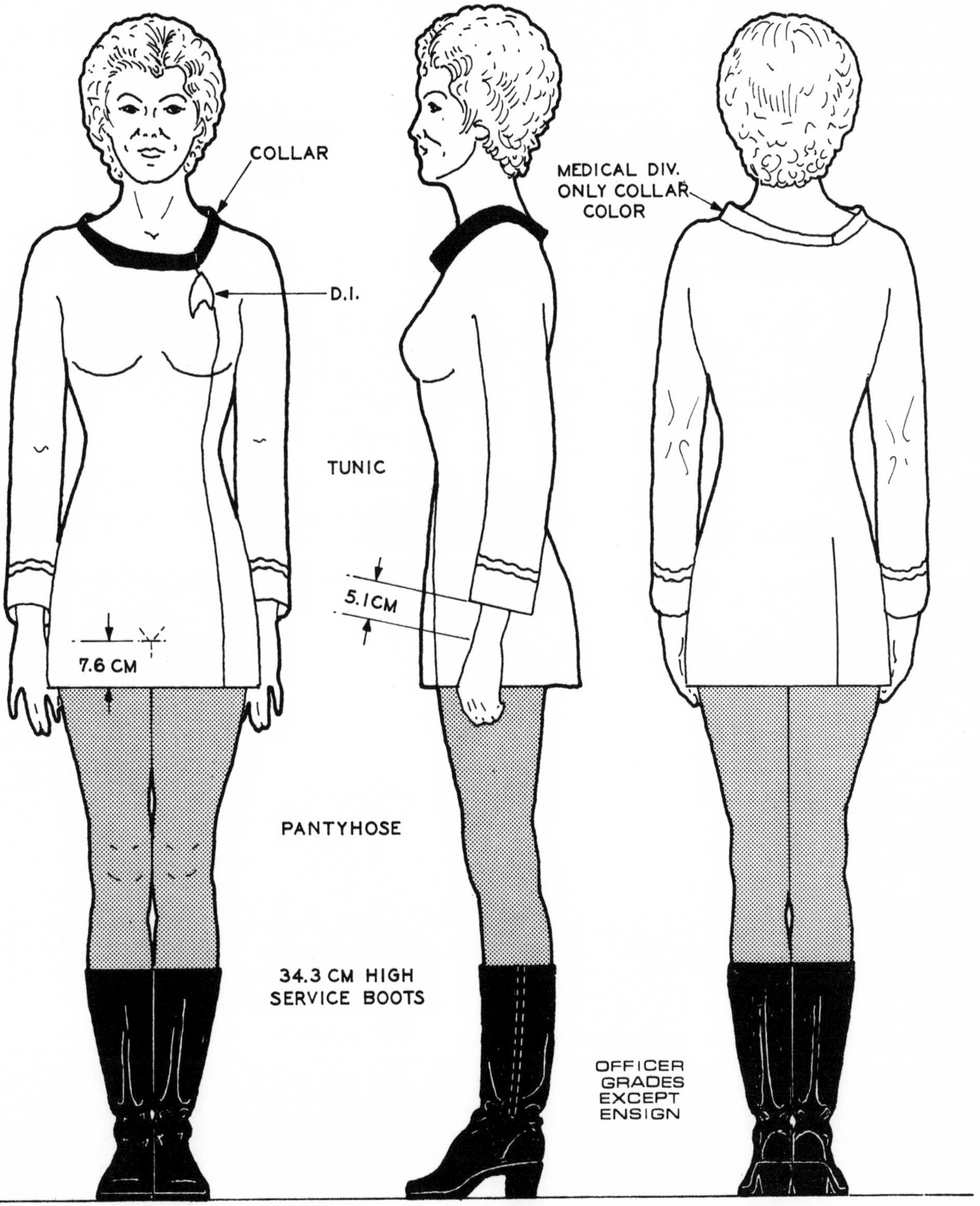

COLLAR

D.I.

MEDICAL DIV.
ONLY COLLAR
COLOR

TUNIC

5.1CM

7.6 CM

PANTYHOSE

34.3 CM HIGH
SERVICE BOOTS

OFFICER
GRADES
EXCEPT
ENSIGN

COLORS:
DIV: COMMAND		TENNE	NºSF13UC		NUDE	NºSF25UC
SCIENCES		BLUE	NºSF17UC		BLACK	NºSF32UC
ENGRG/OTHER		RED	NºSF10UC			

D.I.– DIVISION INSIGNIA (SEE TO:01:03:00)

OFF. UNIFORM PATTERN
FEMALE - FOR NON-COMPUTERIZED FABRICATION

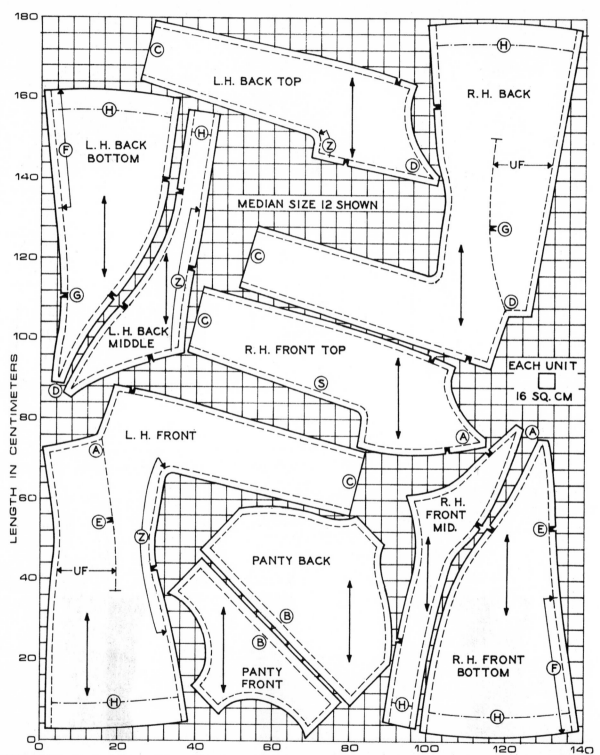

RATIO UNIT UP OR DOWN FOR LARGER OR SMALLER SIZES. MAKE COLLAR FROM 13 X 74 CM BLACK RIBBING. B-WAISTBAND WIDTH-2 CM. C-CUFF. F-FLAP. H-HEM. S-SEAM WIDTH------1.60 CM. UF-UNDER FLAP. Z-INVISIBLE ZIPPER IN SEAM W/TALON UP. ADJUST SEAMS FOR SMOOTH FIT AND FLAP LENGTH FOR FLAT HANG. USE ELASTIC IN PANTY WAISTBAND AND LEG BANDS.

DUTY UNIFORM-FEMALE
STAR FLEET ARMED FORCES

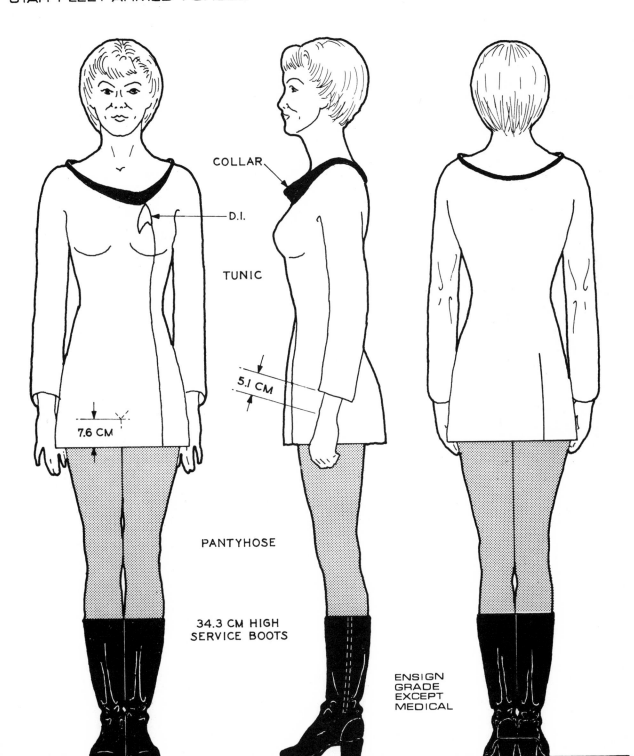

COLLAR

D.I.

TUNIC

5.1 CM

7.6 CM

PANTYHOSE

34.3 CM HIGH
SERVICE BOOTS

ENSIGN
GRADE
EXCEPT
MEDICAL

COLORS:

DIV:			
COMMAND........	☐	TENNE	Nº SF13 UC
SCIENCES........	☐	BLUE	Nº SF17 UC
ENGRG/OTHER...	☐	RED	Nº SF10 UC

NUDE   Nº SF25 UC
BLACK Nº SF32 UC

D.I.-DIVISION INSIGNIA (SEE TO:01:03:00)

ENS. UNIFORM PATTERN
FEMALE -NON-COMPUTERIZED FABRICATION

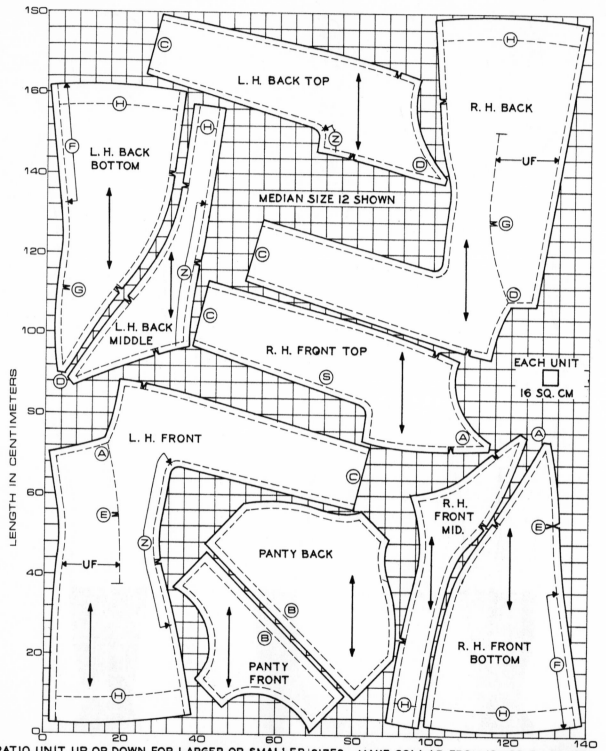

RATIO UNIT UP OR DOWN FOR LARGER OR SMALLER SIZES. MAKE COLLAR FROM 13 x 80 CM BLACK RIBBING. B - WAISTBAND WIDTH - 2 CM. C - CUFF. F - FLAP. H - HEM. S - SEAM WIDTH - 1.6 CM. UF - UNDER FLAP. Z - INVISIBLE ZIPPER IN SEAM W/ TALON UP. ADJUST SEAMS FOR SMOOTH FIT AND FLAP LENGTH FOR FLAT HANG. USE ELASTIC IN PANTY WAISTBAND AND LEG BANDS.

DUTY UNIFORM-FEMALE
STAR FLEET ARMED FORCES

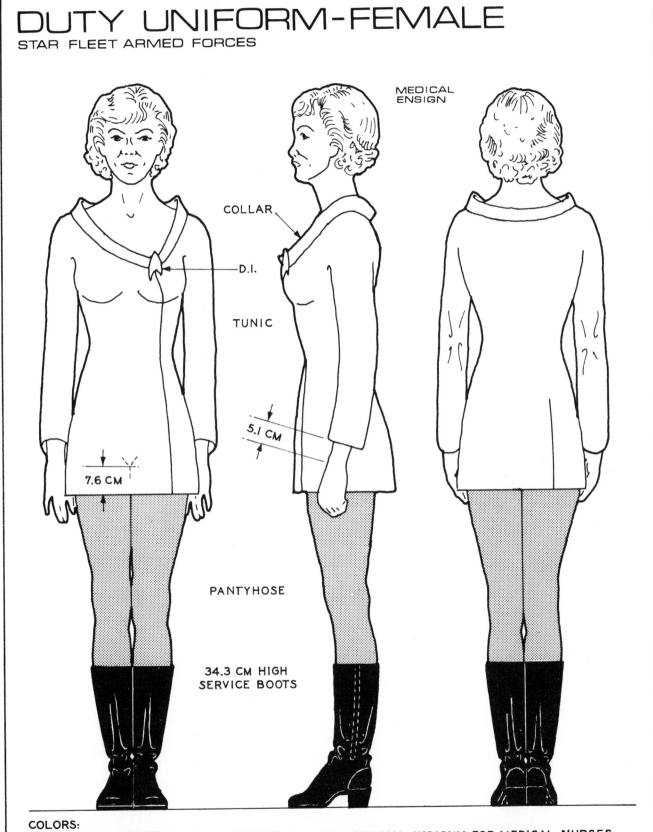

MEDICAL
ENSIGN

COLLAR

D.I.

TUNIC

5.1 CM

7.6 CM

PANTYHOSE

34.3 CM HIGH
SERVICE BOOTS

COLORS:
DIV: SCIENCES

☐	BLUE	N⁰SF17UC
▦	NUDE	N⁰SF25UC
■	BLACK	N⁰SF32UC

D.I. – DIVISION INSIGNIA FOR MEDICAL NURSES
AND ORDERLIES (SEE TO:01:03:01)

MED. UNIFORM PATTERN
FEMALE - NON-COMPUTERIZED FABRICATION

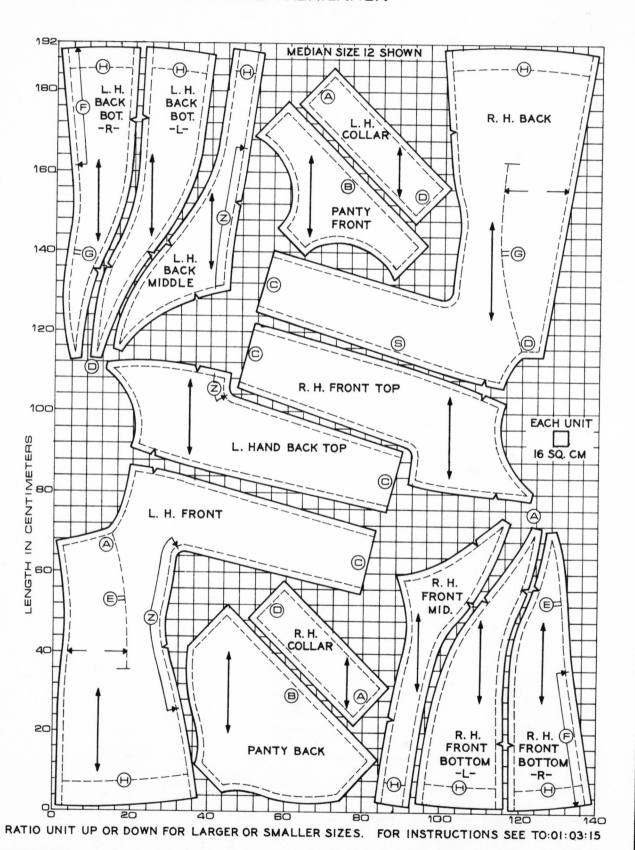

MEDIAN SIZE 12 SHOWN

LENGTH IN CENTIMETERS

L. H. BACK BOT. -R-

L. H. BACK BOT. -L-

L. H. BACK MIDDLE

L. H. COLLAR

PANTY FRONT

R. H. BACK

EACH UNIT
☐ 16 SQ. CM

R. H. FRONT TOP

L. HAND BACK TOP

L. H. FRONT

R. H. COLLAR

PANTY BACK

R. H. FRONT MID.

R. H. FRONT BOTTOM -L-

R. H. FRONT BOTTOM -R-

RATIO UNIT UP OR DOWN FOR LARGER OR SMALLER SIZES. FOR INSTRUCTIONS SEE TO:01:03:15

FLEET SHIP CLASSIFICATIONS
CLASS I STARSHIPS

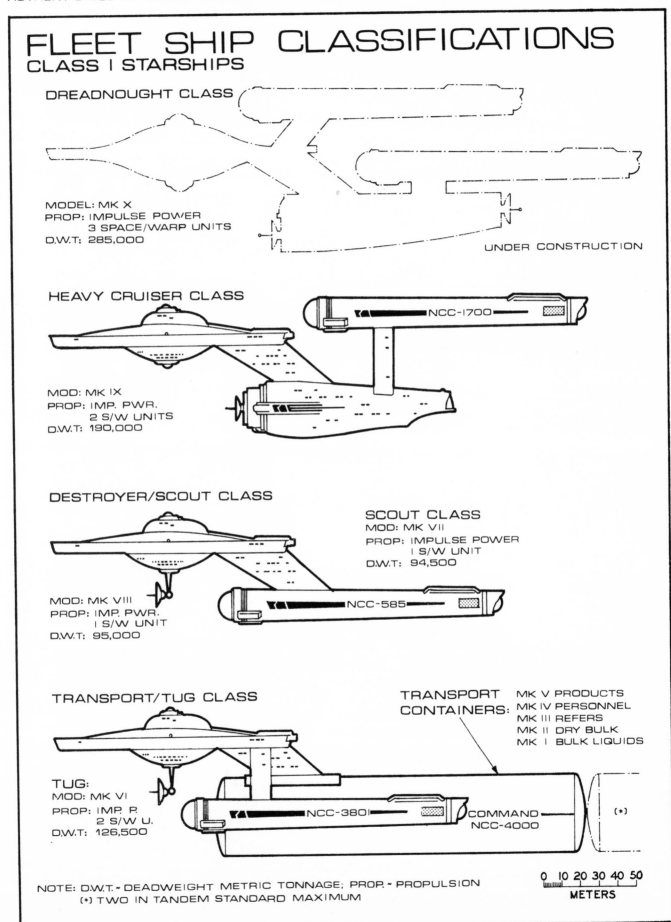

DREADNOUGHT CLASS

MODEL: MK X
PROP: IMPULSE POWER
    3 SPACE/WARP UNITS
D.W.T: 285,000

UNDER CONSTRUCTION

HEAVY CRUISER CLASS

NCC-1700

MOD: MK IX
PROP: IMP. PWR.
    2 S/W UNITS
D.W.T: 190,000

DESTROYER/SCOUT CLASS

SCOUT CLASS
MOD: MK VII
PROP: IMPULSE POWER
    I S/W UNIT
D.W.T: 94,500

NCC-585

MOD: MK VIII
PROP: IMP. PWR.
    I S/W UNIT
D.W.T: 95,000

TRANSPORT/TUG CLASS

TRANSPORT
CONTAINERS:
MK V PRODUCTS
MK IV PERSONNEL
MK III REFERS
MK II DRY BULK
MK I BULK LIQUIDS

TUG:
MOD: MK VI
PROP: IMP. P.
    2 S/W U.
D.W.T: 126,500

NCC-3801

COMMAND
NCC-4000

(*)

NOTE: D.W.T. - DEADWEIGHT METRIC TONNAGE; PROP. - PROPULSION
    (*) TWO IN TANDEM STANDARD MAXIMUM

0 10 20 30 40 50
METERS

CLASS I HEAVY CRUISER
CONSTITUTION CLASS STARSHIPS

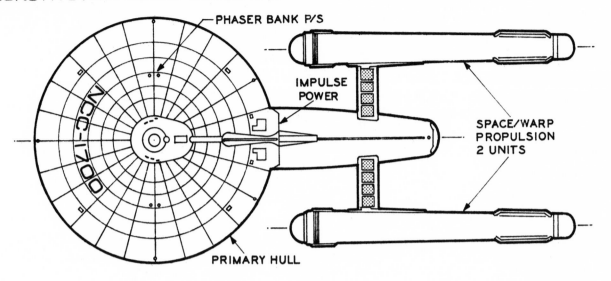

PHASER BANK P/S
IMPULSE POWER
SPACE/WARP PROPULSION 2 UNITS
PRIMARY HULL

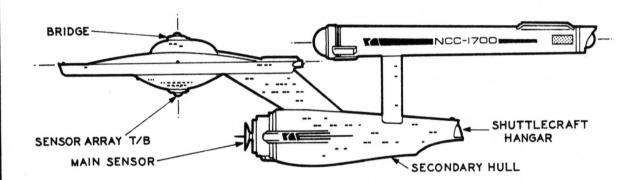

BRIDGE
SENSOR ARRAY T/B
MAIN SENSOR
SHUTTLECRAFT HANGAR
SECONDARY HULL

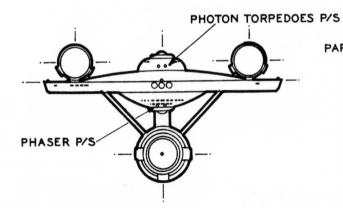

PHOTON TORPEDOES P/S
PHASER P/S

PARTICULARS:

DEADWEIGHT TONNAGE-METRIC	190,000
STD. RANGE	18 YEARS AT L.Y.V.
MAX. SAFE CRUISING SPEED	W/F 6
EMERGENCY SPEED	W/F 8
MAIN PHASERS	3 BANKS/2 EACH
PHOTON TORPEDOES	2 BANKS
LENGTH OVERALL-METERS	288.6
BREADTH OVERALL-METERS	127.1
HEIGHT OVERALL-METERS	72.6
PRIMARY HULL DIA.-METERS	127.1
SEC. HULL LENGTH-METERS	103.6
SEC. HULL MAX. DIA.-METERS	34.1
PROP. UNIT L.O.A.-METERS	153.6
PROP. UNIT DIA.-METERS	17.3

STD. SHIP'S COMPLEMENT:

OFFICERS (COMMAND)	43
CREW (ENSIGN GRADE)	387

0 10 20 30 40 50
METERS

SEE BOOKLET OF GENERAL PLANS FOR DETAILS

HEAVY CRUISER CLASS
AUTHORIZED CONSTRUCTION

THE FOLLOWING SHIPS OF THE MK-IX CLASS WERE AUTHORIZED BY THE ORIGINAL ARTICLES OF FEDERATION OF STARDATE 0965:

CONSTELLATION – NCC-1017**	FARRAGUT – NCC-1702**	POTEMPKIN – NCC-1711
CONSTITUTION – NCC-1700*	HOOD – NCC-1707	REPUBLIC – NCC-1371
ENTERPRISE – NCC-1701	INTREPID – NCC-1708**	VALIANT – NCC-1709**
EXCALIBUR – NCC-1705	KONGO – NCC-1710	YORKTOWN – NCC-1704
EXETER – NCC-1706	LEXINGTON – NCC-1703	

THE FOLLOWING SHIPS OF THE MK-IXA CLASS WERE AUTHORIZED BY THE STAR FLEET APPROPRIATION OF STARDATE 3220:

ARI – NCC-1723	EXCELSIOR – NCC-1718	MONITOR – NCC-1713
BONHOMME RICHARD – NCC-1712*	HORNET – NCC-1714	SARATOGA – NCC-1724
EAGLE – NCC-1719	LAFAYETTE – NCC-1720	TORI – NCC-1725
EL DORADO – NCC-1722	KRIEGER – NCC-1726	WASP – NCC-1721
ENDEAVOR – NCC-1716	MERRIMAC – NCC-1715	DEFIANCE – NCC-1717
ESSEX – NCC-1727		

THE FOLLOWING REPLACEMENTS FOR THE CONSTITUTION CLASS WERE AUTHORIZED BY STAR FLEET APPROPRIATION OF STARDATE 4444:

CONSTELLATION II – NCC-1728	INTREPID II – NCC-1730	
FARRAGUT II – NCC-1729	VALIANT II – NCC-1731	

THE FOLLOWING SHIPS OF THE MK-IXB CLASS WERE AUTHORIZED BY THE STAR FLEET APPROPRIATION OF STARDATE 5930:

ACHERNAR – NCC-1732*	FOMALHAUT – NCC-1804	PILAR – NCC-1746
ACRUX – NCC-1818	GALINA – NCC-1764	POLARIS – NCC-1839
ADHARA – NCC-1827	GHAR – NCC-1786	POLLUX – NCC-1808
AGENA – NCC-1816	GHONDR – NCC-1749	PROCYON – NCC-1756
AHZDAR – NCC-1790	HAJJ – NCC-1782	PROXIMA – NCC-1737
ALAM'AK – NCC-1796	HELIOS – NCC-1825	QUAL'AT – NCC-1776
ALDEBARAN – NCC-1812	HIEMDAL – NCC-1793	QIZAN – NCC-1775
ALFERAZ – NCC-1781	HOR – NCC-1813	QUINDAR – NCC-1736
ALFR – NCC-1741	HOROK – NCC-1748	REGULUS – NCC-1840
ALIOTH – NCC-1828	JASSAN – NCC-1754	RIGEL – NCC-1824
ALKAID – NCC-1829	JENSHAHN – NCC-1791	RIGIL KENTAURUS – NCC-1735
ALNILAM – NCC-1830	JUPITER – NCC-1734	SALAYNA – NCC-1774
ALTAIR – NCC-1803	KARS – NCC-1769	SAMAARA – NCC-1765
ANAK – NCC-1821	KASIMAR – NCC-1784	SARDAR – NCC-1811
ANDROCUS – NCC-1738	KEP SALU – NCC-1767	SHAHR – NCC-1745
ANNOBON – NCC-1752	KESTRAL – NCC-1766	SHAULA – NCC-1841
ANTARES – NCC-1820	KETOI – NCC-1768	SHAANDRA – NCC-1795
ARCTURUS – NCC-1807	K'HOTAN – NCC-1802	SINUIJI – NCC-1770
ARIDED – NCC-1831	K'USHUI – NCC-1801	SIRIUS – NCC-1744
ASTRAD – NCC-1739	LUX – NCC-1823	SOL – NCC-1733
BEHR'AK – NCC-1797	MIAPLACIDAS – NCC-1836	SPICA – NCC-1815
BELLATRIX – NCC-1832	MAAT – NCC-1794	TALI – NCC-1751
BETELGEUSE – NCC-1822	MAZDA – NCC-1778	TAJARHI – NCC-1783
BINAR – NCC-1819	MENGEN – NCC-1773	TEMIR – NCC-1763
CANOPUS – NCC-1814	MIRFAK – NCC-1837	THELONII – NCC-1742
CAPELLA – NCC-1809	MIRAZH – NCC-1788	THOLUS – NCC-1747
CASPAN – NCC-1753	MONDOLOY – NCC-1740	TIKOPAI – NCC-1800*
CASTOR – NCC-1833	MONGO – NCC-1785	TULAN – NCC-1777
CZAR'AK – NCC-1798	MURZIM – NCC-1838	TUTAKAI – NCC-1799
DARION – NCC-1810	NDELE – NCC-1758	VEGA – NCC-1806
DENEB – NCC-1826	NAKARAT – NCC-1805	VENA – NCC-1817
DUBHE – NCC-1834	OOMARU – NCC-1761	WEZEN – NCC-1842
EL NATH – NCC-1835	OBLIK – NCC-1772	XANTHII – NCC-1743
ELOHIM – NCC-1792	PARI – NCC-1787	YAAN – NCC-1762
EKINUS – NCC-1771	PAEGAN – NCC-1755	ZAAHM – NCC-1780
ESABL – NCC-1779	PELIONE – NCC-1750	ZA'FARAN – NCC-1760
ESKIIS – NCC-1789	PHARDOS – NCC-1757	ZINDAR – NCC-1759

*CLASS SHIP. **LOST IN THE LINE OF DUTY. ALL NAMES PRECEDED WITH "U.S.S."

CLASS I DESTROYER
SALADIN CLASS STARSHIPS

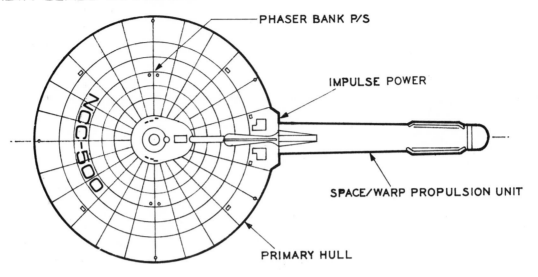

PHASER BANK P/S

IMPULSE POWER

SPACE/WARP PROPULSION UNIT

PRIMARY HULL

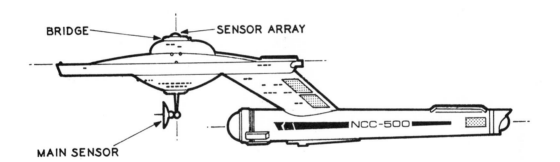

BRIDGE — SENSOR ARRAY

MAIN SENSOR

NCC-500

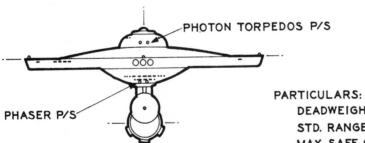

PHOTON TORPEDOS P/S

PHASER P/S

PARTICULARS:

DEADWEIGHT TONNAGE-METRIC	95,000
STD. RANGE	9 YEARS AT L.Y.V.
MAX. SAFE CRUISING SPEED	W/F 6
EMERGENCY SPEED	W/F 8
MAIN PHASERS	3 BANKS/2 EACH
PHOTON TORPEDOES	2 BANKS
LENGTH OVERALL-METERS	242.5
BREADTH OVERALL-METERS	127.1
HEIGHT OVERALL-METERS	60
PRIMARY HULL DIA.-METERS	127.1
PROP. UNIT L.O.A-METERS	153.6
PROP. UNIT DIA.-METERS	17.3

0 10 20 30 40 50
METERS

STD. SHIP'S COMPLEMENT:

OFFICERS (COMMAND)	20
CREW (ENSIGN GRADE)	180

SEE BOOKLET OF GENERAL PLANS FOR DETAILS

DESTROYER CLASS
AUTHORIZED CONSTRUCTION

THE FOLLOWING SHIPS OF THE MK-VIII CLASS WERE AUTHORIZED BY THE ORIGINAL
ARTICLES OF FEDERATION OF STARDATE 0965:

ADAD – NCC-515	HAMILCAR – NCC-518	SHAITAN – NCC-519
AHRIMAN – NCC-513	HANNIBAL – NCC-512	SALADIN – NCC-500*
ALARIC – NCC-503	HASHISHIYUN – NCC-516	SARGON – NCC-504
ALEXANDER – NCC-511	JENGHIZ – NCC-501	SULEIMAN – NCC-508
AZRAEL – NCC-517	KUBLAI – NCC-507	TAMERLANE – NCC-510
DARIUS – NCC-502	POMPEY – NCC-506	XERXES – NCC-505
ETZEL – NCC-509	RAHMAN – NCC-514	

THE FOLLOWING SHIPS OF THE MK-VIIIA CLASS WERE AUTHORIZED BY STAR FLEET
APPROPRIATION OF STARDATE 3030:

ARES – NCC-524	LOKI – NCC-529	SIVA – NCC-520*
HATHOR – NCC-523	LUCIFER – NCC-521	TYR – NCC-526
IBLIS – NCC-528	MARS – NCC-525	
JUGURTHA – NCC-527	MOLOCK – NCC-522	

THE FOLLOWING SHIPS OF THE MK-VIIIB CLASS WERE AUTHORIZED BY STAR FLEET
APPROPRIATION OF STARDATE 4699:

ABU BEKR – NCC-549	COCHISE – NCC-530*	MARTEL – NCC-554
ACHILLES – NCC-551	CORTEZ – NCC-536	NELSON – NCC-546
AJAX – NCC-547	DE RUYTER – NCC-538	NEY – NCC-533
AKBAR – NCC-548	DRAKE – NCC-541	PERSEUS – NCC-544
ALVA – NCC-531	EL CID – NCC-534	PONTIAC – NCC-532
ALVARADO – NCC-537	GERONIMO – NCC-535	SCIPIO – NCC-553
AL MAHDI – NCC-545	HEKTOR – NCC-539	SAMSON – NCC-543
APPOLLYON – NCC-542	IVAN – NCC-550	THESEUS – NCC-552
CIMON – NCC-555	LYSANDER – NCC-540	

*CLASS SHIP.   ALL NAMES PRECEDED WITH "U.S.S."

CLASS I SCOUT
HERMES CLASS STARSHIPS

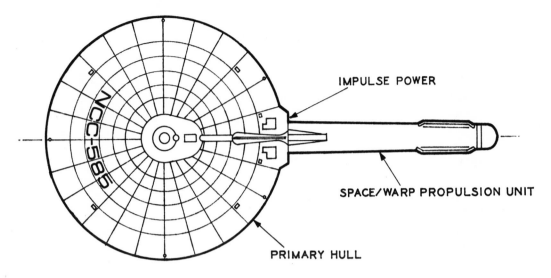

IMPULSE POWER

SPACE/WARP PROPULSION UNIT

PRIMARY HULL

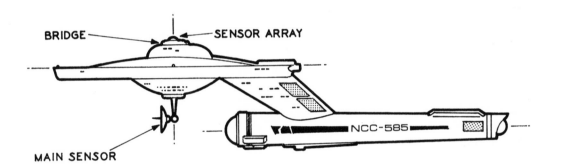

BRIDGE — SENSOR ARRAY

MAIN SENSOR

NCC-585

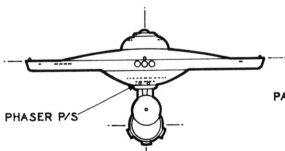

PHASER P/S

PARTICULARS:

DEADWEIGHT TONNAGE-METRIC..........94,500
STD. RANGE........................9 YEARS AT L.Y.V.
MAX. SAFE CRUISING SPEED.................W/F 6
EMERGENCY SPEED.............................W/F 8
MAIN PHASERS....................... I BANK/2 EACH
LENGTH OVERALL-METERS.................242.5
BREADTH OVERALL-METERS...................127.1
HEIGHT OVERALL-METERS.........................60
PRIMARY HULL DIA.-METERS.................127.1
PROP. UNIT L.O.A.-METERS.....................153.6
PROP. UNIT DIA.-METERS.....................17.3

STD. SHIP'S COMPLEMENT:
OFFICERS (COMMAND)......................20
CREW (ENSIGN GRADE)....................175

0 10 20 30 40 50
METERS

SEE BOOKLET OF GENERAL PLANS FOR DETAILS

SCOUT CLASS
AUTHORIZED CONSTRUCTION

THE FOLLOWING SHIPS OF THE MK-VII CLASS WERE AUTHORIZED BY THE ORIGINAL ARTICLES OF FEDERATION OF STARDATE 0965:

AEOLUS – NCC-588	CARSON – NCC-592	QUINTILLUS – NCC-590
ANUBIS – NCC-586	CODY – NCC-594	REVERE – 595
BATIDOR – NCC-593	CROCKETT – NCC-600	SACAJAWEA – NCC-598
BOWIE – NCC-597	DIANA – NCC-589	SPAKER – 596
BRIDGER – NCC-591	HERMES – NCC-585*	TONTI – NCC-599

THE FOLLOWING SHIPS OF THE MK-VIIA CLASS WERE AUTHORIZED BY STAR FLEET APPROPRIATION OF STARDATE 3669:

ARIES – NCC-602	LEO MINOR – NCC-614	PEGASUS – NCC-612
CAMELOPARDUS – NCC-606	LEPUS – NCC-610	TAURUS – NCC-605
CANIS MAJOR – NCC-611	LUPUS – NCC-604	URSA MAJOR – NCC-609
CANIS MINOR – NCC-615	LYNX – NCC-608	URSA MINOR – NCC-616
EQUULUS – NCC-603	MONOCEROS – NCC-601*	VULPECULA – NCC-613
LEO – NCC-607		

THE FOLLOWING SHIPS OF THE MK-VIIB CLASS WERE AUTHORIZED BY STAR FLEET APPROPRIATION OF STARDATE 5099. THEY ARE SPECIALLY OUTFITTED FOR REGULAR DUTY AS COMMAND AND DIPLOMATIC COURRIERS:

APUS – NCC-618	CORVUS – NCC-620	PAVO – NCC-622
AQUILA – NCC-623	CYGNUS – NCC-617*	PHOENIX – NCC-625
COLUMBIA – NCC-621	GRUS – NCC-624	TUCANA – NCC-619

*CLASS SHIP. ALL NAMES PRECEDED WITH "U.S.S."

CLASS I TRANSPORT/TUG
PTOLEMY CLASS STARSHIPS

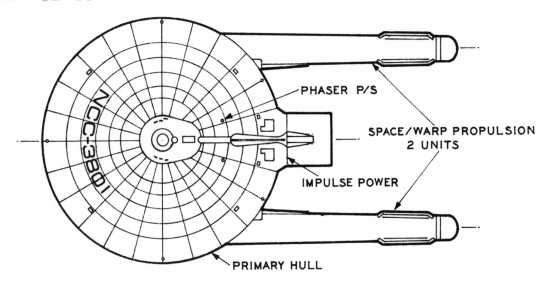

PHASER P/S

SPACE/WARP PROPULSION
2 UNITS

IMPULSE POWER

PRIMARY HULL

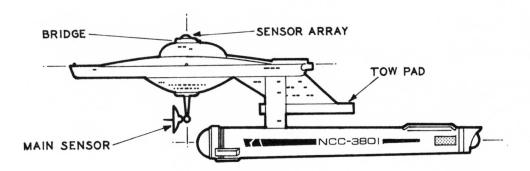

BRIDGE

SENSOR ARRAY

TOW PAD

MAIN SENSOR

NCC-3801

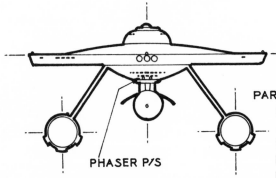

PHASER P/S

PARTICULARS:

DEADWEIGHT TONNAGE -METRIC	126,500
STD. RANGE	9 YEARS AT L.Y.V.
MAX. SAFE CRUISING SPEED	W/F 6
EMERGENCY SPEED	W/F 8
MAIN PHASERS	2 BANKS/2 EACH
LENGTH OVERALL-METERS	222
BREADTH OVERALL-METERS	127.1
HEIGHT OVERALL-METERS	66
PRIMARY HULL DIA.-METERS	127.1
PROP. UNIT L.O.A.-METERS	153.6
PROP. UNIT DIA.-METERS	17.3

STD. SHIP'S COMPLEMENT:
OFFICERS (COMMAND) 22
CREW (ENSIGN GRADE) 198

0 10 20 30 40 50
METERS

SEE BOOKLET OF GENERAL PLANS FOR DETAILS

TRANSP./TUG CLASS
AUTHORIZED CONSTRUCTION

THE FOLLOWING SHIPS OF THE MK-VI CLASS WERE AUTHORIZED BY THE ORIGINAL
ARTICLES OF FEDERATION OF STARDATE 0965:

AL RASHID – NCC-3802	ERATOSTHENES – NCC-3807	PHILOLAUS – NCC-3811
ANAXAGORAS – NCC-3803	GALILEI – NCC-3808	PTOLEMY – NCC-3801 *
ANAXIMANDER – NCC-3804	HEVELIUS – NCC-3814	PYTHAGORAS – NCC-3812
ARISTARCHUS – NCC-3805	HIPPARCHUS – NCC-3809	THALES – NCC-3813
COPERNICUS – NCC-3815	IBN DAUD – NCC-3806	ULUGH BEG – NCC-3810

THE FOLLOWING SHIPS OF THE MK-VIA CLASS WERE AUTHORIZED BY STAR FLEET
APPROPRIATION OF STARDATE 3640:

AMBARTSUMIAN – NCC-3817	FLAMARION – NCC-3818	LUYTEN – NCC-3829
BRAHE – NCC-3821	KEPPLER – NCC-3816 *	NEWTON – NCC-3822
CASSINI – NCC-3824	KIDINNU – NCC-3826	PIAZZI – NCC-3827
DESLANDRES – NCC-3820	LEVERRIER – NCC-3828	RICCIOLI – NCC-3823
DONATI – NCC-3825	MESSIER – NCC-3830	SCHIAPARELLI – NCC-3819

THE FOLLOWING SHIPS OF THE MK-VIB CLASS WERE AUTHORIZED BY STAR FLEET
APPROPRIATION OF STARDATE 4990:

ADAMS – NCC-3925	HALE – NCC-3873	PIERCE – NCC-3931
AIRY – NCC-3842	HALL – NCC-3926	PICKERING – NCC-3864
APIAN – NCC-3896	HALLEY – NCC-3833	POGSON – NCC-3906
BAADE – NCC-3855	HAYASHI – NCC-3887	POPPER – NCC-3878
BAUM – NCC-3935	HENCKE – NCC-3847	PLASKETT – NCC-3918
BAYER – NCC-3869	HENDERSON – NCC-3914	PRITCHETT – NCC-3838
BESSEL – NCC-3911	HERSCHELL – NCC-3860	REBER – NCC-3892
BIELA – NCC-3884	HERTZSPRUNG – NCC-3902	RITTENHOUSE – NCC-3851
BODE – NCC-3922	HIRAYAMA – NCC-3874	ROQUES – NCC-3932
BONDI – NCC-3843	HOYLE – NCC-3928	ROSS – NCC-3865
BROUWER – NCC-3897	HOLDEN – NCC-3834	RUSSELL – NCC-3907
CAMPELL – NCC-3856	HUBBARD – NCC-3888	SABINE – NCC-3879
CARPENTER – NCC-3936	HUBBLE – NCC-3848	SANDAGE – NCC-3919
CARRINGTON – NCC-3870	HUGGINS – NCC-3915	SAVARY – NCC-3839
CHALLIS – NCC-3912	HUMANSON – NCC-3861	SCHEINER – NCC-3893
CHAMBERLAIN – NCC-3883	IRWIN – NCC-3903	SCHMIDT – NCC-3880
CHANDRASEKHER – NCC-3923	JANSKY – NCC-3875	SECCHI – NCC-3852
CHAUVENET – NCC-3844	JEANS – NCC-3929	SHAPLEY – NCC-3933
CLARK – NCC-3898	JEFFREY – NCC-3835	SHKLOVSKY – NCC-3866
COLUMBO – NCC-3857	KAULA – NCC-3889	SLIPHER – NCC-3908
DELAMBRE – NCC-3937	KLEPSTRA – NCC-3862	SCHAWBE – NCC-3920
DOLLFUS – NCC-3885	KOHLSCHUTTER – NCC-3904	STRUVE – NCC-3840
DOLLOND – NCC-3900 *	KRUGER – NCC-3871	SWIFT – NCC-3894
DOPPLER – NCC-3831*	KUIPER – NCC-3836	TODD – NCC-3934
DREYER – NCC-3899	LAGRANGE – NCC-3916	TOMBAUGH – NCC-3853
EDDINGTON – NCC-3845	LAPLACE – NCC-3876	TOSCANELLI – NCC-3867
EICHELBERGER – NCC-3924	LEAVITT – NCC-3849	VAN DE HULST – NCC-3909
ENCKE – NCC-3859	LANGLEY – NCC-3930	VAN DE KAMP – NCC-3881
FLAMSTEED – NCC-3913	LOCKYER – NCC-3890	VAN MAANEN – NCC-3940
FRACASTOR – NCC-3872	LOWELL – NCC-3939	VOGEL – NCC-3841
FROST – NCC-3938	MITCHELL – NCC-3863	VON ZACH – NCC-3882
GAILLOT – NCC-3832	MOULTON – NCC-3905	WALKER – NCC-3895
GALLE – NCC-3886	NEWCOMB – NCC-3877	WOLASTON – NCC-3854
GAUTIER – NCC-3846	OLBERS – NCC-3917	WOLF – NCC-3921
GOLD – NCC-3927	OORT – NCC-3837	WRIGHT – NCC-3868
GOLDRICKE – NCC-3859	PALITZSCH – NCC-3891	YOUNG – NCC-3910
GOLDREICH – NCC-3901	PEALE – NCC-3850	

*CLASS SHIP. ALL NAMES PRECEDED WITH "U.S.S."

TRANSPORT CONTAINERS
CLASS I STARSHIPS – USE WITH CLASS I TUG

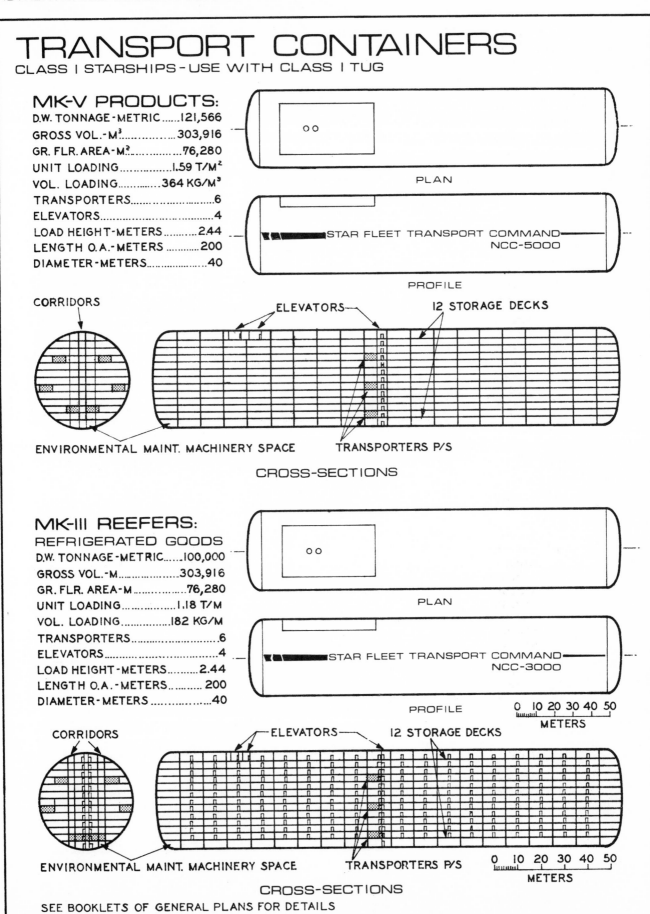

MK-V PRODUCTS:

D.W. TONNAGE - METRIC	121,566
GROSS VOL. - M³	303,916
GR. FLR. AREA - M²	76,280
UNIT LOADING	1.59 T/M²
VOL. LOADING	364 KG/M³
TRANSPORTERS	6
ELEVATORS	4
LOAD HEIGHT - METERS	2.44
LENGTH O.A. - METERS	200
DIAMETER - METERS	40

PLAN

STAR FLEET TRANSPORT COMMAND
NCC-5000

PROFILE

CORRIDORS

ELEVATORS

12 STORAGE DECKS

ENVIRONMENTAL MAINT. MACHINERY SPACE

TRANSPORTERS P/S

CROSS-SECTIONS

MK-III REEFERS:
REFRIGERATED GOODS

D.W. TONNAGE - METRIC	100,000
GROSS VOL. - M	303,916
GR. FLR. AREA - M	76,280
UNIT LOADING	1.18 T/M
VOL. LOADING	182 KG/M
TRANSPORTERS	6
ELEVATORS	4
LOAD HEIGHT - METERS	2.44
LENGTH O.A. - METERS	200
DIAMETER - METERS	40

PLAN

STAR FLEET TRANSPORT COMMAND
NCC-3000

PROFILE

0 10 20 30 40 50
METERS

CORRIDORS

ELEVATORS

12 STORAGE DECKS

ENVIRONMENTAL MAINT. MACHINERY SPACE

TRANSPORTERS P/S

0 10 20 30 40 50
METERS

CROSS-SECTIONS

SEE BOOKLETS OF GENERAL PLANS FOR DETAILS

TRANSPORT CONTAINERS
CLASS I STARSHIPS-USE WITH CLASS I TUG

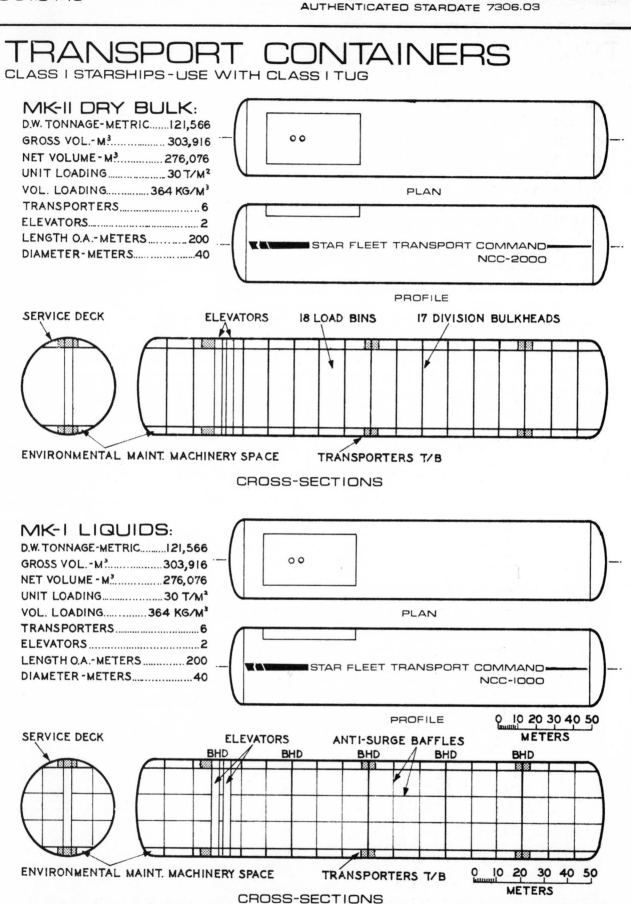

MK-II DRY BULK:

D.W. TONNAGE-METRIC	121,566
GROSS VOL.-M^3	303,916
NET VOLUME-M^3	276,076
UNIT LOADING	30 T/M^2
VOL. LOADING	364 KG/M^3
TRANSPORTERS	6
ELEVATORS	2
LENGTH O.A.-METERS	200
DIAMETER-METERS	40

PLAN

STAR FLEET TRANSPORT COMMAND
NCC-2000

PROFILE

SERVICE DECK   ELEVATORS   18 LOAD BINS   17 DIVISION BULKHEADS

ENVIRONMENTAL MAINT. MACHINERY SPACE   TRANSPORTERS T/B

CROSS-SECTIONS

MK-I LIQUIDS:

D.W. TONNAGE-METRIC	121,566
GROSS VOL.-M^3	303,916
NET VOLUME-M^3	276,076
UNIT LOADING	30 T/M^2
VOL. LOADING	364 KG/M^3
TRANSPORTERS	6
ELEVATORS	2
LENGTH O.A.-METERS	200
DIAMETER-METERS	40

PLAN

STAR FLEET TRANSPORT COMMAND
NCC-1000

PROFILE

0 10 20 30 40 50
METERS

SERVICE DECK   ELEVATORS   ANTI-SURGE BAFFLES

BHD   BHD   BHD   BHD   BHD

ENVIRONMENTAL MAINT. MACHINERY SPACE   TRANSPORTERS T/B

0 10 20 30 40 50
METERS

CROSS-SECTIONS

SEE BOOKLETS OF GENERAL PLANS FOR DETAILS

TRANSPORT CONTAINER
CLASS I STARLINERS-USE WITH CLASS I TUG

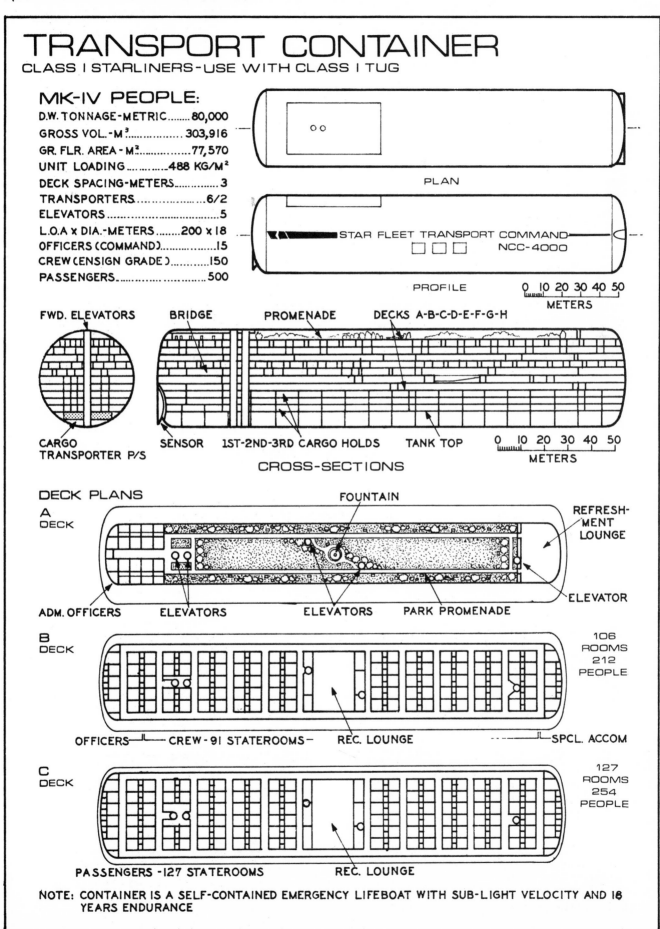

MK-IV PEOPLE:

D.W. TONNAGE-METRIC	80,000
GROSS VOL.-M³	303,916
GR. FLR. AREA-M²	77,570
UNIT LOADING	488 KG/M²
DECK SPACING-METERS	3
TRANSPORTERS	6/2
ELEVATORS	5
L.O.A x DIA.-METERS	200 x 18
OFFICERS (COMMAND)	15
CREW (ENSIGN GRADE)	150
PASSENGERS	500

PLAN

STAR FLEET TRANSPORT COMMAND
NCC-4000

PROFILE

0 10 20 30 40 50
METERS

FWD. ELEVATORS   BRIDGE   PROMENADE   DECKS A-B-C-D-E-F-G-H

CARGO TRANSPORTER P/S   SENSOR   1ST-2ND-3RD CARGO HOLDS   TANK TOP

0 10 20 30 40 50
METERS

CROSS-SECTIONS

DECK PLANS

A DECK

FOUNTAIN

REFRESH-MENT LOUNGE

ADM. OFFICERS   ELEVATORS   ELEVATORS   PARK PROMENADE

ELEVATOR

B DECK

106 ROOMS 212 PEOPLE

OFFICERS — CREW-91 STATEROOMS —   REC. LOUNGE   — SPCL. ACCOM

C DECK

127 ROOMS 254 PEOPLE

PASSENGERS -127 STATEROOMS   REC. LOUNGE

NOTE: CONTAINER IS A SELF-CONTAINED EMERGENCY LIFEBOAT WITH SUB-LIGHT VELOCITY AND 18 YEARS ENDURANCE

MK-IV STARLINER
DECK PLANS

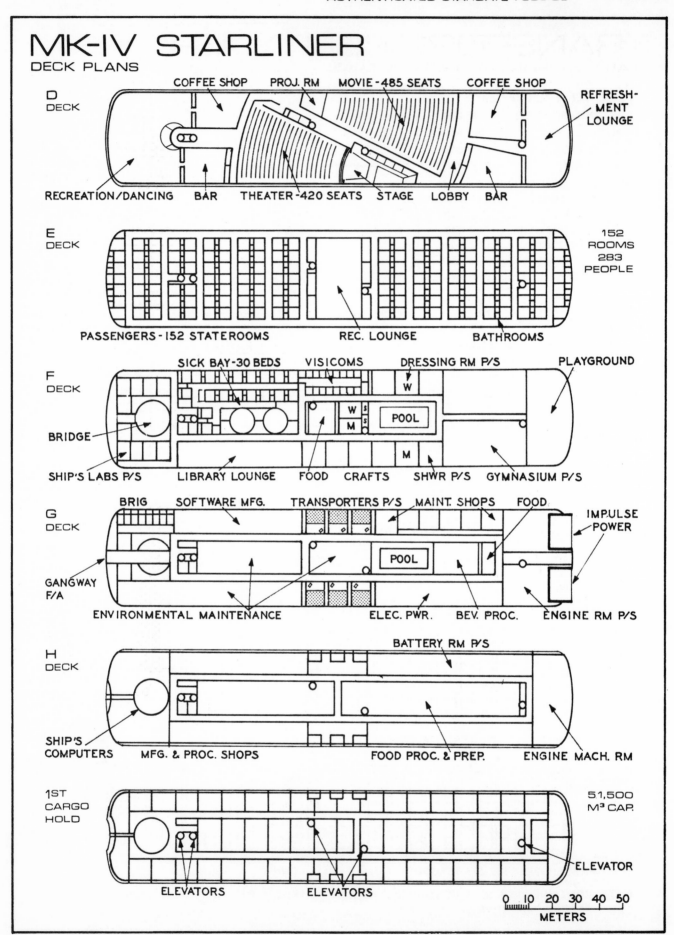

D DECK — COFFEE SHOP, PROJ. RM, MOVIE - 485 SEATS, COFFEE SHOP, REFRESHMENT LOUNGE, RECREATION/DANCING, BAR, THEATER - 420 SEATS, STAGE, LOBBY, BAR

E DECK — 152 ROOMS 283 PEOPLE, PASSENGERS - 152 STATEROOMS, REC. LOUNGE, BATHROOMS

F DECK — SICK BAY - 30 BEDS, VISICOMS, DRESSING RM P/S, PLAYGROUND, W, POOL, W S S M, M, BRIDGE, SHIP'S LABS P/S, LIBRARY LOUNGE, FOOD, CRAFTS, SHWR P/S, GYMNASIUM P/S

G DECK — BRIG, SOFTWARE MFG., TRANSPORTERS P/S, MAINT. SHOPS, FOOD, IMPULSE POWER, POOL, GANGWAY F/A, ENVIRONMENTAL MAINTENANCE, ELEC. PWR., BEV. PROC., ENGINE RM P/S

H DECK — BATTERY RM P/S, SHIP'S COMPUTERS, MFG. & PROC. SHOPS, FOOD PROC. & PREP., ENGINE MACH. RM

1ST CARGO HOLD — 51,500 M³ CAP., ELEVATORS, ELEVATORS, ELEVATOR

0 10 20 30 40 50
METERS

MK-IV STARLINER
DECK PLANS AND DETAILS

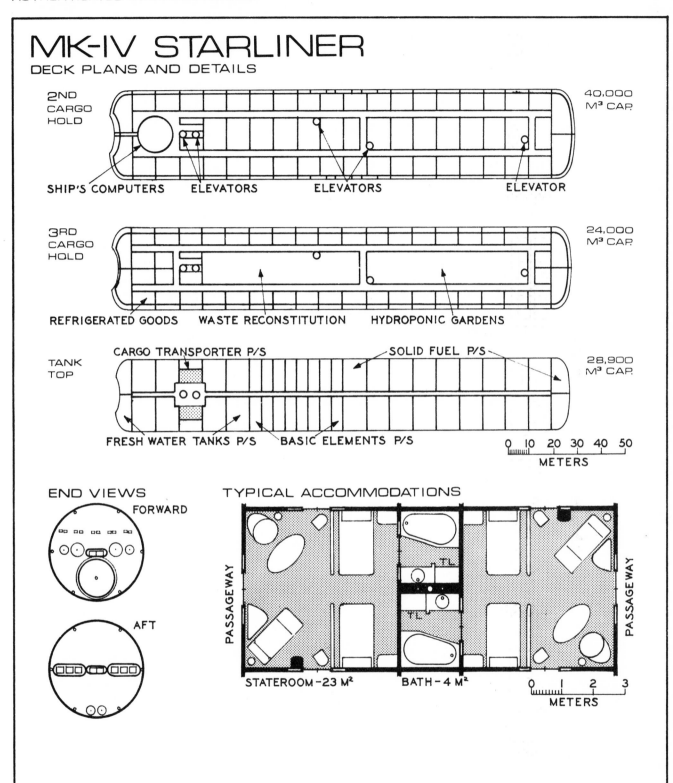

2ND CARGO HOLD

40,000 M³ CAP.

SHIP'S COMPUTERS   ELEVATORS   ELEVATORS   ELEVATOR

3RD CARGO HOLD

24,000 M³ CAP.

REFRIGERATED GOODS   WASTE RECONSTITUTION   HYDROPONIC GARDENS

TANK TOP

CARGO TRANSPORTER P/S   SOLID FUEL P/S

28,900 M³ CAP.

FRESH WATER TANKS P/S   BASIC ELEMENTS P/S

0 10 20 30 40 50
METERS

END VIEWS
FORWARD

AFT

TYPICAL ACCOMMODATIONS

PASSAGEWAY

TL

TL

PASSAGEWAY

STATEROOM - 23 M²   BATH - 4 M²

0 1 2 3
METERS

CLASS I DREADNOUGHT
FEDERATION CLASS STARSHIPS

MK-X

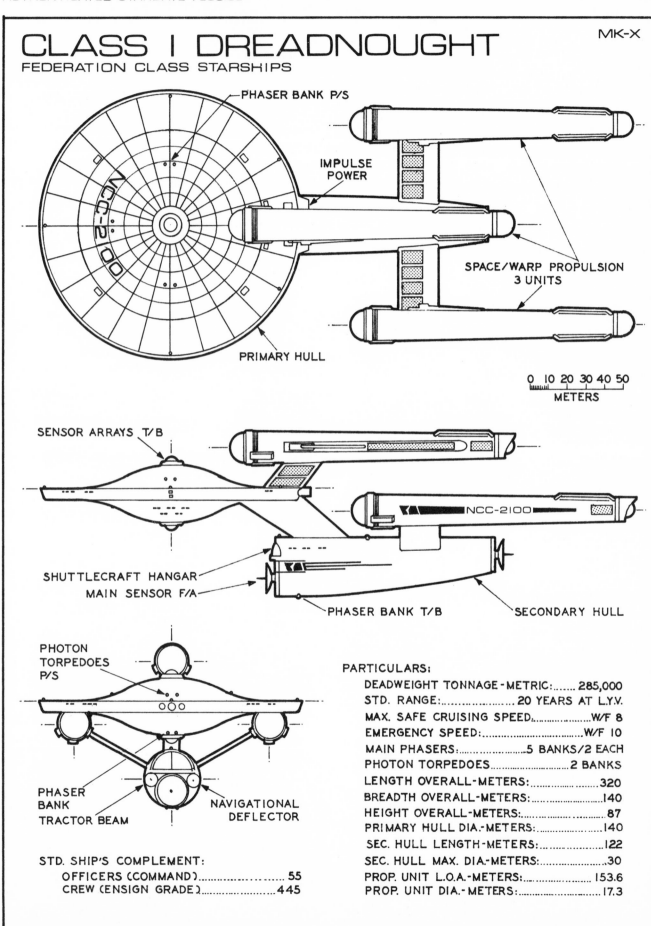

PHASER BANK P/S

IMPULSE POWER

SPACE/WARP PROPULSION 3 UNITS

PRIMARY HULL

0 10 20 30 40 50
METERS

SENSOR ARRAYS T/B

NCC-2100

SHUTTLECRAFT HANGAR
MAIN SENSOR F/A

PHASER BANK T/B

SECONDARY HULL

PHOTON TORPEDOES P/S

PHASER BANK
TRACTOR BEAM

NAVIGATIONAL DEFLECTOR

PARTICULARS:

DEADWEIGHT TONNAGE - METRIC:........ 285,000
STD. RANGE:....................... 20 YEARS AT L.Y.V.
MAX. SAFE CRUISING SPEED:.....................W/F 8
EMERGENCY SPEED:................................W/F 10
MAIN PHASERS:.....................5 BANKS/2 EACH
PHOTON TORPEDOES...................... 2 BANKS
LENGTH OVERALL-METERS:.....................320
BREADTH OVERALL-METERS:....................140
HEIGHT OVERALL-METERS:..................... 87
PRIMARY HULL DIA.-METERS:..................140
SEC. HULL LENGTH-METERS:...................122
SEC. HULL MAX. DIA.-METERS:.................30
PROP. UNIT L.O.A.-METERS:.................. 153.6
PROP. UNIT DIA.- METERS:....................17.3

STD. SHIP'S COMPLEMENT:
OFFICERS (COMMAND)........................ 55
CREW (ENSIGN GRADE).................445

DREADNOUGHT CLASS
AUTHORIZED CONSTRUCTION

THE FOLLOWING SHIPS OF THE MK-X CLASS WERE AUTHORIZED BY STAR FLEET
APPROPRIATION OF STARDATE 6066:

AFFILIATION – NCC-2108	CORPORATION – NCC-2104	STAR EMPIRE – NCC-2116
ALLIANCE – NCC-2113	DIRECTORATE – NCC-2110	STAR LEAGUE – NCC-2101
ASSOCIATION – NCC-2118	DOMINION – NCC-2115	STAR SYSTEM – NCC-2107
COMPACTAT – NCC-2103	ENTENTE – NCC-2120	STAR UNION – NCC-2112
CONCORDAT – NCC-2109	FEDERATION – NCC-2100 *	TRUSTEESHIP – NCC-2117
CONFEDERATION – NCC-2114	KONKORDIUM – NCC-2106	UNIFICATUM – NCC-2102
CONSORTIUM – NCC-2119	ORGANIZATION – NCC-2111	

*CLASS SHIP.   ALL NAMES PRECEDED WITH "U.S.S."

SHUTTLECRAFT
7 PERSON - EXTERNAL ARRANGEMENT

TYPE: SPCR 48A
MK   12B
80   5621

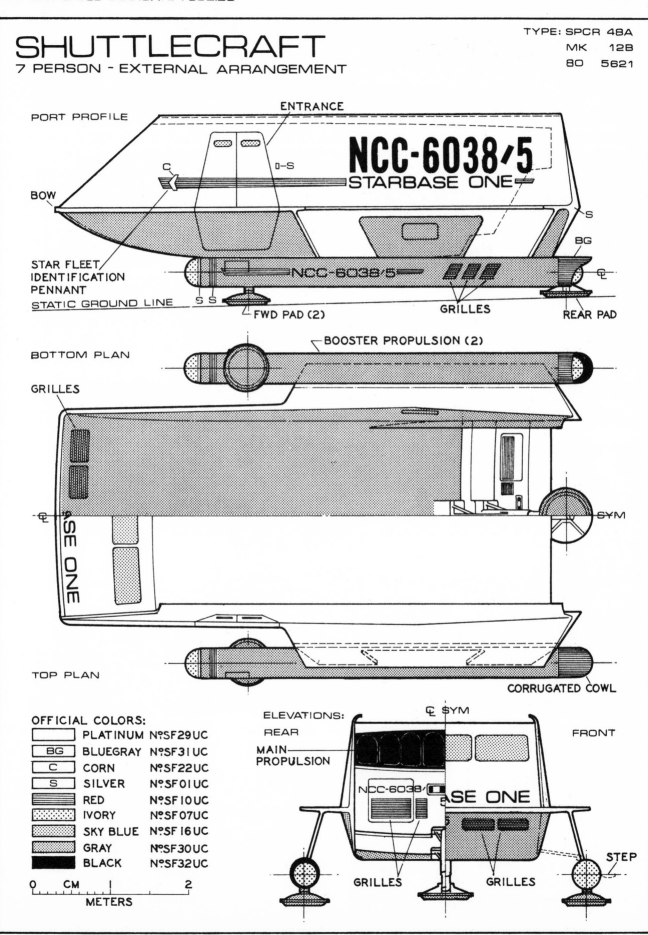

PORT PROFILE

ENTRANCE

NCC-6038/5
STARBASE ONE

BOW

C

□-S

S

BG

CL

STAR FLEET
IDENTIFICATION
PENNANT

NCC-6038/5

GRILLES

STATIC GROUND LINE

S S

FWD PAD (2)

REAR PAD

BOTTOM PLAN

BOOSTER PROPULSION (2)

GRILLES

ASE ONE

CL

SYM

TOP PLAN

CORRUGATED COWL

OFFICIAL COLORS:

	PLATINUM	Nº SF29UC
BG	BLUEGRAY	Nº SF31UC
C	CORN	Nº SF22UC
S	SILVER	Nº SF01UC
	RED	Nº SF10UC
	IVORY	Nº SF07UC
	SKY BLUE	Nº SF16UC
	GRAY	Nº SF30UC
	BLACK	Nº SF32UC

ELEVATIONS:

REAR

CL SYM

FRONT

MAIN
PROPULSION

NCC-6038/

ASE ONE

0   CM   1   2

METERS

GRILLES

GRILLES

STEP

SHUTTLECRAFT
INTERNAL GENERAL ARRANGEMENT

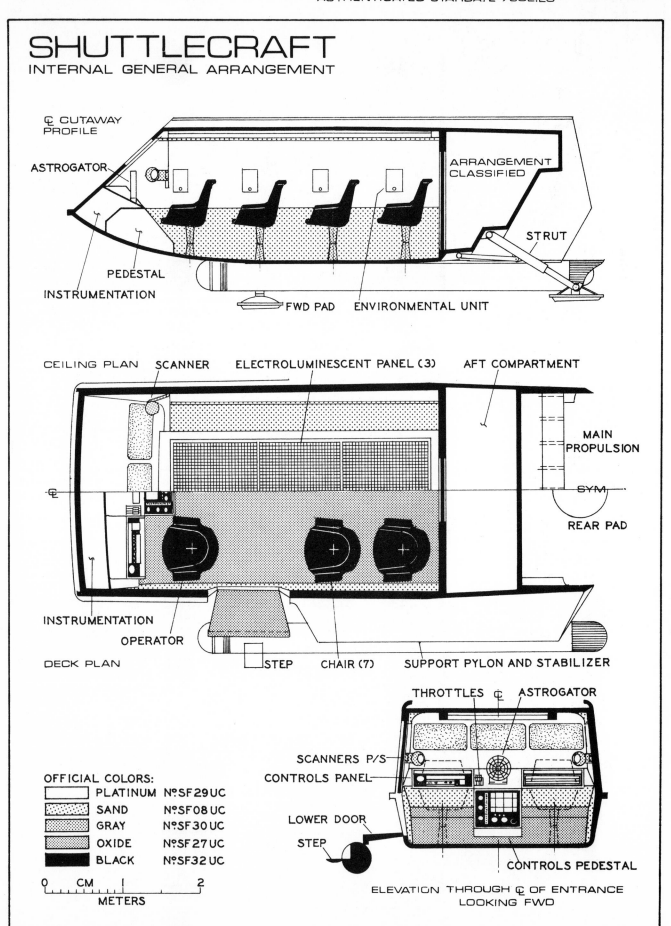

℄ CUTAWAY PROFILE

ASTROGATOR

ARRANGEMENT CLASSIFIED

STRUT

PEDESTAL

INSTRUMENTATION

FWD PAD   ENVIRONMENTAL UNIT

CEILING PLAN   SCANNER   ELECTROLUMINESCENT PANEL (3)   AFT COMPARTMENT

MAIN PROPULSION

℄

SYM

REAR PAD

INSTRUMENTATION

OPERATOR

DECK PLAN

STEP   CHAIR (7)   SUPPORT PYLON AND STABILIZER

THROTTLES   ℄   ASTROGATOR

SCANNERS P/S

CONTROLS PANEL

LOWER DOOR

STEP

CONTROLS PEDESTAL

ELEVATION THROUGH ℄ OF ENTRANCE
LOOKING FWD

OFFICIAL COLORS:

	PLATINUM	Nº SF 29 UC
	SAND	Nº SF 08 UC
	GRAY	Nº SF 30 UC
	OXIDE	Nº SF 27 UC
	BLACK	Nº SF 32 UC

0   CM   1   2
METERS

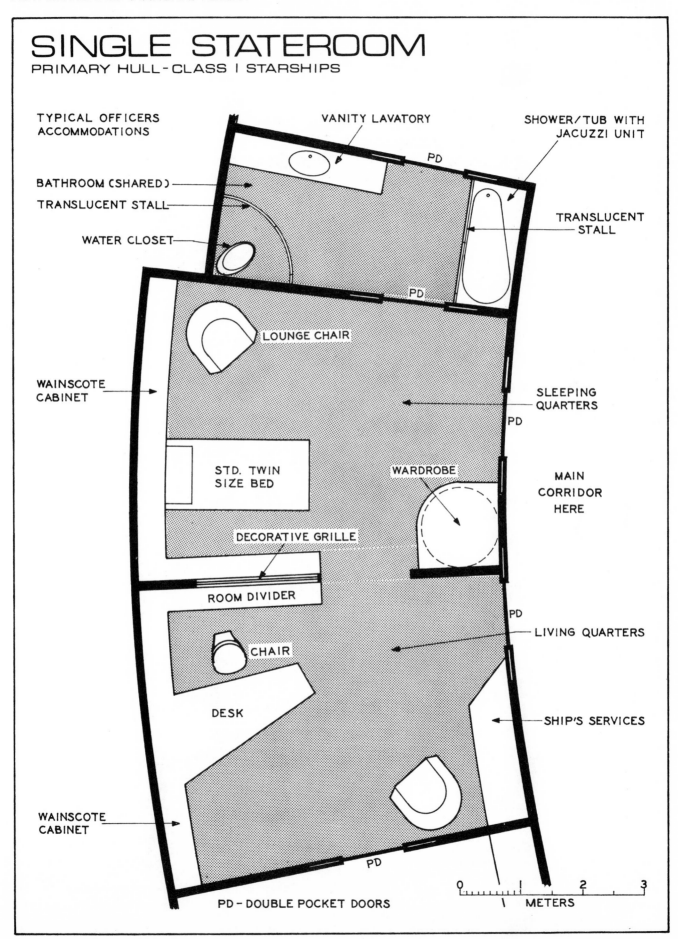

SINGLE STATEROOM
PRIMARY HULL-CLASS I STARSHIPS

TYPICAL OFFICERS ACCOMMODATIONS

VANITY LAVATORY

SHOWER/TUB WITH JACUZZI UNIT

BATHROOM (SHARED)

TRANSLUCENT STALL

TRANSLUCENT STALL

WATER CLOSET

PD

PD

LOUNGE CHAIR

WAINSCOTE CABINET

SLEEPING QUARTERS

PD

STD. TWIN SIZE BED

WARDROBE

MAIN CORRIDOR HERE

DECORATIVE GRILLE

ROOM DIVIDER

CHAIR

PD

LIVING QUARTERS

DESK

SHIP'S SERVICES

WAINSCOTE CABINET

PD

PD - DOUBLE POCKET DOORS

0 1 2 3
METERS

DOUBLE STATEROOM
PRIMARY HULL - CLASS I STARSHIPS

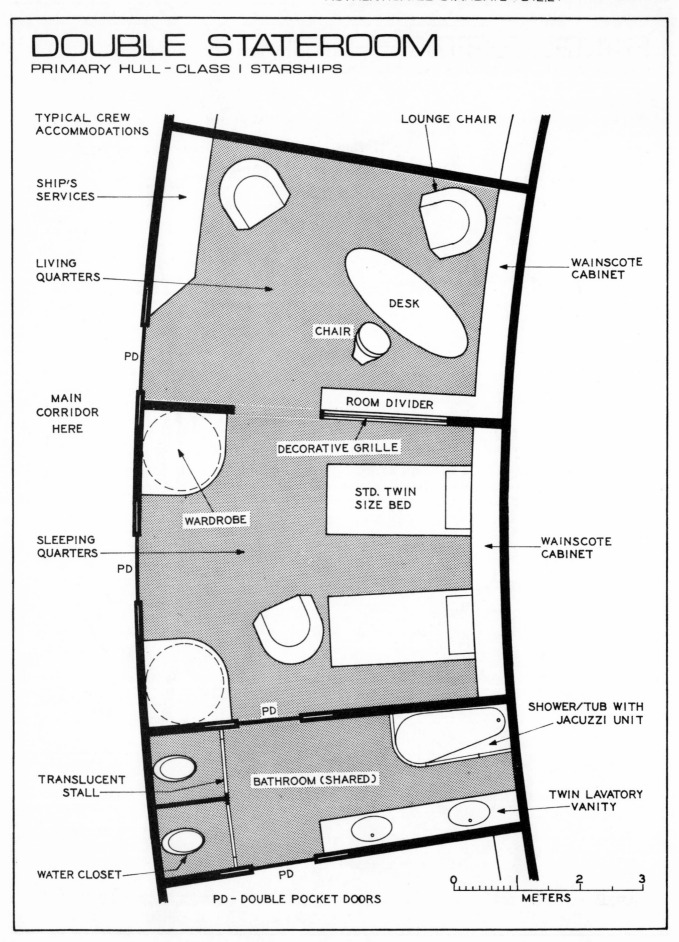

TYPICAL CREW
ACCOMMODATIONS

LOUNGE CHAIR

SHIP'S
SERVICES

WAINSCOTE
CABINET

LIVING
QUARTERS

DESK

CHAIR

MAIN
CORRIDOR
HERE

PD

ROOM DIVIDER

DECORATIVE GRILLE

STD. TWIN
SIZE BED

WARDROBE

WAINSCOTE
CABINET

SLEEPING
QUARTERS

PD

PD

SHOWER/TUB WITH
JACUZZI UNIT

TRANSLUCENT
STALL

BATHROOM (SHARED)

TWIN LAVATORY
VANITY

WATER CLOSET

PD

PD — DOUBLE POCKET DOORS

0   1   2   3
METERS

MAIN BRIDGE
DECK 1 PLAN - PRIMARY HULL - CLASS I STARSHIPS

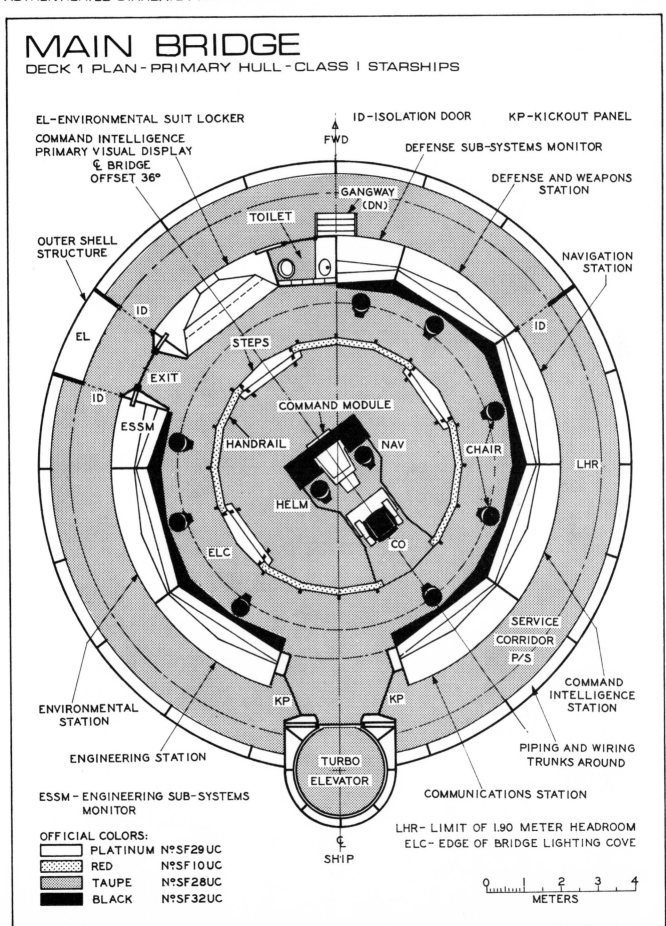

EL-ENVIRONMENTAL SUIT LOCKER

COMMAND INTELLIGENCE
PRIMARY VISUAL DISPLAY
₵ BRIDGE
OFFSET 36°

ID-ISOLATION DOOR   KP-KICKOUT PANEL

FWD

DEFENSE SUB-SYSTEMS MONITOR

DEFENSE AND WEAPONS
STATION

OUTER SHELL
STRUCTURE

GANGWAY
(DN)

TOILET

NAVIGATION
STATION

ID

EL

ID

STEPS

EXIT

ID

COMMAND MODULE

ESSM

NAV

CHAIR

LHR

HANDRAIL

HELM

CO

ELC

SERVICE
CORRIDOR
P/S

COMMAND
INTELLIGENCE
STATION

KP   KP

ENVIRONMENTAL
STATION

PIPING AND WIRING
TRUNKS AROUND

ENGINEERING STATION

TURBO
ELEVATOR

COMMUNICATIONS STATION

ESSM - ENGINEERING SUB-SYSTEMS
MONITOR

₵
SHIP

LHR- LIMIT OF 1.90 METER HEADROOM
ELC- EDGE OF BRIDGE LIGHTING COVE

OFFICIAL COLORS:

PLATINUM   N°SF29UC
RED   N°SF10UC
TAUPE   N°SF28UC
BLACK   N°SF32UC

0 1 2 3 4
METERS

MAIN BRIDGE
PRINCIPAL CROSS-SECTIONS

COMMAND INTELLIGENCE PRIM. VISUAL DISPLAY

HIGH ENERGY LAB AREA

SECONDARY EXIT

GANGWAY

COMMAND MODULE

ZZ' AXIS PRIMARY HULL

DECK STRUCTURE

LONGITUDINAL-LOOKING TO PORT

DOME TRANSPARENT TO ALL FORMS OF ELECTROMAGNETIC RADIATION

TURBO ELEV.

DECK 1:

PHYSICS LAB AREA

TURBO ELEVATOR

T/E SHAFT

DOME PIPING AND WIRING TRUNK AROUND

OUTER HULL STRUCTURE

SERVICE CORRIDOR

GEOLOGY LAB AREA

BRIDGE STATIONS

GANGWAY TO BRIDGE

¢ SHIP

TRANSVERSE-LOOKING FWD

BRIDGE DOME LIGHTING COVE

DECK 0: UPPER SPACE SENSOR PLATFORM

ISOLATION DOOR

BIOLOGY LAB AREA

ENVIRONMENTAL SUIT LOCKER

OFFICIAL COLORS:
PLATINUM N°SF29UC
N°SF11UC ORANGE
N°SF30UC GRAY
N°SF32UC BLACK

0 1 2 3 4
METERS

COMMAND MODULE
MAIN BRIDGE STATION - CLASS I STARSHIPS

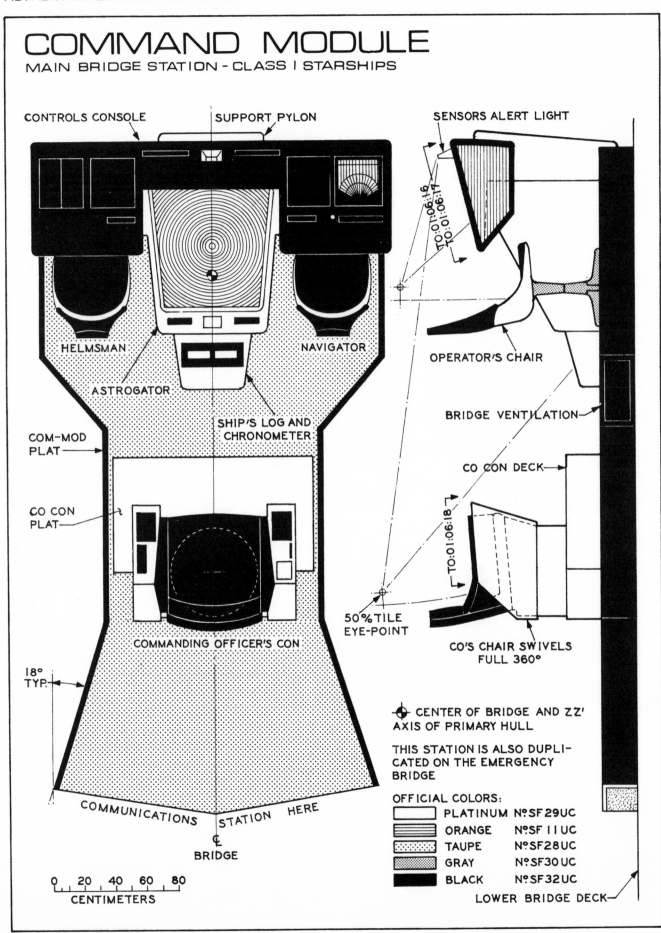

CONTROLS CONSOLE

SUPPORT PYLON

SENSORS ALERT LIGHT

TO:01:06:16
TO:01:06:17

HELMSMAN

NAVIGATOR

ASTROGATOR

OPERATOR'S CHAIR

SHIP'S LOG AND CHRONOMETER

COM-MOD PLAT

BRIDGE VENTILATION

CO CON PLAT

CO CON DECK

TO:01:06:18

COMMANDING OFFICER'S CON

50% TILE EYE-POINT

CO'S CHAIR SWIVELS FULL 360°

18° TYP.

CENTER OF BRIDGE AND ZZ' AXIS OF PRIMARY HULL

THIS STATION IS ALSO DUPLICATED ON THE EMERGENCY BRIDGE

COMMUNICATIONS STATION HERE

℄ BRIDGE

OFFICIAL COLORS:

	PLATINUM	Nº SF 29 UC
	ORANGE	Nº SF 11 UC
	TAUPE	Nº SF 28 UC
	GRAY	Nº SF 30 UC
	BLACK	Nº SF 32 UC

0 20 40 60 80
CENTIMETERS

LOWER BRIDGE DECK

COMMAND MODULE
FRONT AND REAR ELEVATIONS

SHIP'S CONTROLS CONSOLE:

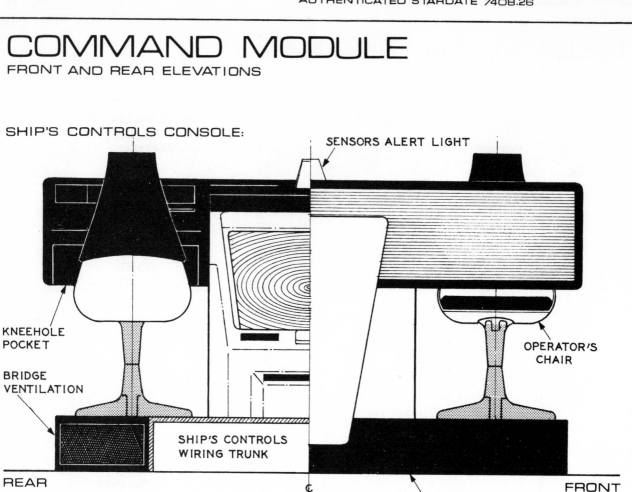

SENSORS ALERT LIGHT

KNEEHOLE
POCKET

BRIDGE
VENTILATION

SHIP'S CONTROLS
WIRING TRUNK

OPERATOR'S
CHAIR

REAR

CL

COM-MOD PLAT

FRONT

COMMAND CON:

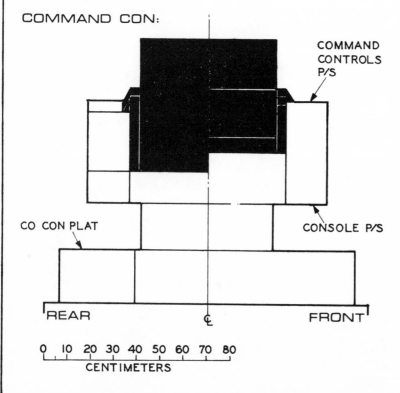

COMMAND
CONTROLS
P/S

CO CON PLAT

CONSOLE P/S

REAR

CL

FRONT

SEE MANUAL SECTIONS 2 AND 3
FOR VITAL FUNCTIONS AND MAIN
SCHEMATICS

COMMANDING OFFICER'S CON IS
THE FUNCTIONAL CENTER OF THE
BRIDGE. ALL OTHER STATIONS
SUPPORT THIS POSITION

0 10 20 30 40 50 60 70 80
CENTIMETERS

OFFICIAL COLORS:

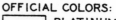

PLATINUM	Nº SF 29 UC
ORANGE	Nº SF 11 UC
GRAY	Nº SF 30 UC
BLACK	Nº SF 32 UC

HELMSMAN'S STATION
COMMAND MODULE-MAIN BRIDGE

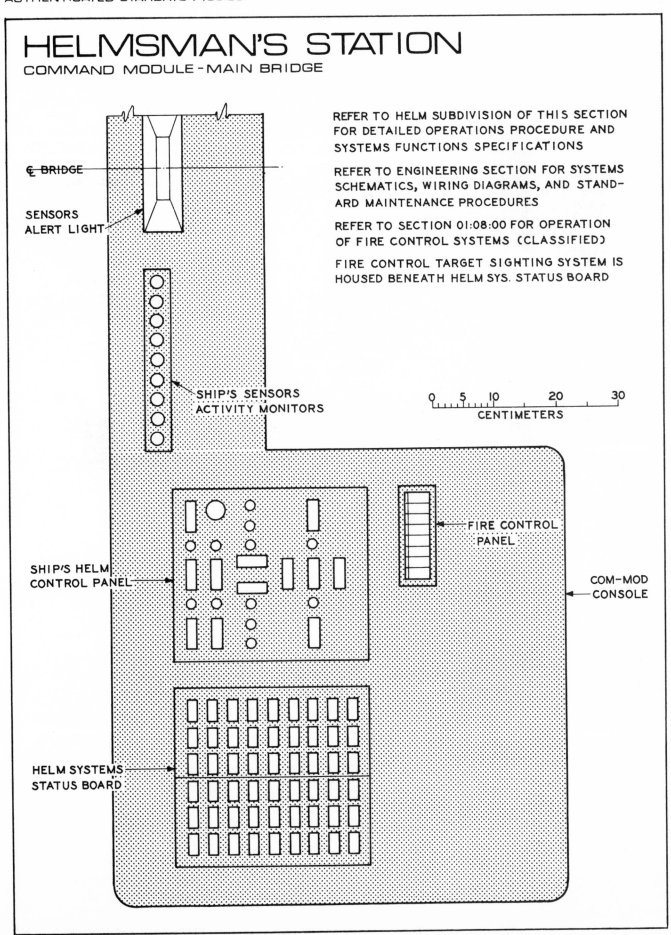

REFER TO HELM SUBDIVISION OF THIS SECTION FOR DETAILED OPERATIONS PROCEDURE AND SYSTEMS FUNCTIONS SPECIFICATIONS

REFER TO ENGINEERING SECTION FOR SYSTEMS SCHEMATICS, WIRING DIAGRAMS, AND STANDARD MAINTENANCE PROCEDURES

REFER TO SECTION 01:08:00 FOR OPERATION OF FIRE CONTROL SYSTEMS (CLASSIFIED)

FIRE CONTROL TARGET SIGHTING SYSTEM IS HOUSED BENEATH HELM SYS. STATUS BOARD

¢ BRIDGE

SENSORS ALERT LIGHT

SHIP'S SENSORS ACTIVITY MONITORS

0 5 10   20   30
CENTIMETERS

FIRE CONTROL PANEL

SHIP'S HELM CONTROL PANEL

COM-MOD CONSOLE

HELM SYSTEMS STATUS BOARD

NAVIGATOR'S STATION
COMMAND MODULE-MAIN BRIDGE

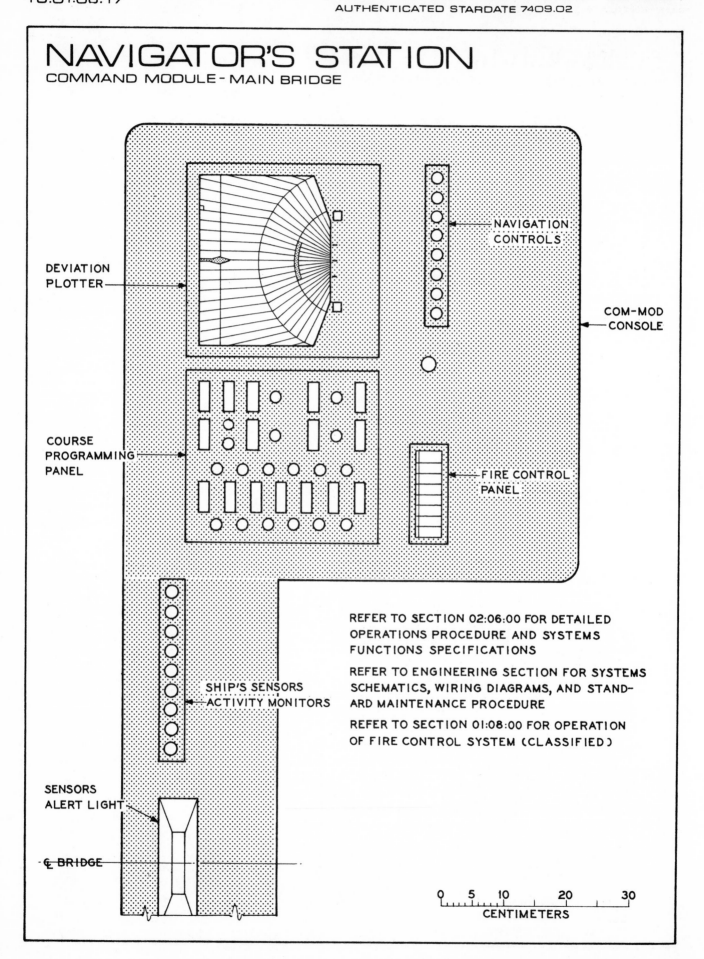

NAVIGATION CONTROLS

DEVIATION PLOTTER

COM-MOD CONSOLE

COURSE PROGRAMMING PANEL

FIRE CONTROL PANEL

SHIP'S SENSORS
ACTIVITY MONITORS

REFER TO SECTION 02:06:00 FOR DETAILED
OPERATIONS PROCEDURE AND SYSTEMS
FUNCTIONS SPECIFICATIONS

REFER TO ENGINEERING SECTION FOR SYSTEMS
SCHEMATICS, WIRING DIAGRAMS, AND STAND-
ARD MAINTENANCE PROCEDURE

REFER TO SECTION 01:08:00 FOR OPERATION
OF FIRE CONTROL SYSTEM (CLASSIFIED)

SENSORS
ALERT LIGHT

BRIDGE

0   5   10   20   30
CENTIMETERS

COMMAND CON
COMMAND MODULE - MAIN BRIDGE

PORT CONSOLE:

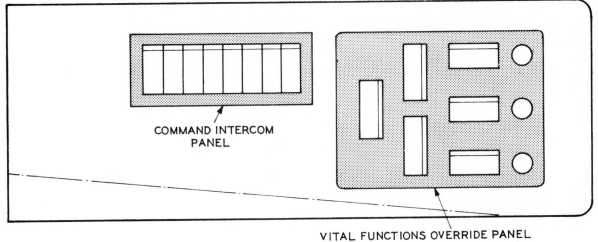

COMMAND INTERCOM
PANEL

VITAL FUNCTIONS OVERRIDE PANEL

—|— CON PIVOT CENTER

STARBOARD CONSOLE:

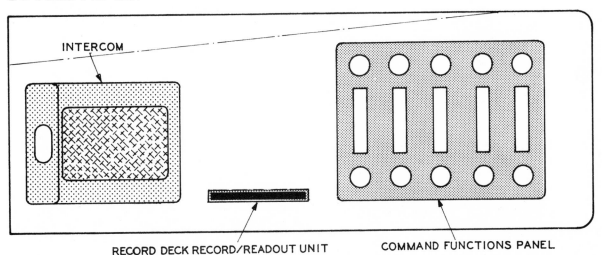

INTERCOM

RECORD DECK RECORD/READOUT UNIT

COMMAND FUNCTIONS PANEL

REFER TO SECTION 01:06:30 FOR DETAILED
OPERATIONS PROCEDURE AND SYSTEMS
FUNCTIONS SPECIFICATIONS

REFER TO ENGINEERING SECTION FOR SYS-
TEMS SCHEMATICS, WIRING DIAGRAMS, AND
STANDARD MAINTENANCE PROCEDURES

OFFICIAL COLOR:
░░░ SKY BLUE N°SF16UC

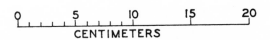

0   5   10   15   20
CENTIMETERS

ASTROGATOR
COMMAND MODULE - MAIN BRIDGE

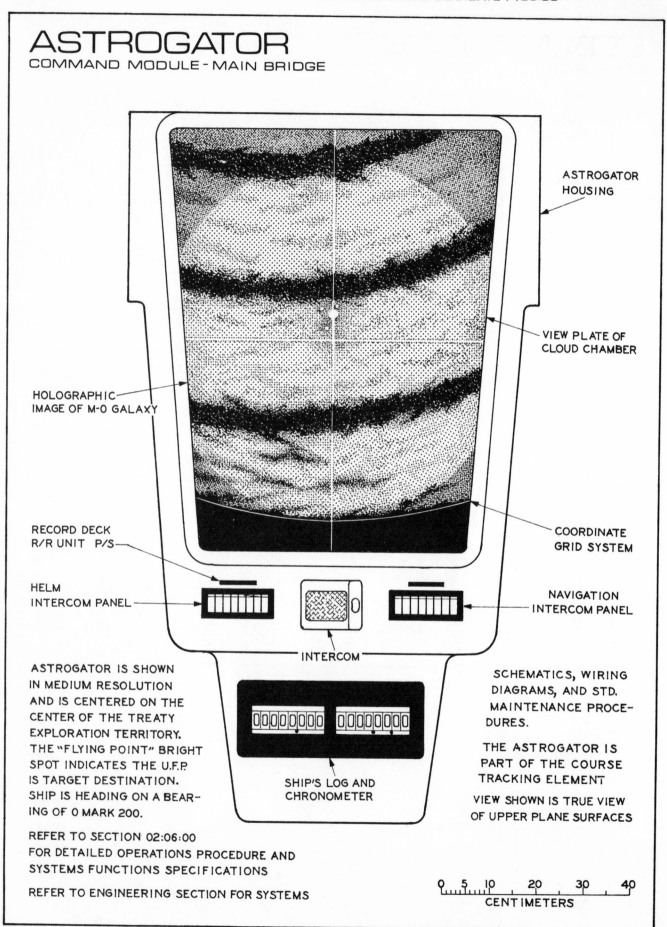

ASTROGATOR HOUSING

VIEW PLATE OF CLOUD CHAMBER

HOLOGRAPHIC IMAGE OF M-0 GALAXY

COORDINATE GRID SYSTEM

RECORD DECK R/R UNIT P/S

HELM INTERCOM PANEL

NAVIGATION INTERCOM PANEL

INTERCOM

SHIP'S LOG AND CHRONOMETER

ASTROGATOR IS SHOWN IN MEDIUM RESOLUTION AND IS CENTERED ON THE CENTER OF THE TREATY EXPLORATION TERRITORY. THE "FLYING POINT" BRIGHT SPOT INDICATES THE U.F.P. IS TARGET DESTINATION. SHIP IS HEADING ON A BEARING OF 0 MARK 200.

REFER TO SECTION 02:06:00 FOR DETAILED OPERATIONS PROCEDURE AND SYSTEMS FUNCTIONS SPECIFICATIONS

REFER TO ENGINEERING SECTION FOR SYSTEMS

SCHEMATICS, WIRING DIAGRAMS, AND STD. MAINTENANCE PROCE-DURES.

THE ASTROGATOR IS PART OF THE COURSE TRACKING ELEMENT

VIEW SHOWN IS TRUE VIEW OF UPPER PLANE SURFACES

0 5 10   20   30   40
CENTIMETERS

SECURITY SECTION
PRIMARY HULL - CLASS I STARSHIPS

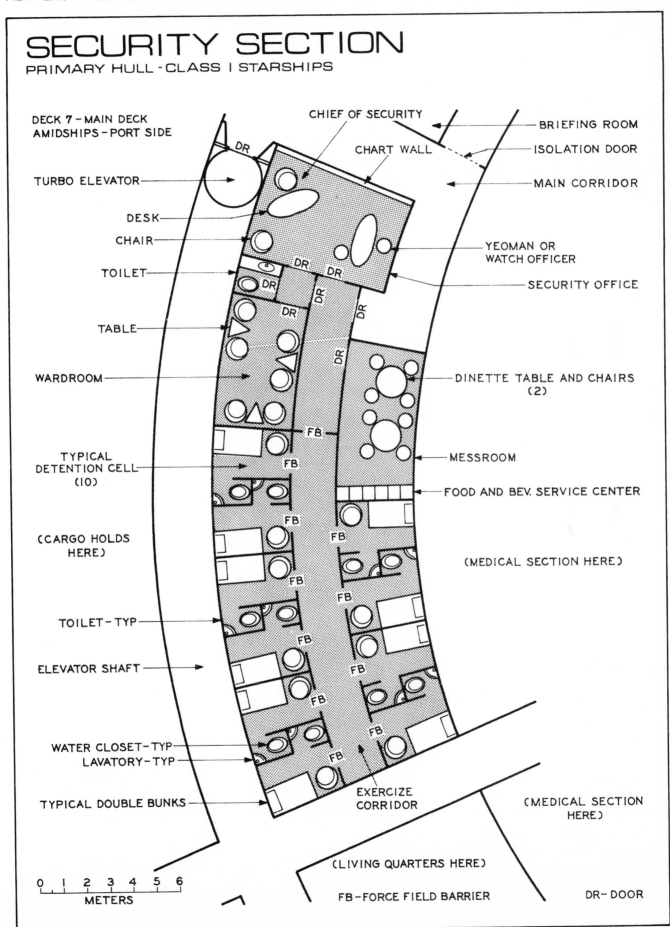

DECK 7 - MAIN DECK
AMIDSHIPS - PORT SIDE

CHIEF OF SECURITY

CHART WALL

BRIEFING ROOM

ISOLATION DOOR

MAIN CORRIDOR

TURBO ELEVATOR

DR

DESK

CHAIR

TOILET

YEOMAN OR
WATCH OFFICER

SECURITY OFFICE

DR

DR

DR

DR

DR

DR

TABLE

WARDROOM

DINETTE TABLE AND CHAIRS
(2)

FB

FB

TYPICAL
DETENTION CELL
(10)

MESSROOM

FOOD AND BEV. SERVICE CENTER

(CARGO HOLDS
HERE)

FB

FB

(MEDICAL SECTION HERE)

FB

FB

TOILET - TYP

FB

ELEVATOR SHAFT

FB

FB

FB

WATER CLOSET - TYP

LAVATORY - TYP

FB

TYPICAL DOUBLE BUNKS

EXERCIZE
CORRIDOR

(MEDICAL SECTION
HERE)

(LIVING QUARTERS HERE)

0 1 2 3 4 5 6
METERS

FB - FORCE FIELD BARRIER

DR - DOOR

HAND PHASER-TYPE I

EFF. RANGES IN METERS:
OVERLOAD BLAST RADIUS.....40
DE-MATERIALIZE...................10
DISRUPT...........................20
HEAT.................................2
STUN................................30

COLORS:
☐ BR. ANTIMONY №SF02UC
▨ GLOSS BLACK №SF32UC

DIM: W.O.A.....49.40 MM   D.O.A.....27.00 MM
L.O.A.....107.20 MM

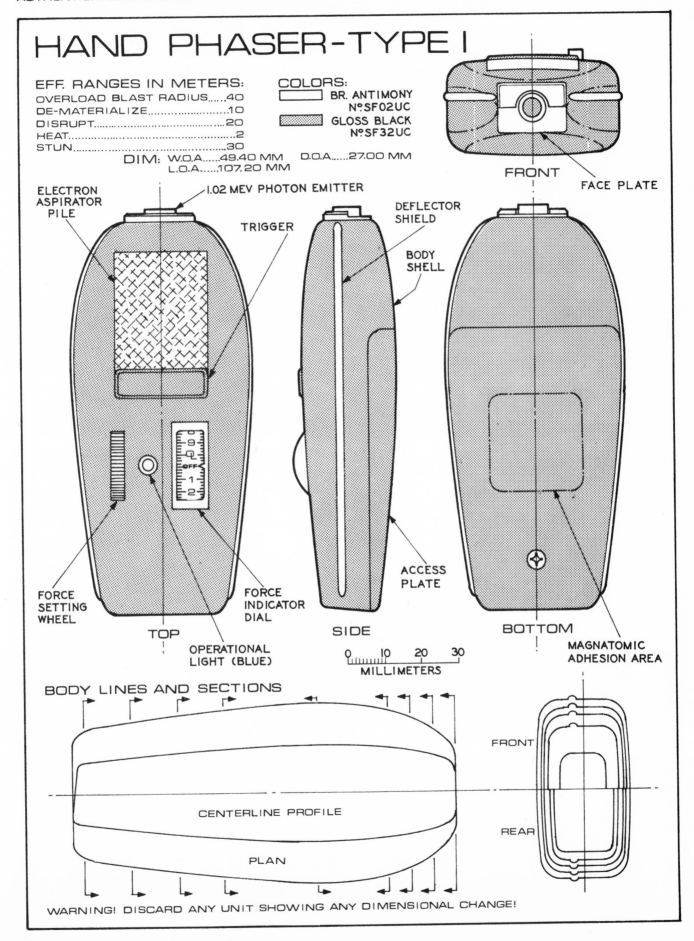

FRONT

FACE PLATE

ELECTRON ASPIRATOR PILE

1.02 MEV PHOTON EMITTER

TRIGGER

DEFLECTOR SHIELD

BODY SHELL

FORCE SETTING WHEEL

FORCE INDICATOR DIAL

TOP

OPERATIONAL LIGHT (BLUE)

ACCESS PLATE

SIDE

BOTTOM

MAGNATOMIC ADHESION AREA

0   10   20   30
MILLIMETERS

BODY LINES AND SECTIONS

FRONT

CENTERLINE PROFILE

REAR

PLAN

WARNING! DISCARD ANY UNIT SHOWING ANY DIMENSIONAL CHANGE!

HAND PHASER-TYPE II

EFF. RANGES IN METERS:
OVERLOAD BLAST RADIUS....135
DE-MATERIALIZE......................30
DISRUPT................................60
HEAT..6
STUN......................................90

DIM:
L.O.A.....221.00 MM
W.O.A.....49.40 MM
D.O.A.....157.50 MM

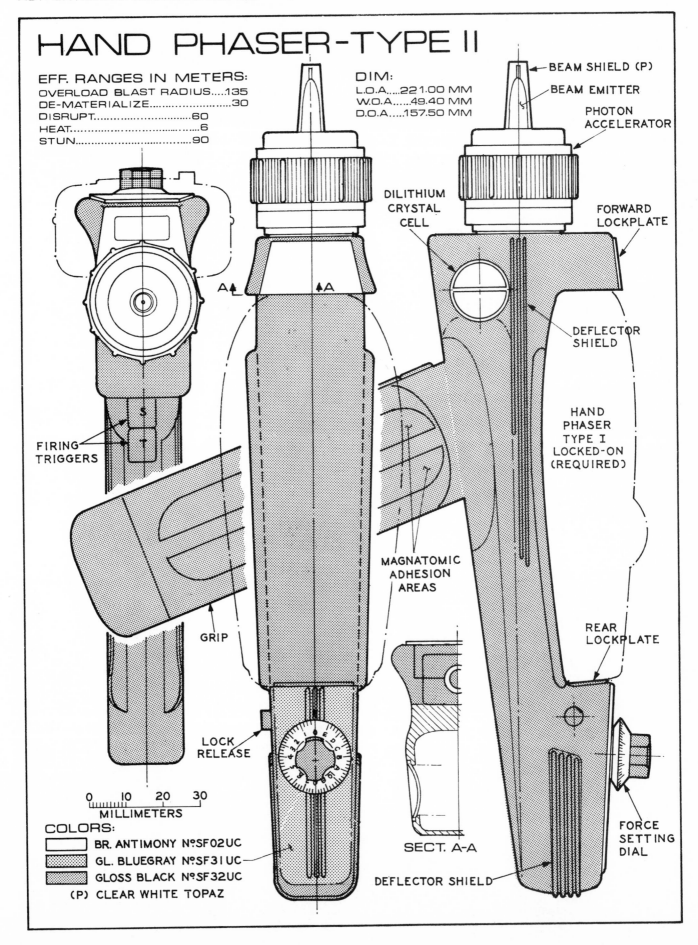

BEAM SHIELD (P)

BEAM EMITTER

PHOTON ACCELERATOR

DILITHIUM CRYSTAL CELL

FORWARD LOCKPLATE

DEFLECTOR SHIELD

HAND PHASER TYPE I LOCKED-ON (REQUIRED)

FIRING TRIGGERS

MAGNATOMIC ADHESION AREAS

REAR LOCKPLATE

GRIP

LOCK RELEASE

SECT. A-A

DEFLECTOR SHIELD

FORCE SETTING DIAL

A

0   10   20   30
MILLIMETERS

COLORS:
☐ BR. ANTIMONY NºSF02UC
▨ GL. BLUEGRAY NºSF31UC
▦ GLOSS BLACK NºSF32UC
(P) CLEAR WHITE TOPAZ

HAND PHASER-TYPE II

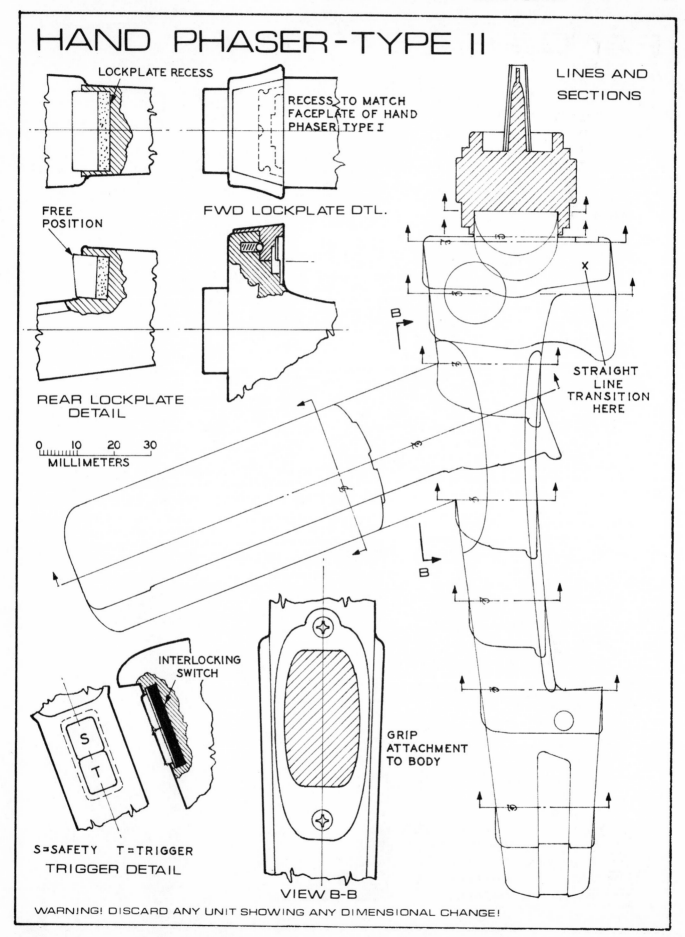

LOCKPLATE RECESS

RECESS TO MATCH FACEPLATE OF HAND PHASER TYPE I

LINES AND SECTIONS

FREE POSITION

FWD LOCKPLATE DTL.

REAR LOCKPLATE DETAIL

STRAIGHT LINE TRANSITION HERE

```
0    10    20    30
|||||||||||||||||||
   MILLIMETERS
```

INTERLOCKING SWITCH

S

S
T

S=SAFETY   T=TRIGGER
TRIGGER DETAIL

GRIP ATTACHMENT TO BODY

VIEW B-B

RAY GUN
OFFENSIVE/DEFENSIVE AREA WEAPON

SPECIFICATION:
MODEL: TYPE I
OFFENSIVE (DISRUPT) RANGE (M)_____90
EFFECTIVE AREA AT RANGE (M)_____3
DEFENSIVE (STUN) RANGE (M)_____180
EFFECTIVE AREA AT RANGE (M)_____8
LENGTH OVERALL (CM)_____23.5
MAXIMUM DIAMETER (CM)_____8.4
WEIGHT (GM)_____630

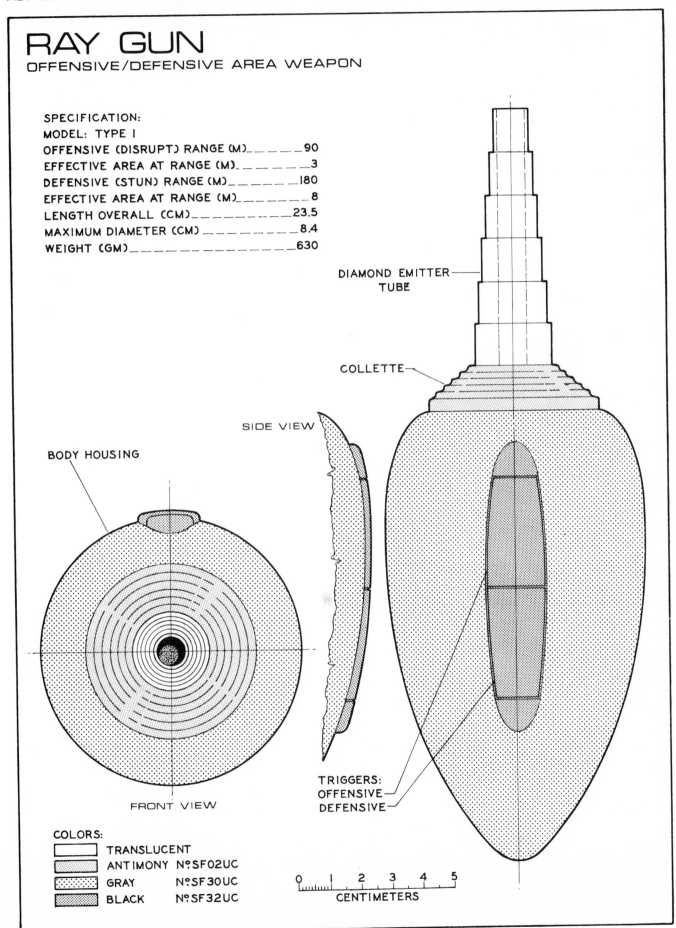

DIAMOND EMITTER TUBE

COLLETTE

SIDE VIEW

BODY HOUSING

FRONT VIEW

TRIGGERS:
OFFENSIVE
DEFENSIVE

COLORS:
TRANSLUCENT
ANTIMONY NºSF02UC
GRAY   NºSF30UC
BLACK   NºSF32UC

0 1 2 3 4 5
CENTIMETERS

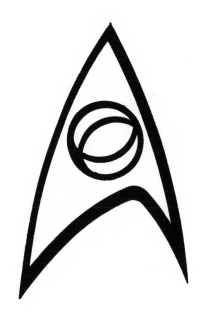

SCIENCES   SECTION

SECTION INDEX

TO. NO:	SUBJECT	CURRENT	REPLACES
02:00:00	SCIENCES SECTION FLYSHEET	7305.30	
» » :02	FOREWORD	*	
» » :04	SECTION INDEX	7309.10	
» :01:00	COMMAND INTELLIGENCE STATION - MAIN BRIDGE	7408.23	
» » :01	CONTROLS CONSOLE	7409.14	
» :04:00	SCIENCE TRICORDER - EXTERNAL ARRANGEMENT	7305.02	
» » :01	» » - OPEN ARR.	»	
» » :02	» » - INTERNAL ARR.	»	
» » :03	» » - DETAILS	7305.02	
» :06:00	NAVIGATION STATION - MAIN BRIDGE	*	
» » :01	CONTROLS CONSOLE	*	
» :06:10	GALACTIC COORDINATE SYSTEM	7305.06	
» » :12	S.I.N.S BASE DATUM	7306.05	
» » :13	COURSE TRACKING ELEMENT	7502.15	
» :06:20	VELOCITY/TIME RELATIONSHIP	7305.14	
» :06:30	STANDARD ORBITS - CLASS I STARSHIPS	7502.06	
» :07:00	MILKY WAY GALAXY	7305.19	
» » :01	KNOWN GALACTIC REGION	7305.16	
» » :02	UNITED FEDERATION OF PLANETS	7305.17	
» » :03	*	*	
» » :04	SOL SYSTEM (UN - EARTH)	*	
» » :05	» » - PLANETARY DATA	*	
» » :06	40 ERIDANI SYSTEM	*	
» » :07	» » » - PLANETARY DATA	*	
» » :08	61 CYGNI SYSTEM	*	
» » :09	» » » - PLANETARY DATA	*	
» » :10	EPSILON INDII SYSTEM	*	
» » :11	» » » - PLANETARY DATA	*	
» » :12	ALPHA CENTAURI SYSTEM	*	
» » :13	» » » - PLANETARY DATA	*	
» :10:00	MEDICAL SECTION - PRIMARY HULL - CLASS I STARSHIPS	7512.21	
» » :01	» » - SECONDARY HULL - MK-IX MODEL	*	
» :11:00	MEDICAL TRICORDER - EXTERNAL ARRANGEMENT	7305.03	
» » :01	» » - OPEN ARR.	»	
» » :02	» » - INTERNAL ARR.	»	
» » :03	» » - DETAILS	7305.03	
» » :04	HEARTBEAT READER	7503.06	
» » :05	FIELD READER TUBE	*	
» » :06	SPRAY APPLICATOR	7503.06	
» » :07	MEDICAL SCANNER	»	
» » :08	LANDING PARTY MEDICAL POUCH	*	
» » :09	NON-COMPUTERIZED FABRICATION PATTERN	*	
» » :10	MEDICAL HYPO	*	
» » :11	» »	*	

NOTE (*). NO CURRENT PRINT-OUT FROM MASTERCOM DATABANKS/SFHQ

SECTION INDEX

TO. NO:	SUBJECT	CURRENT	REPLACES
02:00:05	SECTION INDEX	7309.10	
» :11:12	ANABOLIC PROTOPLASER – LARGE VERSION	7503.04	
» » :13	» » – SMALL VERSION	»	
» » :14	SURGICAL SCALPELS	7503.03	

NOTE (*): NO CURRENT PRINT-OUT FROM MASTERCOM DATABANKS/SFHQ

COMMAND INTELLIGENCE
MAIN BRIDGE STATION - CLASS I STARSHIPS

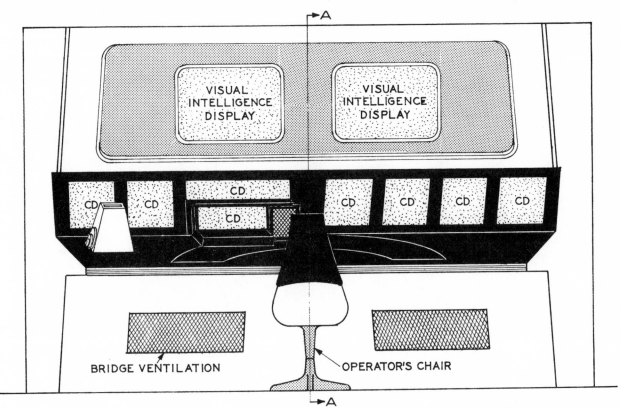

FRONT ELEVATION

VIEW A-A:

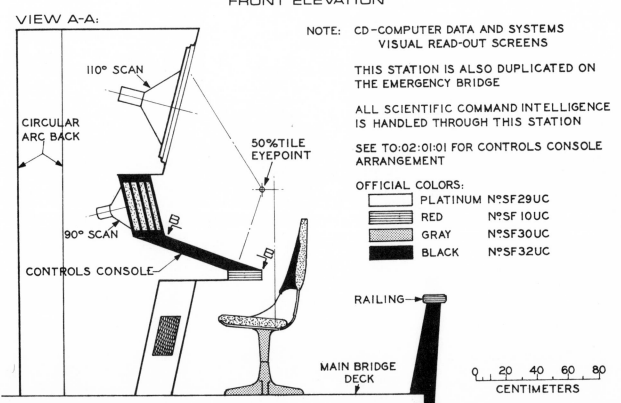

NOTE: CD-COMPUTER DATA AND SYSTEMS
VISUAL READ-OUT SCREENS

THIS STATION IS ALSO DUPLICATED ON
THE EMERGENCY BRIDGE

ALL SCIENTIFIC COMMAND INTELLIGENCE
IS HANDLED THROUGH THIS STATION

SEE TO:02:01:01 FOR CONTROLS CONSOLE
ARRANGEMENT

OFFICIAL COLORS:

	PLATINUM	Nº SF29UC
	RED	Nº SF10UC
	GRAY	Nº SF30UC
	BLACK	Nº SF32UC

CENTIMETERS
0   20   40   60   80

CONTROLS CONSOLE
VIEW B-B OF TO·02:01:00

REFER ELSEWHERE IN THIS SECTION FOR
DETAILED OPERATIONS PROCEDURES,
AND SYSTEMS FUNCTIONS SPECIFICA-
TIONS.

REFER TO ENGINEERING SECTION FOR
SYSTEMS SCHEMATICS, WIRING DIA-
GRAMS, AND STANDARD MAINTENANCE
PROCEDURES.

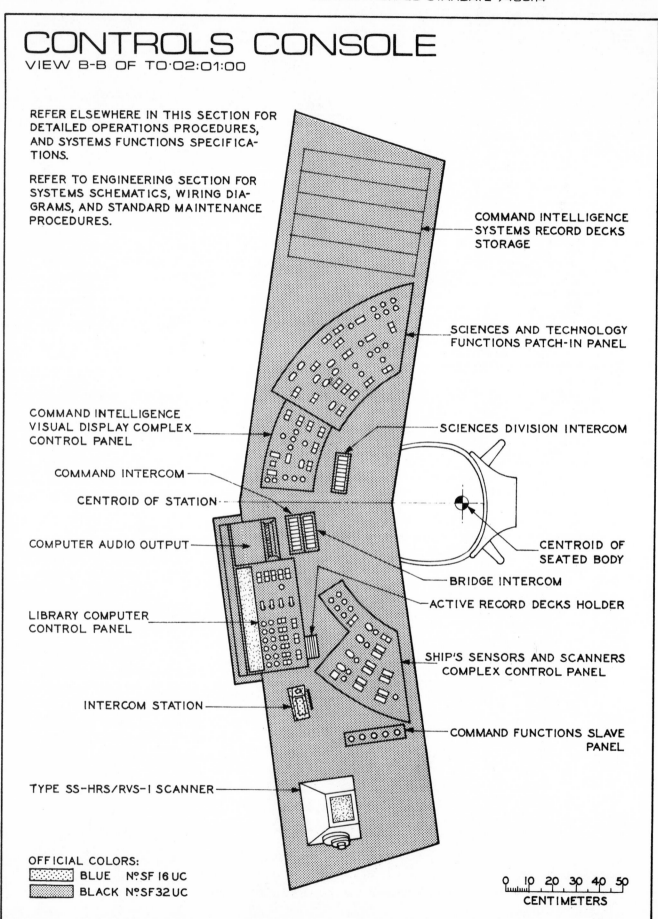

COMMAND INTELLIGENCE
SYSTEMS RECORD DECKS
STORAGE

SCIENCES AND TECHNOLOGY
FUNCTIONS PATCH-IN PANEL

COMMAND INTELLIGENCE
VISUAL DISPLAY COMPLEX
CONTROL PANEL

SCIENCES DIVISION INTERCOM

COMMAND INTERCOM

CENTROID OF STATION

COMPUTER AUDIO OUTPUT

CENTROID OF
SEATED BODY

BRIDGE INTERCOM

ACTIVE RECORD DECKS HOLDER

LIBRARY COMPUTER
CONTROL PANEL

SHIP'S SENSORS AND SCANNERS
COMPLEX CONTROL PANEL

INTERCOM STATION

COMMAND FUNCTIONS SLAVE
PANEL

TYPE SS-HRS/RVS-I SCANNER

OFFICIAL COLORS:
BLUE   N° SF 16 UC
BLACK   N° SF 32 UC

0 10 20 30 40 50
CENTIMETERS

SCIENCES TRICORDER

TYPE I

SELECTIVELY SENSE, MEASURE, ANALYZE, COMPARE, AND
IDENTIFY SURROUNDING ENVIRONMENTAL CONDITION.
MULTIPLE CHANNEL RECORD OR READOUT CAPABILITY
WITH MULTI-MODE DISPLAY CHOICE.

OFFICIAL COLORS:

	ANTIMONY	Nº SF 02 UC
	OLIVE	Nº SF 14 UC
	BLACK	Nº SF 32 UC

₵ SYMMETRY

DISPLAY-CONTROL
HEAD COVER

DISPLAY HEAD OPEN

127 CM LONG
NAUGAHYDE
SHOULDER
STRAP

RECORD-COMPARE
SECTION LID

CIRCUITRY-POWER SUPPLY
SECTION (IN BODY)

SIDE BODY
STORAGE
SHELLS

CASE
FRAMES
(BRUSHED)

(PEBBLED)

(PEBBLED)

FULL SIZE. DIMENSIONS: H.O.A.(CLOSED)~177.8 MM; W.O.A.~114.3 MM; D.O.A.~48.3 MM;

SCIENCES TRICORDER

ARRANGEMENT - UNIT OPEN

TYPE I

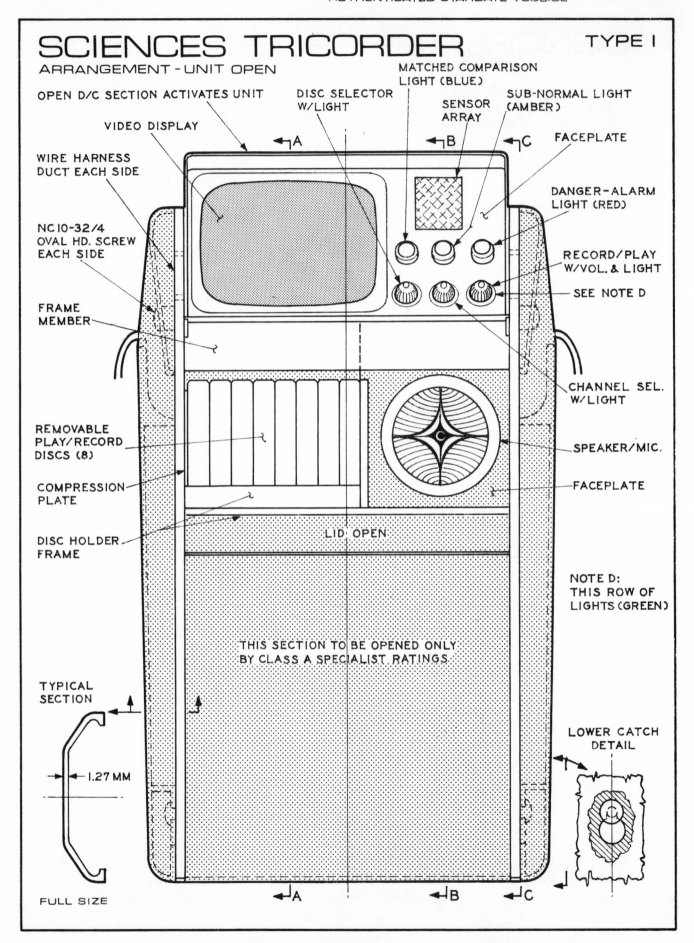

OPEN D/C SECTION ACTIVATES UNIT

VIDEO DISPLAY

WIRE HARNESS
DUCT EACH SIDE

NC 10-32/4
OVAL HD. SCREW
EACH SIDE

FRAME
MEMBER

REMOVABLE
PLAY/RECORD
DISCS (8)

COMPRESSION
PLATE

DISC HOLDER
FRAME

MATCHED COMPARISON
LIGHT (BLUE)

DISC SELECTOR
W/LIGHT

SENSOR
ARRAY

SUB-NORMAL LIGHT
(AMBER)

FACEPLATE

DANGER-ALARM
LIGHT (RED)

RECORD/PLAY
W/VOL. & LIGHT

SEE NOTE D

CHANNEL SEL.
W/LIGHT

SPEAKER/MIC.

FACEPLATE

LID OPEN

NOTE D:
THIS ROW OF
LIGHTS (GREEN)

THIS SECTION TO BE OPENED ONLY
BY CLASS A SPECIALIST RATINGS.

TYPICAL
SECTION

1.27 MM

FULL SIZE

LOWER CATCH
DETAIL

SCIENCES TRICORDER
INTERNAL ARRANGEMENT*

TYPE I

SENSOR ARRAY:
DENSITY –GAS –PRESSURE –RADIATION–
SPECTRAL –AND THERMAL SENSORS.

VIEW A-A

VIEW B-B

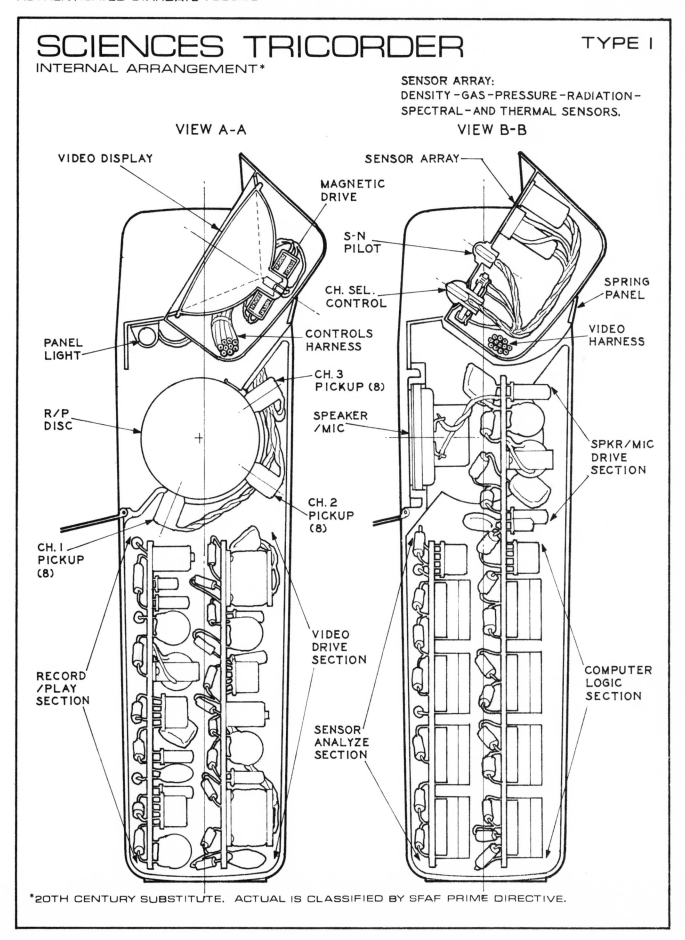

VIDEO DISPLAY

MAGNETIC DRIVE

SENSOR ARRAY

S-N PILOT

CH. SEL. CONTROL

SPRING PANEL

VIDEO HARNESS

PANEL LIGHT

CONTROLS HARNESS

CH. 3 PICKUP (8)

R/P DISC

SPEAKER /MIC

SPKR/MIC DRIVE SECTION

CH. 2 PICKUP (8)

CH. I PICKUP (8)

VIDEO DRIVE SECTION

COMPUTER LOGIC SECTION

RECORD /PLAY SECTION

SENSOR ANALYZE SECTION

*20TH CENTURY SUBSTITUTE. ACTUAL IS CLASSIFIED BY SFAF PRIME DIRECTIVE.

SCIENCES TRICORDER
CASE DETAILS

TYPE I

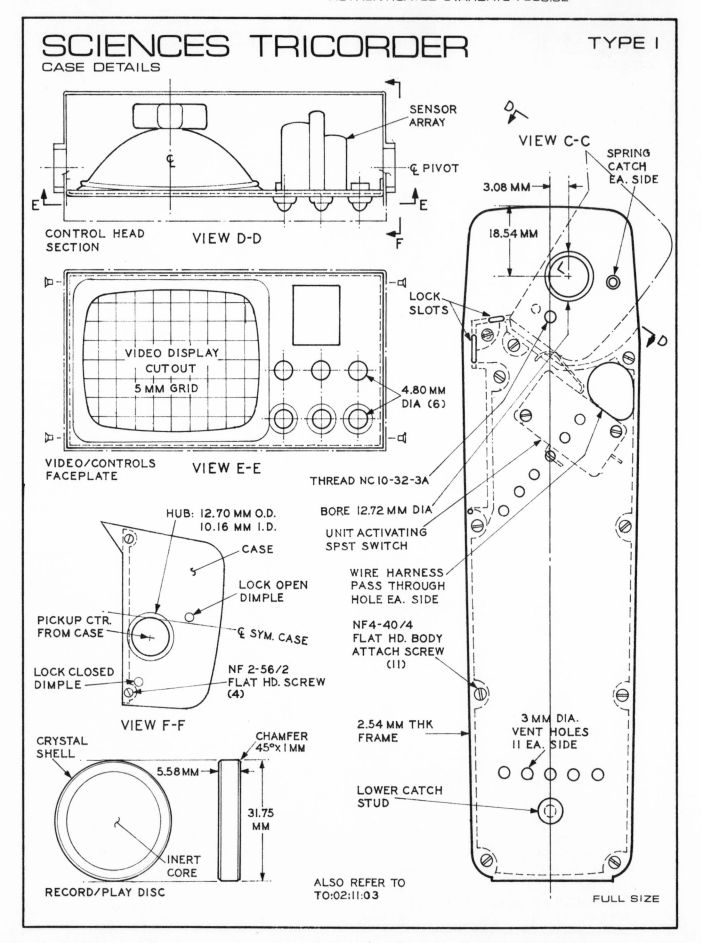

SENSOR ARRAY

ℂ PIVOT

VIEW C-C

SPRING CATCH EA. SIDE

3.08 MM

18.54 MM

CONTROL HEAD SECTION

VIEW D-D

LOCK SLOTS

VIDEO DISPLAY CUT OUT
5 MM GRID

4.80 MM DIA (6)

VIDEO/CONTROLS FACEPLATE

VIEW E-E

THREAD NC 10-32-3A

BORE 12.72 MM DIA

UNIT ACTIVATING SPST SWITCH

HUB: 12.70 MM O.D.
10.16 MM I.D.

CASE

LOCK OPEN DIMPLE

PICKUP CTR. FROM CASE

ℂ SYM. CASE

WIRE HARNESS PASS THROUGH HOLE EA. SIDE

NF4-40/4 FLAT HD. BODY ATTACH SCREW (II)

LOCK CLOSED DIMPLE

NF 2-56/2 FLAT HD. SCREW (4)

VIEW F-F

2.54 MM THK FRAME

3 MM DIA. VENT HOLES II EA. SIDE

CRYSTAL SHELL

CHAMFER 45° x I MM

5.58 MM

31.75 MM

LOWER CATCH STUD

INERT CORE

RECORD/PLAY DISC

ALSO REFER TO TO:02:11:03

FULL SIZE

GALACTIC COORD. SYSTEM
GREAT SPIRAL MILKY WAY GALAXY M-0

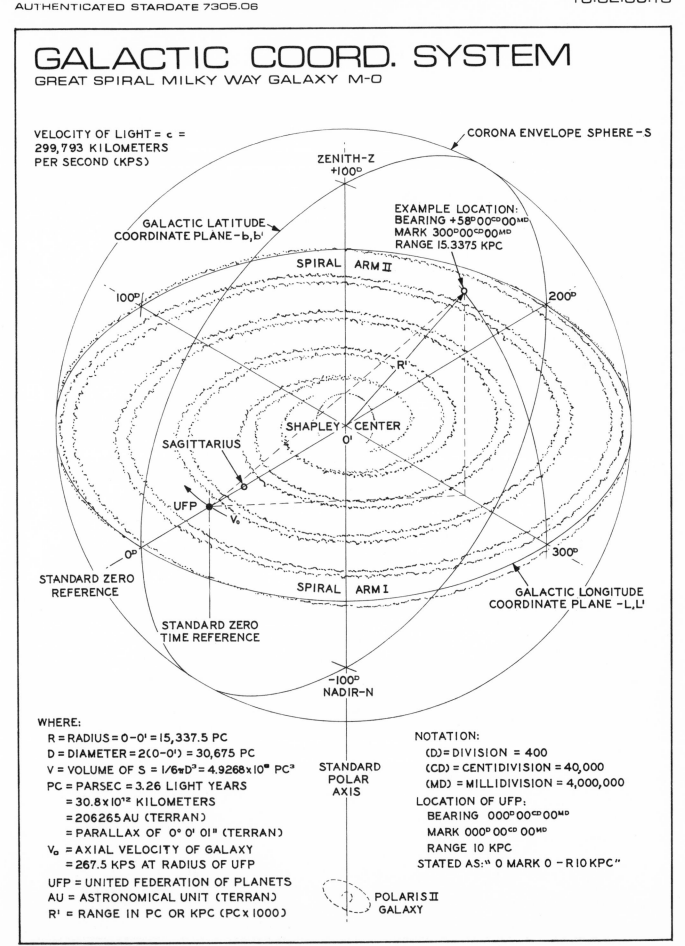

VELOCITY OF LIGHT = c =
299,793 KILOMETERS
PER SECOND (KPS)

CORONA ENVELOPE SPHERE – S

ZENITH-Z
+100ᴰ

GALACTIC LATITUDE
COORDINATE PLANE – b,b'

EXAMPLE LOCATION:
BEARING +58ᴰ00ᶜᴰ00ᴹᴰ
MARK 300ᴰ00ᶜᴰ00ᴹᴰ
RANGE 15.3375 KPC

SPIRAL   ARM II

100ᴰ

200ᴰ

R'

SHAPLEY   CENTER
0'

SAGITTARIUS

UFP
V₀

0ᴰ

300ᴰ

STANDARD ZERO
REFERENCE

STANDARD ZERO
TIME REFERENCE

SPIRAL   ARM I

GALACTIC LONGITUDE
COORDINATE PLANE – L,L'

-100ᴰ
NADIR-N

STANDARD
POLAR
AXIS

POLARIS II
GALAXY

WHERE:
R = RADIUS = 0-0' = 15,337.5 PC
D = DIAMETER = 2(0-0') = 30,675 PC
V = VOLUME OF S = $\frac{1}{6}\pi D^3$ = 4.9268 × 10⁸ PC³
PC = PARSEC = 3.26 LIGHT YEARS
    = 30.8 × 10¹² KILOMETERS
    = 206265 AU (TERRAN)
    = PARALLAX OF 0° 0' 01" (TERRAN)
V₀ = AXIAL VELOCITY OF GALAXY
    = 267.5 KPS AT RADIUS OF UFP
UFP = UNITED FEDERATION OF PLANETS
AU = ASTRONOMICAL UNIT (TERRAN)
R' = RANGE IN PC OR KPC (PC × 1000)

NOTATION:
    (D) = DIVISION = 400
    (CD) = CENTIDIVISION = 40,000
    (MD) = MILLIDIVISION = 4,000,000
LOCATION OF UFP:
    BEARING 000ᴰ00ᶜᴰ00ᴹᴰ
    MARK 000ᴰ 00ᶜᴰ 00ᴹᴰ
    RANGE 10 KPC
    STATED AS: " 0 MARK 0 – R 10 KPC"

S.I.N.S.* BASE DATUM
IN GALACTIC COORDINATE SYSTEM

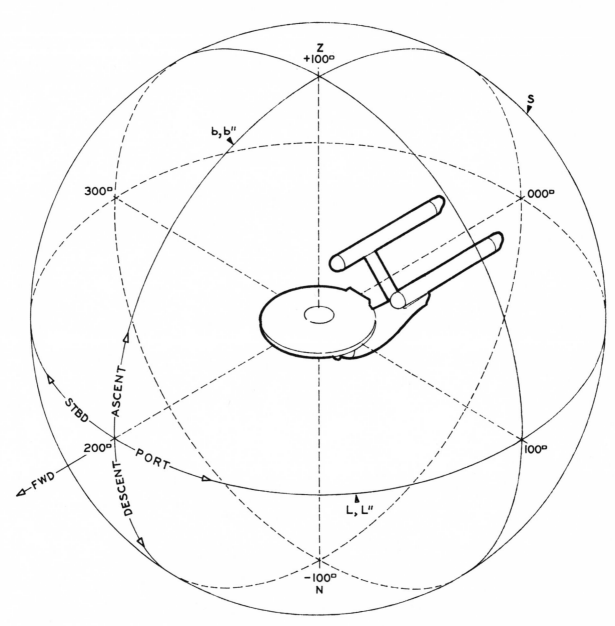

WHERE:

THE SPACE·INERTIAL·NAVIGATION·SYSTEM* IS THE FUNDAMENTAL GUIDANCE BASE FOR THE
ONBOARD NAVIGATIONAL COMPUTER COMPLEX.   IT IS ACTIVATED AND ACCURATELY ALIGNED
IN THE GALACTIC COORDINATE SYSTEM AT COMMISSIONING IN PLANETARY ORBIT AND THERE-
AFTER MAINTAINS THIS ALIGNMENT WITHOUT ERROR.   THE STARSHIP CARRIES THIS DATUM
WITH IT (FWD) WHEREVER IT GOES AND MOVES WITHIN THIS REFERENCE FRAMEWORK: TO
PORT OR STARBOARD AND UP OR DOWN IN ANY COMBINATION.

b, b" – DECLINATION PLANE
L, L" – AZIMUTH PLANE
N – NADIR AT b, b" –100°
Z – ZENITH AT b, b" +100°

S – SPHERICAL ENVELOPE CONTAINING ALL
NUMERICAL COMBINATIONS OF b,b" & L, L"

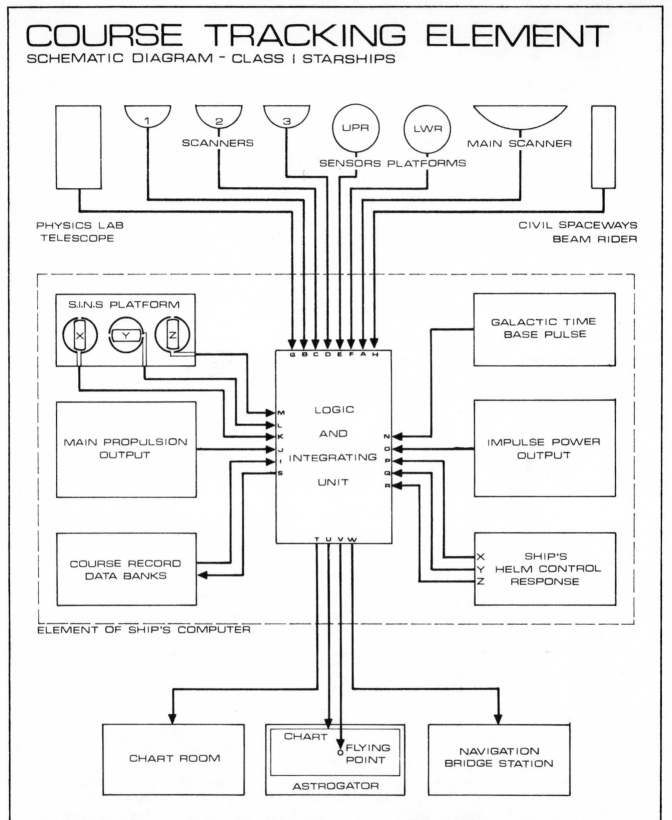

COURSE TRACKING ELEMENT
SCHEMATIC DIAGRAM - CLASS I STARSHIPS

SCANNERS

1 2 3

UPR LWR

MAIN SCANNER

SENSORS PLATFORMS

PHYSICS LAB
TELESCOPE

CIVIL SPACEWAYS
BEAM RIDER

S.I.N.S PLATFORM

X Y Z

GALACTIC TIME
BASE PULSE

G B C D E F A H

LOGIC

AND

INTEGRATING

UNIT

MAIN PROPULSION
OUTPUT

M
L
K
J
I
S

N
O
P
Q
R

IMPULSE POWER
OUTPUT

COURSE RECORD
DATA BANKS

T U V W

X
Y
Z

SHIP'S
HELM CONTROL
RESPONSE

ELEMENT OF SHIP'S COMPUTER

CHART ROOM

CHART

FLYING
POINT

ASTROGATOR

NAVIGATION
BRIDGE STATION

THE COURSE TRACKING ELEMENT IS THE VITAL HEART OF THE STARSHIP'S NAVIGATION
SYSTEM. IT IS ACTIVATED UPON COMMISIONING IN PLANETARY ORBIT AND THEREAFTER IT
MAINTAINS AN ACCURATE CONSTANT RECORD AND PLOT OF THE SHIP'S COURSE AND LOCA-
TION WITHIN THE GALAXY. FROM ANY LOCATION IT WILL GIVE A DIRECT BEARING TO THE
SHIP'S HOME BASE, ITS DESTINATION, OR ANY OTHER DIVERSIONARY POINT.

VELOCITY/TIME RELATIONSHIP
INTERSTELLAR SPACE/WARP TECHNOLOGY

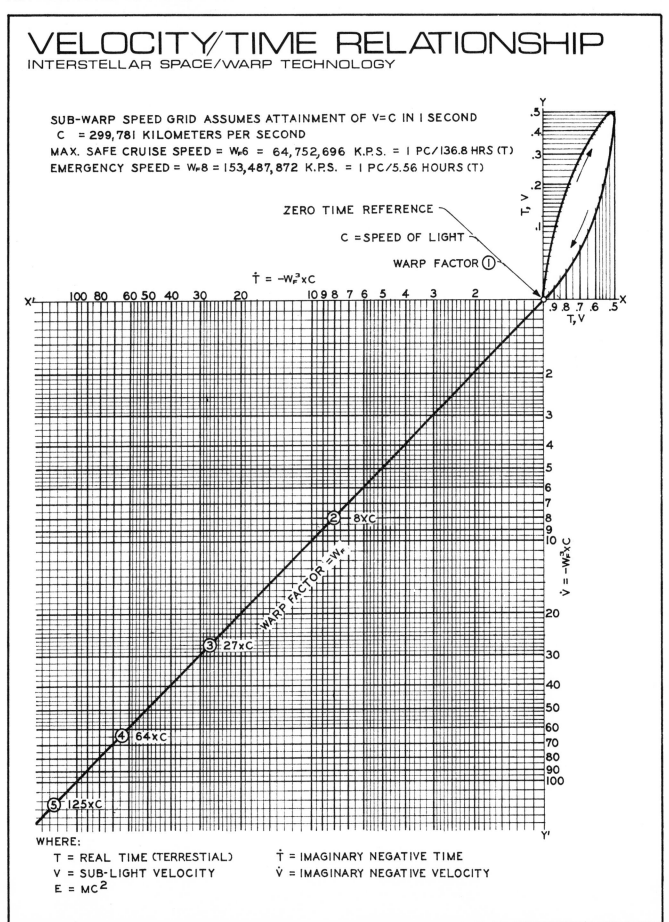

SUB-WARP SPEED GRID ASSUMES ATTAINMENT OF V=C IN I SECOND

C = 299,781 KILOMETERS PER SECOND

MAX. SAFE CRUISE SPEED = W_F6 = 64,752,696 K.P.S. = I PC/136.8 HRS (T)

EMERGENCY SPEED = W_F8 = 153,487,872 K.P.S. = I PC/5.56 HOURS (T)

ZERO TIME REFERENCE

C = SPEED OF LIGHT

WARP FACTOR ①

$\dot{T} = -W_F^3 \times C$

$\dot{V} = -W_F^3 \times C$

WARP FACTOR = W_F

② 8XC
③ 27XC
④ 64XC
⑤ 125XC

WHERE:

T = REAL TIME (TERRESTIAL) $\dot{T}$ = IMAGINARY NEGATIVE TIME

V = SUB-LIGHT VELOCITY $\dot{V}$ = IMAGINARY NEGATIVE VELOCITY

$E = MC^2$

STANDARD ORBITS
CLASS I STARSHIPS

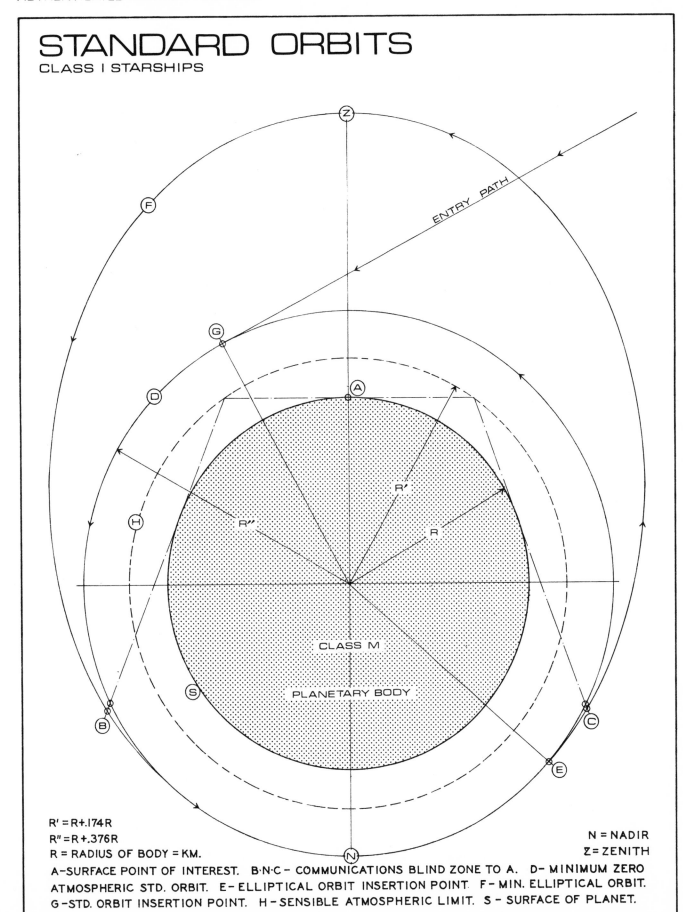

$R' = R + .174R$

$R'' = R + .376R$

$R = \text{RADIUS OF BODY} = \text{KM.}$

N = NADIR

Z = ZENITH

A—SURFACE POINT OF INTEREST.   B·N·C — COMMUNICATIONS BLIND ZONE TO A.   D— MINIMUM ZERO ATMOSPHERIC STD. ORBIT.   E— ELLIPTICAL ORBIT INSERTION POINT.   F— MIN. ELLIPTICAL ORBIT. G—STD. ORBIT INSERTION POINT.   H— SENSIBLE ATMOSPHERIC LIMIT.   S — SURFACE OF PLANET.

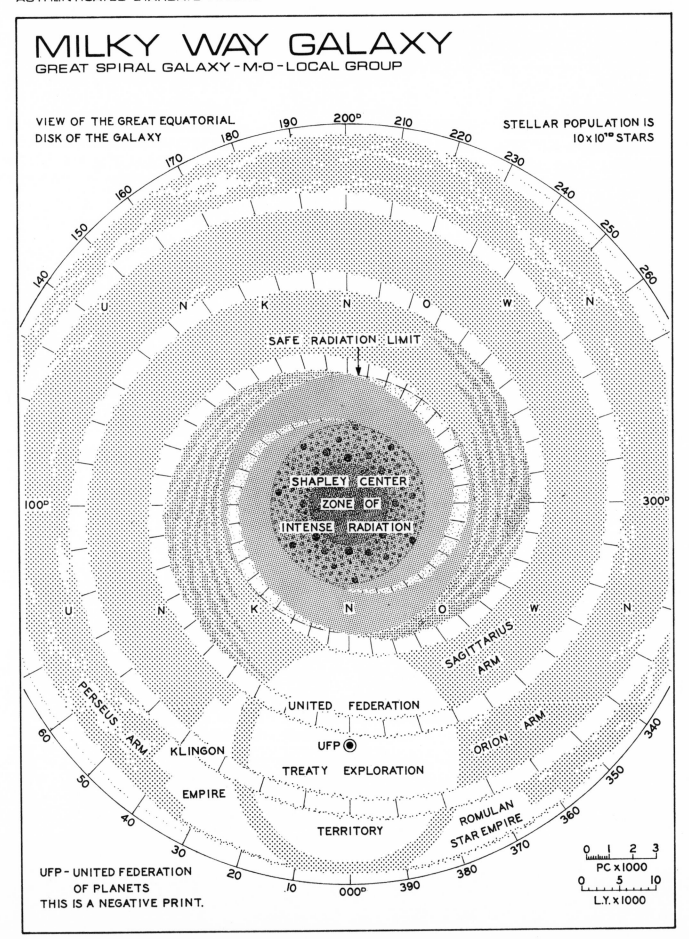

MILKY WAY GALAXY
GREAT SPIRAL GALAXY - M·0 - LOCAL GROUP

VIEW OF THE GREAT EQUATORIAL
DISK OF THE GALAXY

STELLAR POPULATION IS
10 x 10^10 STARS

200°
190   210
180   220
170   230
160   240
150   250
140   260

U   N   K   N   O   W   N

SAFE RADIATION LIMIT

100°   300°

SHAPLEY CENTER
ZONE OF
INTENSE RADIATION

U   N   K   N   O   W   N

SAGITTARIUS ARM

PERSEUS ARM

UNITED FEDERATION

UFP ⊙

KLINGON

ORION ARM

TREATY   EXPLORATION

EMPIRE

ROMULAN
STAR EMPIRE

TERRITORY

60
50
40
30
20
10   000°   390
380   370   360   350   340

0 1 2 3
PC x 1000

0   5   10
L.Y. x 1000

UFP - UNITED FEDERATION
OF PLANETS
THIS IS A NEGATIVE PRINT.

KNOWN GALACTIC REGION
UFP TREATY EXPLORATION TERRITORY

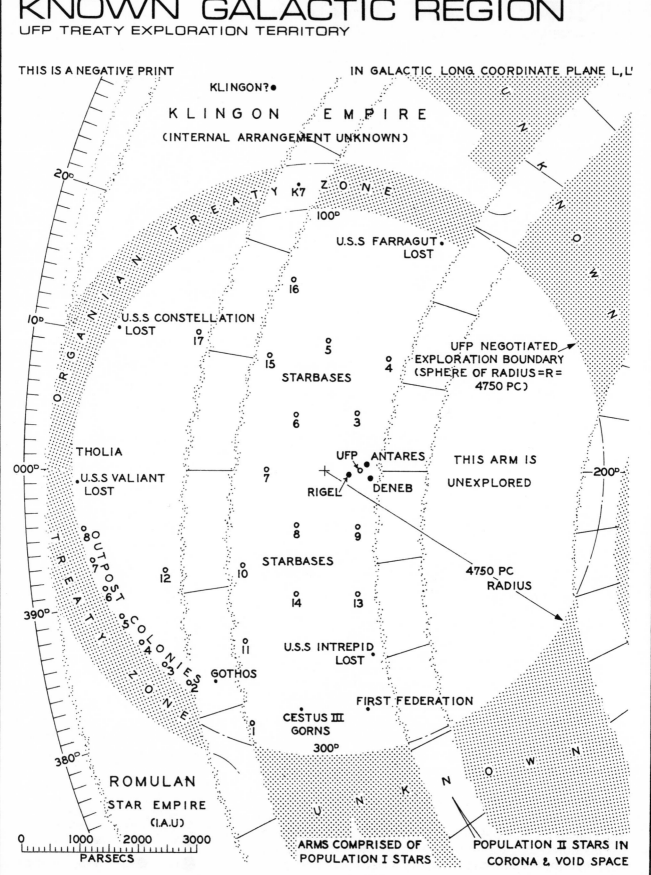

THIS IS A NEGATIVE PRINT

IN GALACTIC LONG COORDINATE PLANE L, L'

KLINGON? •

KLINGON EMPIRE
(INTERNAL ARRANGEMENT UNKNOWN)

UNKNOWN

ORGANIAN TREATY ZONE

20°

K7 • ZONE

100°

U.S.S FARRAGUT •
LOST

○ 16

10°

• U.S.S CONSTELLATION
• LOST
○ 17

○ 5

UFP NEGOTIATED
EXPLORATION BOUNDARY
(SPHERE OF RADIUS=R=
4750 PC)

○ 15

STARBASES

○ 4

○ 6   ○ 3

000°

THOLIA

• U.S.S VALIANT
LOST

○ 7

UFP ○ ANTARES
RIGEL ○
• DENEB

THIS ARM IS

UNEXPLORED

200°

+

○ 8   ○ 9

TREATY

○ 8
○ 7
OUTPOST ○ 6
○ 5 COLONIES
○ 4
ZONE ○ 3
○ 2

○ 12

○ 10

STARBASES

○ 14   ○ 13

4750 PC
RADIUS

390°

○ 11

U.S.S INTREPID
LOST

• GOTHOS

FIRST FEDERATION •

380°

○ 1

CESTUS III •
GORNS

300°

ROMULAN

STAR EMPIRE
(I.A.U)

UNKNOWN

0   1000   2000   3000
ᴵᴵᴵᴵᴵᴵᴵᴵᴵᴵ
PARSECS

ARMS COMPRISED OF
POPULATION I STARS

POPULATION II STARS IN
CORONA & VOID SPACE

UNITED FEDERATION
OF PLANETS - PRINCIPAL STELLAR SYSTEMS

VIEWED FROM ZENITH LOOKING
DOWN ON PROJECTION OF
GALACTIC LONGITUDE
COORDINATE PLANE
L, L'.

THE FEDERATION BOUNDARY IS A
SPHERE OF RADIUS -R = 7 PC
CENTERED ON SOL.
VOL-V = 1434 PC³

200
180
220
160
240
140
260
120
280
100
300
80
320
60
340
40
360
20
380
0

TO
SHAPLEY
CENTER

VEGA

HIEMDAL
MAAT

ALTAIR

OBLIK
PARI
TAJARHI

CASPAN
JASSAN
PAEGAN

STARBASE 1

STARBASE 2

HOROK

JENSHAHN ZAAHM

ALFERAZ
HAJJ

KESTRAL
MIRAZH

AHZDAR

ESKIIS
ZINDAR
ZA'FARAN

QIZAN
QAL'AT

RIGIL
QUINDAR
PROXIMA

ANDROCUS
ASTRAD

KEP SALU
KETOI

ANNOBON

MONGO

FOMALHAUT
NAKARAT

NDELE

TALI
KASIMAR

GHONDR
GALINA

ELOHIM
SHAANDRA

OOMARU
YAAN

MAZDA

TUTAKAI
TIKOPAI

MONDOLOY

THELONII
XANTHII
ALFR

SOL
JUPITER

PILAR
THOLUS

MENGEN

TULAN

TEMIR

GHAR

3
2

4

K'USHUI
K'HOTAN

ESABL

SIRIUS
SHAHR

5

KARS

PELIONE

PROCYON
PHARDOS

6

SAMAARA

SINUIJI
EKINUS

SALAYNA

7

ALAM'AK
BEHR'AK
CZAR'AK

RANGE IN
PARSECS-PC

STAR FLEET
HEADQUARTERS

THE FEDERATION ORBITS
THE GALACTIC CENTER WITH A
UNIT VELOCITY -V = 267.5 KPS IN
DIRECTION OF ARROW.

DOUBLE NAMES ARE
BINARIES, TRIPLE NAMES
ARE TRINARIES, AND THE
MAGNITUDE ● SHOWN IS FOR THE
LARGEST MEMBER (OR TOP NAME). SOL/
JUPITER AND ANDROCUS/ASTRAD MAY BE PROTO-BINARIES AS
THE LATER MEMBER OF EACH APPEAR TO BE "FAILED" STARS.
THE PROPER LONGITUDE NOTATION IS 000ᴰ00ᶜᴰ00ᴹᴰ WHERE:
(D)-DIVISION (400); (CD)-CENTIDIVISION (40,000); AND (MD)-
MILLIDIVISION (4,000,000). THIS IS A NEGATIVE PRINT.

RELATIVE RANGE OF
ABSOLUTE VISUAL MAGNETUDES
● 0   ● +2   ● +4   ● +6
● +1   ● +3   ● +5   ● +7 & <

MEDICAL SECTION
DECK 7 - PLAN - PRIMARY HULL - CLASS I STARSHIPS

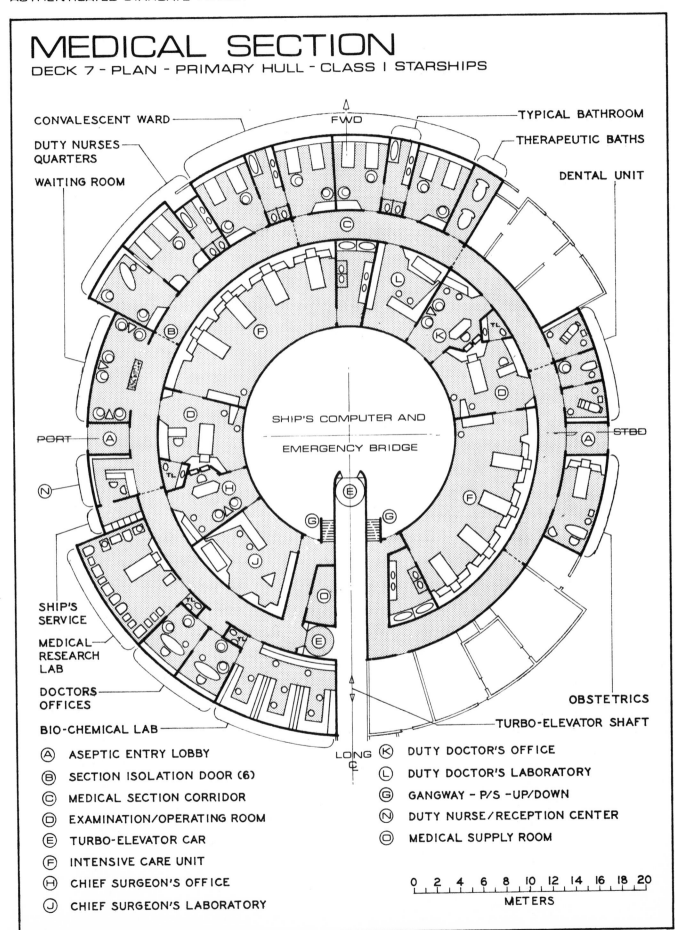

CONVALESCENT WARD

DUTY NURSES QUARTERS

WAITING ROOM

TYPICAL BATHROOM

THERAPEUTIC BATHS

DENTAL UNIT

FWD

SHIP'S COMPUTER AND EMERGENCY BRIDGE

PORT

STBD

SHIP'S SERVICE

MEDICAL RESEARCH LAB

DOCTORS OFFICES

BIO-CHEMICAL LAB

OBSTETRICS

TURBO-ELEVATOR SHAFT

LONG ℄

(A) ASEPTIC ENTRY LOBBY

(B) SECTION ISOLATION DOOR (6)

(C) MEDICAL SECTION CORRIDOR

(D) EXAMINATION/OPERATING ROOM

(E) TURBO-ELEVATOR CAR

(F) INTENSIVE CARE UNIT

(H) CHIEF SURGEON'S OFFICE

(J) CHIEF SURGEON'S LABORATORY

(K) DUTY DOCTOR'S OFFICE

(L) DUTY DOCTOR'S LABORATORY

(G) GANGWAY – P/S –UP/DOWN

(N) DUTY NURSE/RECEPTION CENTER

(O) MEDICAL SUPPLY ROOM

0 2 4 6 8 10 12 14 16 18 20
METERS

MEDICAL TRICORDER
STANDARD FIELD EQUIPMENT ITEM – TYPE I

SPECIFICATION:
L.O.A. – 177.8MM _ _ _ _ W.O.A – 114.3MM _ _ _ _ D.O.A. – 48.3MM _ _ _ _ WT. – 900GM

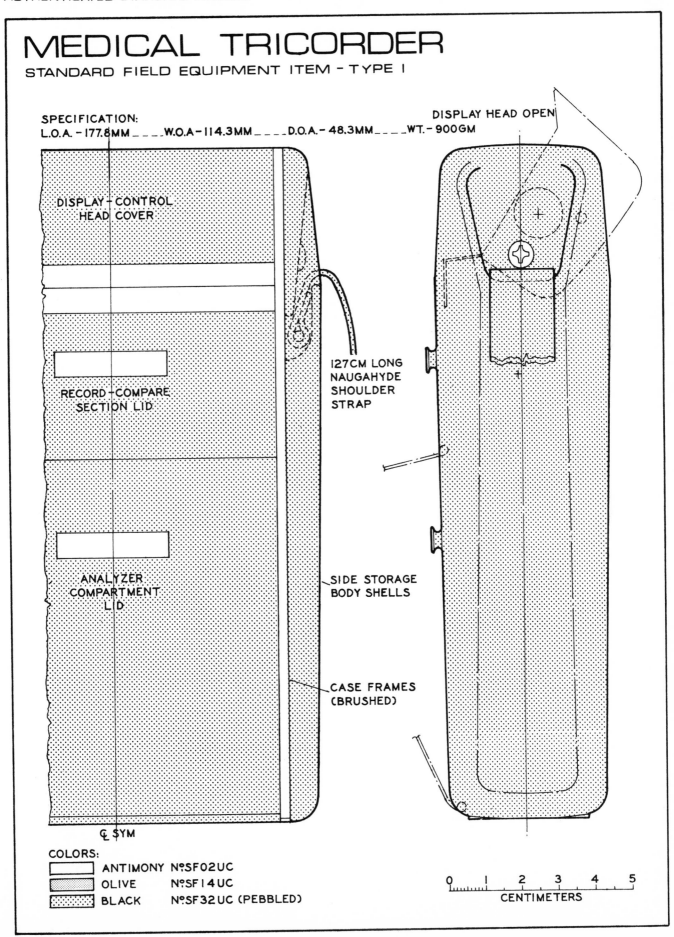

DISPLAY HEAD OPEN

DISPLAY – CONTROL HEAD COVER

RECORD – COMPARE SECTION LID

ANALYZER COMPARTMENT LID

127CM LONG NAUGAHYDE SHOULDER STRAP

SIDE STORAGE BODY SHELLS

CASE FRAMES (BRUSHED)

℄ SYM

COLORS:
ANTIMONY № SF02UC
OLIVE № SF14UC
BLACK № SF32UC (PEBBLED)

0 1 2 3 4 5
CENTIMETERS

MEDICAL TRICORDER
OPEN ARRANGEMENT

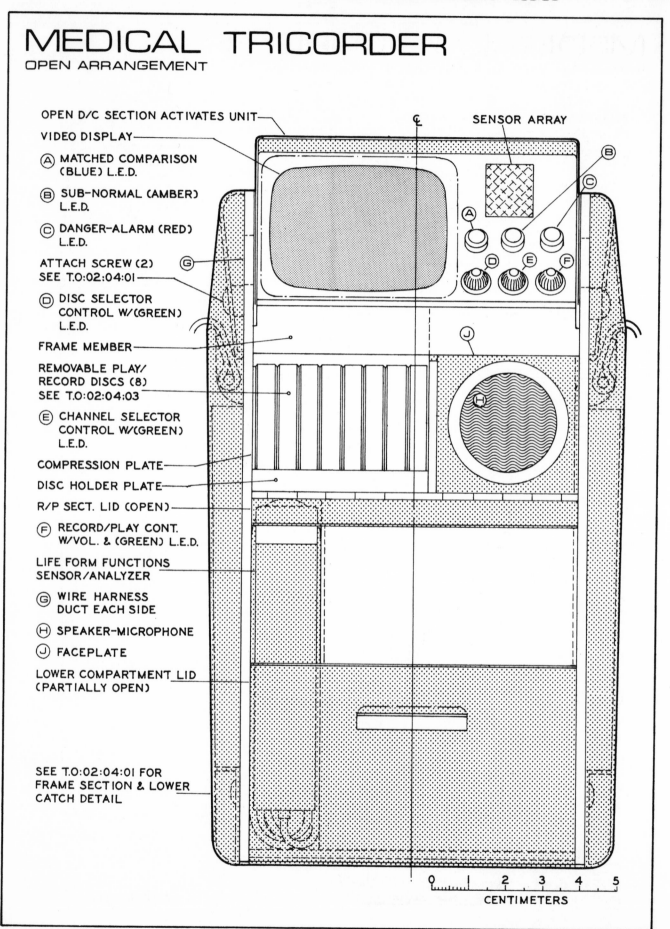

OPEN D/C SECTION ACTIVATES UNIT

VIDEO DISPLAY

(A) MATCHED COMPARISON (BLUE) L.E.D.

(B) SUB-NORMAL (AMBER) L.E.D.

(C) DANGER-ALARM (RED) L.E.D.

ATTACH SCREW (2) SEE T.O:02:04:01

(D) DISC SELECTOR CONTROL W/(GREEN) L.E.D.

FRAME MEMBER

REMOVABLE PLAY/ RECORD DISCS (8) SEE T.O:02:04:03

(E) CHANNEL SELECTOR CONTROL W/(GREEN) L.E.D.

COMPRESSION PLATE

DISC HOLDER PLATE

R/P SECT. LID (OPEN)

(F) RECORD/PLAY CONT. W/VOL. & (GREEN) L.E.D.

LIFE FORM FUNCTIONS SENSOR/ANALYZER

(G) WIRE HARNESS DUCT EACH SIDE

(H) SPEAKER-MICROPHONE

(J) FACEPLATE

LOWER COMPARTMENT LID (PARTIALLY OPEN)

SEE T.O:02:04:01 FOR FRAME SECTION & LOWER CATCH DETAIL

SENSOR ARRAY

0 1 2 3 4 5
CENTIMETERS

MEDICAL TRICORDER
INTERNAL ARRANGEMENT

SELECTIVELY MEASURE, COMPARE, AND DIAGNOSE LIFE FORM
VITAL SIGNS, ALSO SENSE, MEASURE, AND COMPARE HEALTH
CONDITION OF ENVIRONMENT. 24 CHANNEL CAPABILITY IN-
PUT OR RECORD WITH MULTI-MODE DISPLAY READOUT.

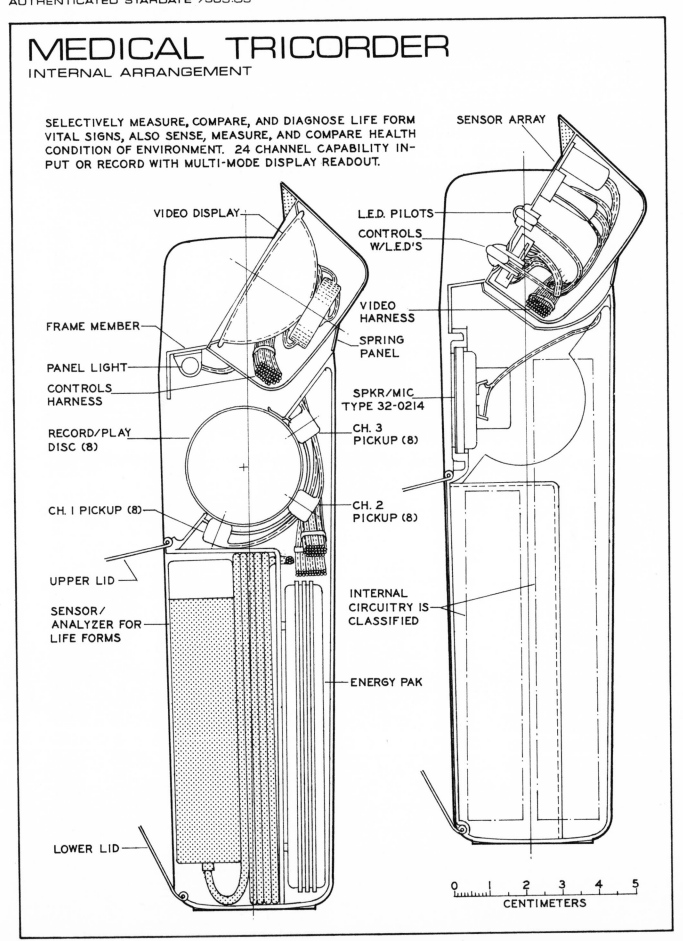

SENSOR ARRAY

VIDEO DISPLAY

L.E.D. PILOTS

CONTROLS
W/L.E.D'S

FRAME MEMBER

VIDEO
HARNESS

SPRING
PANEL

PANEL LIGHT

CONTROLS
HARNESS

SPKR/MIC
TYPE 32-0214

RECORD/PLAY
DISC (8)

CH. 3
PICKUP (8)

CH. I PICKUP (8)

CH. 2
PICKUP (8)

UPPER LID

INTERNAL
CIRCUITRY IS
CLASSIFIED

SENSOR/
ANALYZER FOR
LIFE FORMS

ENERGY PAK

LOWER LID

0 1 2 3 4 5
CENTIMETERS

MEDICAL TRICORDER
DETAILS

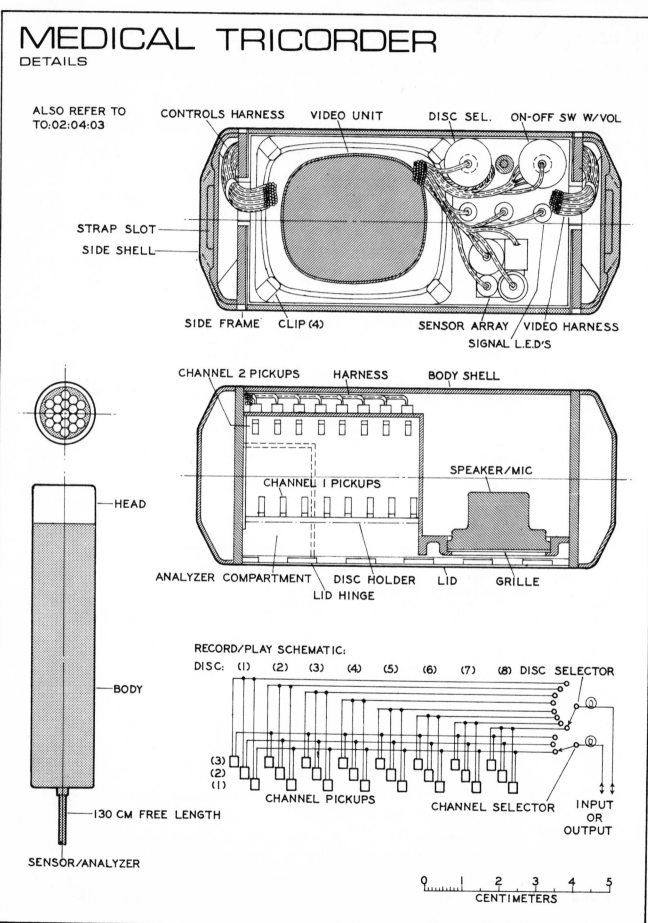

ALSO REFER TO
TO:02:04:03

CONTROLS HARNESS   VIDEO UNIT   DISC SEL.   ON-OFF SW W/VOL

STRAP SLOT
SIDE SHELL

SIDE FRAME   CLIP (4)   SENSOR ARRAY   VIDEO HARNESS
SIGNAL L.E.D'S

CHANNEL 2 PICKUPS   HARNESS   BODY SHELL

SPEAKER/MIC

CHANNEL I PICKUPS

HEAD

ANALYZER COMPARTMENT   DISC HOLDER   LID   GRILLE
LID HINGE

BODY

RECORD/PLAY SCHEMATIC:
DISC: (1)   (2)   (3)   (4)   (5)   (6)   (7)   (8) DISC SELECTOR

(3)
(2)
(1)
CHANNEL PICKUPS   CHANNEL SELECTOR   INPUT
OR
OUTPUT

130 CM FREE LENGTH

SENSOR/ANALYZER

0   1   2   3   4   5
CENTIMETERS

HEARTBEAT READER
STAR FLEET COLLEGE OF MEDICINE STANDARD

USED TO INSTANTANEOUSLY READ
THE INDIVIDUAL OR COLLECTIVE
HEARTBEATS OF ONE OR A GROUP
OF INTELLIGENT LIFE FORMS

GROUP READINGS ARE USEFUL
IN DETERMING NORMS FOR
NEWLY DISCOVERED LIFE FORMS
OR FOR DETECTING AN ALIEN LIFE
FORM DISGUISED IN A KNOWN GROUP

MODEL: SFAF/SG-MK06-TYPE M

GUARD AND ANTI-STRAY
AUDIBLE NOISE SCREEN

CLAMP BAND

GROUND PLANE SCREEN

OMNIDIRECTIONAL SENSOR

MULTIPLE READING
CANCEL INDICATOR

UNIT GO INDICATOR

DIGITAL READOUT WITH
FLOATING DECIMAL

SLIDE SWITCHES

B.P.M

OFF
ACTIVATE

OFF
AUDIBLE

SPECIFICATION:
LENGTH OVERALL (CM)____17.75
MAXIMUM DIAMETER (CM)___5.2
WEIGHT (GM)_____230

SECTION

TO IDENTIFY AN ALIEN IN A GROUP HOLD
UNIT CLOSE TO FIRST INDIVIDUAL AND
REDUCE MULTIPLE SELECTOR UNTIL
CANCEL INDICATOR GOES OUT. THAT
HEARTBEAT IS NOW REMOVED FROM GROUP
READING. CANCEL INDICATOR WILL GLOW
AGAIN WHEN UNIT IS MOVED TO ANOTHER
INDIVIDUAL. REPEAT PROCESS UNTIL
FLUCTUATING READOUT AND AUDIBLE IS
REMOVED, OR IS LAST REMAINING
INDIVIDUAL IN GROUP

BODY SHELL

SOLO/MULTIPLE
READING SELECTOR

S   M
SAMPLE

VOL   10

END VIEW

AUDIBLE VOLUME CONTROL

COLORS:

BLUE   ⎫
RED   ⎬ L.E.D'S
ANTIMONY Nº SF02UC
BLACK   Nº SF32UC

0   1   2   3   4
CENTIMETERS

SPRAY APPLICATOR
STAR FLEET COLLEGE OF MEDICINE STANDARD

THIS DISPENSER IS USED TO APPLY
EXTERNAL MEDICATIONS, ANTIBIOTICS,
AND PROTECTIVE DRESSINGS TO SMALL
WOUNDS AND CONTUSIONS

SPECIFICATION:
    MODEL: SFAF/SG-MK01-70
    SIZE: 70
    LENGTH OVERALL-LOADED (CM)__6.5
    MAXIMUM DIAMETER (CM)_____1.9
    WEIGHT-LOADED (GM)_____160

Ⓐ APPLICATOR BODY

Ⓑ SPRAY TRIGGER (PRESS TO SPRAY)

Ⓒ INTERCHANGABLE VIAL

Ⓓ DISPENSING TEAT

Ⓔ INTERCHANGABLE NOZZLE

NOZZLES AVAILABLE:
    SIZE: ORIFICE DIA/MM
    EXTRA FINE_____.0025
    FINE_____.025
    MEDIUM _____.20
    COARSE_____(SPECIAL ORDER)

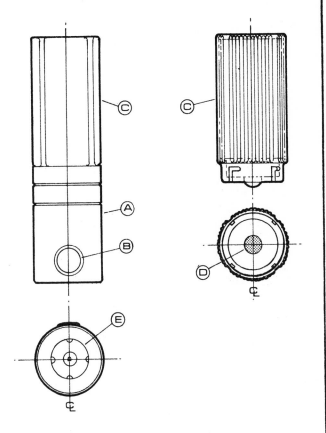

TRANSPARENT PRESSURIZED VIAL. REFER
TO UNIFORM PHARMACEUTICALS CODE
SPECIFICATION FOR PRELOADED VIALS
AVAILABLE FROM STANDARD STOCK

SPECIFICATION:
    FLUID CAPACITY (CC)_____70
    WEIGHT-LOADED (GM)_____80
    PRESSURIZED TO (KG/CM^2)_____1.30

COLORS:
    ANTIMONY N°SF02UC BASIC. OTHERWISE
    MATCHES COLOR CODE OF VIAL CONTENTS

CENTIMETERS

MEDICAL SCANNER
STAR FLEET COLLEGE OF MEDICINE STANDARD

USED FOR FIELD DETERMINATION OF GEN.
MEDICAL CONDITION OF INTELLIGENT
LIFE FORMS BY SENSING BODY EMANATIONS
IN EMISSION GROUPS OF: ALPHA, BETA,
GAMMA, KIRLIAN, THETA, AND XI RAYS

REFER TO COLLEGE OF MEDICINE STD.
DIAGNOSTIC PRACTISES JOURNAL FOR
SCALE CALIBRATIONS AND CURRENT
INTERPRETATIONG OF READINGS

SPECIFICATION:
    LENGTH OVERALL (CM)_ _ _ _ _ _6.05
    MAXIMUM DIAMETER (CM)_ _ _ _ _ _3.5
    WEIGHT (GM)_ _ _ _ _ _ _ _ _ _ _230
    SENSITIVITY (EmV/AU²)_ _ _ _ _TO .0001
    READING GROUPS_ _ _ _ _A, B, Γ, K, Θ, Ξ

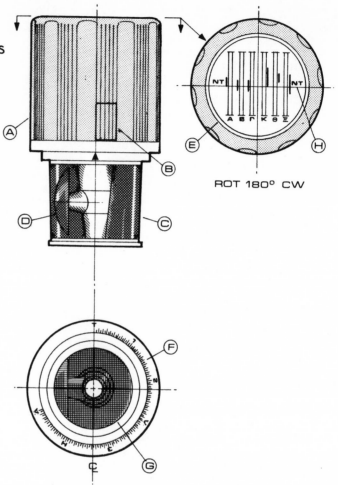

ROT 180° CW

Ⓐ COMPUTER HOUSING

Ⓑ ACTIVATING SWITCH (PRESS ON – OFF)

Ⓒ SCANNER HOUSING (48 MESH SCREEN)

Ⓓ ROTATING SCANNER

Ⓔ READINGS DIAL (INCREASE FROM
    BOTTOM TO TOP)

Ⓕ LIFE FORM TYPE SELECTION SCALE

Ⓖ GROUND PLANE SCREEN (48 MESH)

Ⓗ NT – NORMAL TERRAN RANGE

COLORS:
    ☐ ANTIMONY N°SF02UC
    ▨ GRAY   N°SF30UC
    ■ BLACK   N°SF32UC

0 1 2 3 4
CENTIMETERS

ANABOLIC PROTOPLASER
STAR FLEET COLLEGE OF MEDICINE STANDARD

PORTABLE WOUND HEALER. MINOR
INJURY VERSION. STANDARD FIELD
EQUIPMENT UNIT.

SPECIFICATION:
   MODEL: SFAF/SG-MK08-0
   SIZE: 0
   INTENSITY SCALE: 0-100 EmV/AU²
   LENGTH OVERALL (CM) _ _ _ _ _ _ 25
   WIDTH OVERALL (CM) _ _ _ _ _ _ _ 3.8
   HEIGHT OVERALL (CM) _ _ _ _ _ _ 4.2
   WEIGHT (GM) _ _ _ _ _ _ _ _ _ 450

(A) HOUSING

(B) REMOVABLE BOTTOM PANEL

(C) SPECIFICATIONS PLATE

(D) ACTIVATING SWITCH AND INTENSITY
    CONTROL - DEPRESS TO OPERATE

(E) EFFECTIVITY SENSOR

(F) DNA MATCH SYNTHESIZATION UNIT

(G) RAY EMISSION DUCT

(H) RECHARGING CHAMBER

(J) INTENSITY FORCE LIGHT:

0   25   50   75   100
OFF   SCALE   FULL

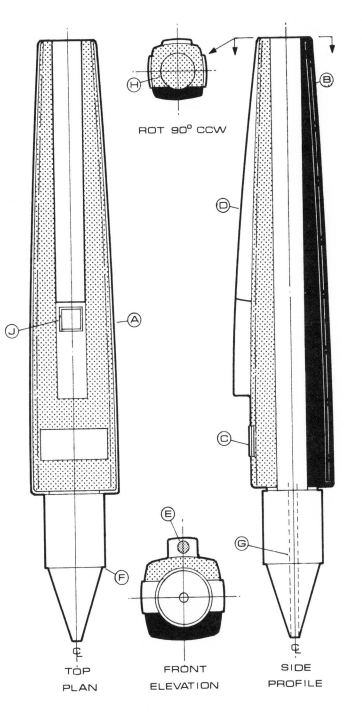

ROT 90° CCW

TOP
PLAN

FRONT
ELEVATION

SIDE
PROFILE

COLORS:

	ANTIMONY	N°SF02UC
	GRAY	N°SF30UC
	RED	N°SF10UC
	BLACK	N°SF32UC

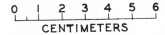

0 1 2 3 4 5 6
CENTIMETERS

ANABOLIC PROTOPLASER
STAR FLEET COLLEGE OF MEDICINE STANDARD

PORTABLE WOUND HEALER – MASSIVE
INJURY VERSION. STANDARD FIELD
EQUIPMENT ITEM.

SPECIFICATION:

MODEL: SFAF/SG-MK08-2
SIZE: 2
INTENSITY RANGE: 0 – 500 EmV/AU^2
LENGTH OVERALL (CM)_ _ _ _ _ _35
WIDTH OVERALL (CM)_ _ _ _ _ _ _5.6
HEIGHT OVERALL (CM)_ _ _ _ _6.95
WEIGHT (GM)_ _ _ _ _ _ _ _ _ _680

Ⓐ HOUSING

Ⓑ REMOVABLE BOTTOM PANEL

Ⓒ ACTIVATING SWITCH – BLACK-OFF
RED-ON (PUSH FORWARD)

Ⓓ INTENSITY CONTROL (DEPRESS TO
INCREASE INTENSITY)

Ⓔ EFFECTIVITY SENSOR

Ⓕ DNA MATCH SYNTHESIZATION UNIT

Ⓖ RAY EMISSION DUCT

Ⓗ RECHARGING CHAMBER

Ⓙ SPECIFICATIONS PLATE

Ⓚ INTENSITY FORCE LIGHT:

0   100   200   300   400   500
OFF   SCALE   FULL

COLORS:

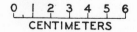

ANTIMONY №SF02UC
GRAY   №SF30UC
RED   №SF10UC
BLACK   №SF32UC

0 1 2 3 4 5 6
CENTIMETERS

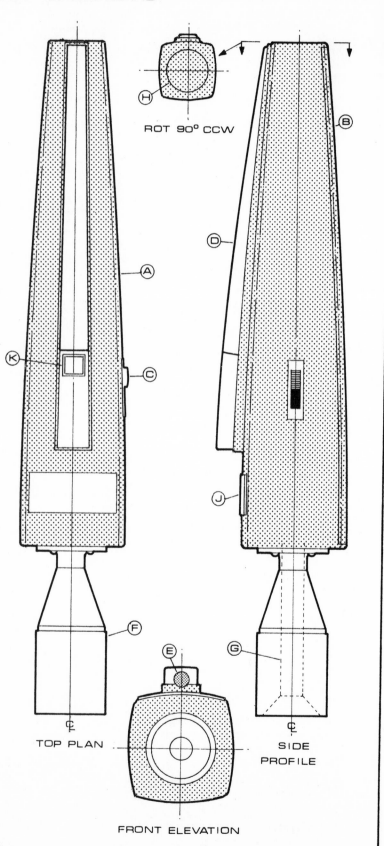

ROT 90° CCW

TOP PLAN

FRONT ELEVATION

SIDE
PROFILE

SURGICAL SCALPELS
STAR FLEET COLLEGE OF MEDICINE STANDARD

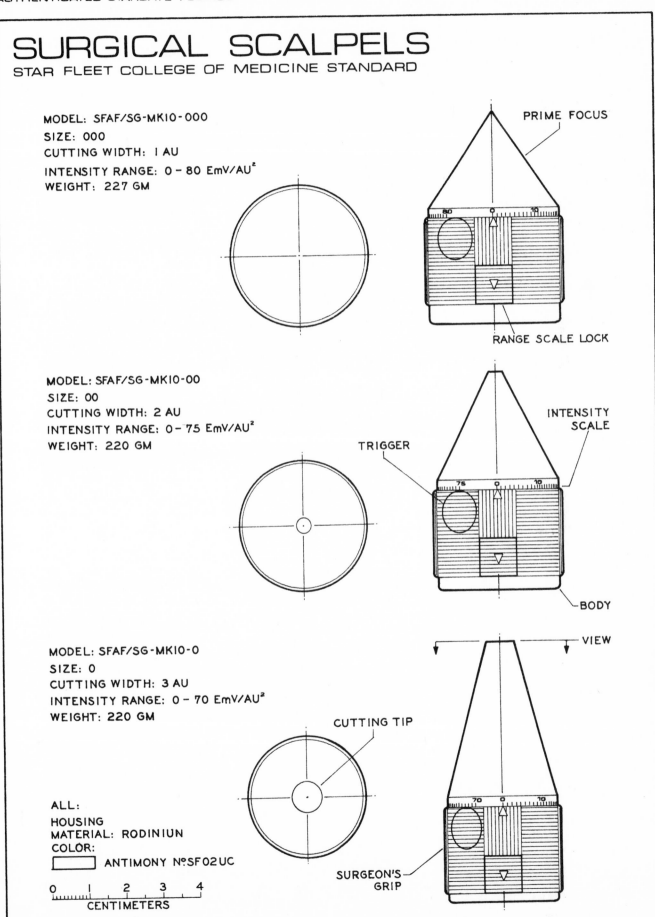

MODEL: SFAF/SG-MK10-000
SIZE: 000
CUTTING WIDTH: I AU
INTENSITY RANGE: 0 – 80 EmV/AU^2
WEIGHT: 227 GM

PRIME FOCUS

RANGE SCALE LOCK

MODEL: SFAF/SG-MK10-00
SIZE: 00
CUTTING WIDTH: 2 AU
INTENSITY RANGE: 0 – 75 EmV/AU^2
WEIGHT: 220 GM

TRIGGER

INTENSITY SCALE

BODY

MODEL: SFAF/SG-MK10-0
SIZE: 0
CUTTING WIDTH: 3 AU
INTENSITY RANGE: 0 – 70 EmV/AU^2
WEIGHT: 220 GM

VIEW

CUTTING TIP

ALL:
HOUSING
MATERIAL: RODINIUN
COLOR:
ANTIMONY N°SF02UC

SURGEON'S GRIP

0   1   2   3   4
CENTIMETERS

SUPPORT SERVICES SECTION

SECTION INDEX

TO. NO:	SUBJECT	CURRENT	REPLACES
03:00:00	SUPPORT SERVICES SECTION FLYSHEET	7305.30	
" " :02	FOREWORD	*	
" " :04	SUPPORT SERVICES SECTION INDEX	7504.08	
" :01:00	COMMUNICATIONS STATION - MAIN BRIDGE	7408.23	
" " :01	CONTROLS CONSOLE	7409.20	
" :02:00	COMMUNICATOR - TYPE I	7304.20	
" " :01	COMMUNICATOR CIRCUITRY	7304.20	
" " :02	BRIDGE EAR RECEIVER - MK05	7503.07	
" " :03	B.E.R. CIRCUITRY	*	
" " :04	UNIVERSAL TRANSLATOR - TYPE I	7503.07	
" " :05	U/T CIRCUITRY	*	
" :05:00	ENVIRONMENTAL STATION - MAIN BRIDGE	*	
" " :01	CONTROLS CONSOLE	*	
" :08:00	ENGINEERING STATION - MAIN BRIDGE	7408.23	
" " :01	CONTROLS CONSOLE	7409.14	
" " :10	ENGINEERING SECTION - PRIMARY HULL - CLASS I STARSHIPS	7312.21	
" " :11	ENGINEERING SECTION - SECONDARY HULL - MK-IX ONLY	*	
" :10:20	IMPULSE POWER - EXTERNAL PLAN & PROFILE	7312.21	
" " :21	IMPULSE POWER - INTERNAL PLAN & PROFILE	CLASSIFIED	
" :11:20	MAIN PROPULSION - EXTERNAL PLAN & PROFILE	7312.21	
" " :21	MAIN PROPULSION - INTERNAL PLAN & PROFILE	CLASSIFIED	
" :16:30	TRANSPORTER - STANDARD 6 PERSON - PLAN	7312.21	
" " :31	ELEVATIONS	*	
" " :50	TRANSPORTER - EMERGENCY - PLAN	7312.21	
" " :51	ELEVATIONS	*	
" " :70	TRANSPORTER - CARGO - PLAN	7312.21	
" " :71	ELEVATIONS	*	
" :17:00	HANGAR DECK - PLAN - MK-IX ONLY	7312.21	
" " :01	ELEVATION	7312.21	
" :98:10	VULCAN LYRETTE	7503.10	
" " :11		*	
" " :30	TRIDIMENSIONAL CHESS	7503.12	
" " :31	CHESSMEN	7503.14	

NOTE (*): NO CURRENT PRINT-OUT FROM MASTERCOM DATABANKS/SFHQ

COMMUNICATIONS
MAIN BRIDGE STATION - CLASS I STARSHIPS

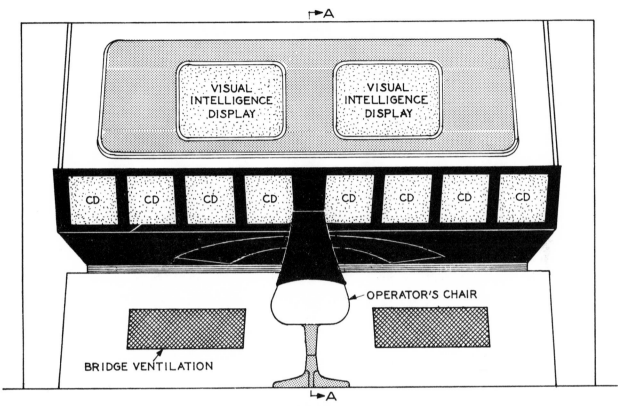

►A

VISUAL INTELLIGENCE DISPLAY

VISUAL INTELLIGENCE DISPLAY

CD CD CD CD CD CD CD CD

OPERATOR'S CHAIR

BRIDGE VENTILATION

►A

FRONT ELEVATION

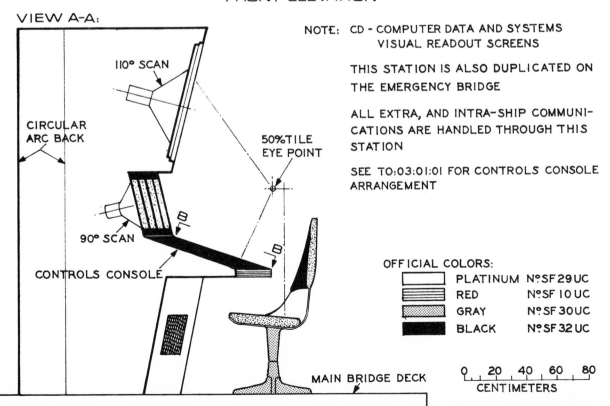

VIEW A-A:

110° SCAN

CIRCULAR ARC BACK

50% TILE EYE POINT

B

90° SCAN

CONTROLS CONSOLE

B

MAIN BRIDGE DECK

NOTE: CD - COMPUTER DATA AND SYSTEMS VISUAL READOUT SCREENS

THIS STATION IS ALSO DUPLICATED ON THE EMERGENCY BRIDGE

ALL EXTRA, AND INTRA-SHIP COMMUNICATIONS ARE HANDLED THROUGH THIS STATION

SEE TO:03:01:01 FOR CONTROLS CONSOLE ARRANGEMENT

OFFICIAL COLORS:

PLATINUM	N°SF 29 UC
RED	N°SF 10 UC
GRAY	N°SF 30 UC
BLACK	N°SF 32 UC

0 20 40 60 80
CENTIMETERS

CONTROLS CONSOLE
VIEW B-B OF TO:03:01:00

REFER ELSEWHERE IN THIS SECTION
FOR DETAILED OPERATIONS PROCED-
URES, AND SYSTEMS FUNCTIONS
SPECIFICATIONS.

REFER TO ENGINEERING SECTION
FOR SYSTEMS SCHEMATICS, WIRING
DIAGRAMS, AND STANDARD MAIN-
TENANCE PROCEDURES.

REFER TO COMMAND SECTION FOR
STAR FLEET SUB-SPACE COMMUNI-
CATIONS CODES (CLASSIFIED).

COMMUNICATIONS SYSTEMS
RECORD DECKS STORAGE
EACH SIDE

ALTERNATE CIRCUITRY AND
EMERGENCY OVERRIDE PANEL

SPECIAL COMMUNICATIONS
FUNCTIONS PATCH-IN PANEL

COMMUNICATIONS INTERCOM

CENTROID OF STATION

SHIP'S INTERNAL COMMUNI-
CATIONS PANEL

CENTROID OF
SEATED BODY

ACTIVE RECORD DECK HOLDER

BRIDGE INTERCOM

SPACE NOISE EMISSIONS
BLANKING CONTROL

EXTERNAL COMMUNICATIONS
PANEL

INTERCOM STATION

OFFICIAL COLORS:
BLUE   N°SF16UC
BLACK N°SF32UC

0 10 20 30 40 50
CENTIMETERS

TYPE I

COMMUNICATOR
STANDARD FIELD EQUIPMENT ITEM

SPECIFICATION:
L.O.A.__113.5MM   W.O.A.__63.5MM   H.O.A.__28MM
WEIGHT__200GM   RANGE__12000KM

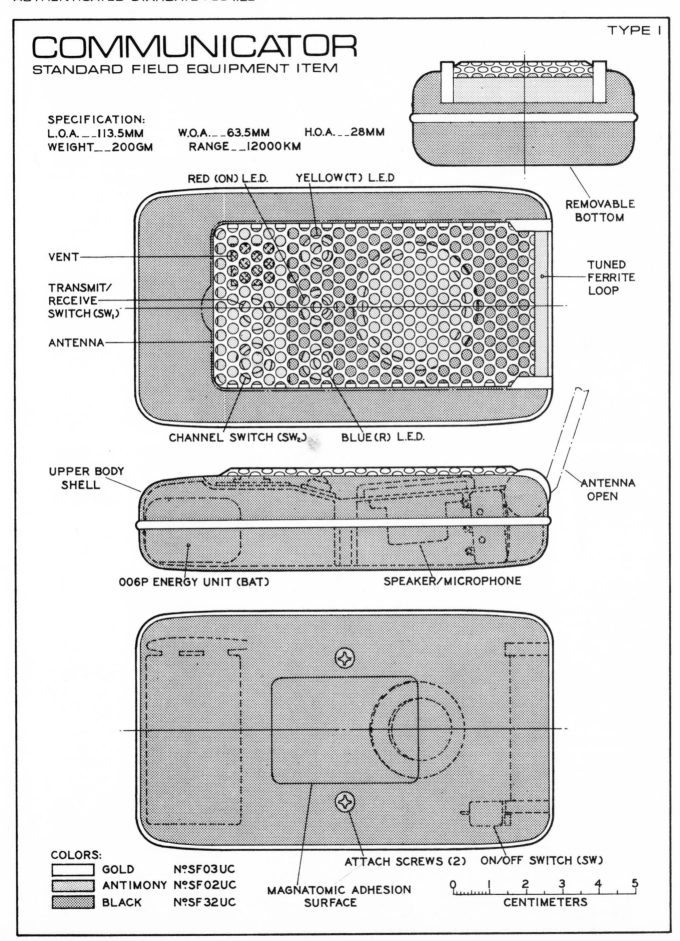

RED (ON) L.E.D.   YELLOW (T) L.E.D

REMOVABLE BOTTOM

VENT

TUNED FERRITE LOOP

TRANSMIT/ RECEIVE SWITCH (SW₁)

ANTENNA

CHANNEL SWITCH (SW₂)   BLUE (R) L.E.D.

UPPER BODY SHELL

ANTENNA OPEN

006P ENERGY UNIT (BAT)   SPEAKER/MICROPHONE

COLORS:
GOLD   №SF03UC
ANTIMONY   №SF02UC
BLACK   №SF32UC

ATTACH SCREWS (2)   ON/OFF SWITCH (SW)

MAGNATOMIC ADHESION SURFACE

0   1   2   3   4   5
CENTIMETERS

COMMUNICATOR

CIRCUITRY DIAGRAM - TYPE I*

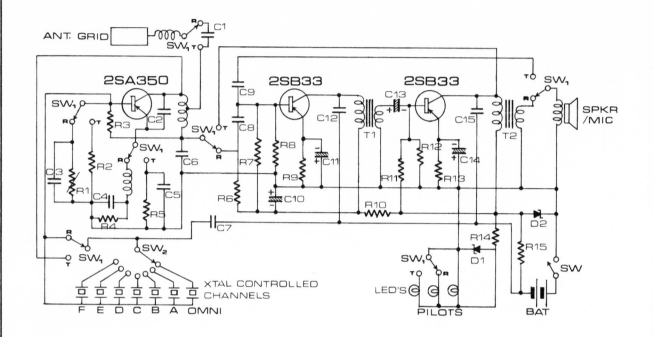

ANTENNA – (COVER GRID) – WITH TUNED FERRITE LOOP

SW – ON-OFF SWITCH COVER ACTUATED – TYPE MICRO 1SMI

SW₁ – NORMAL RECEIVE (R) PRESS TO TRANSMIT (T) (7 CONTACT)

SW₂ – ROTARY 7 CONTACT RF SWITCH

SPKR/MIC – SPEAKER/MICROPHONE – TYPE 32-0214/8Ω/0.1W

CHANNELS	
CH	MHZ
OMNI	27.125
A	49.91
B	49.93
C	49.95
D	49.97
E	49.99
F	N.A

VALUES				
CHANNEL	OMNI	OTHERS		
ENERGY VDC	9	9	15	22.5
C1 CAPAC'T'R pF	100			
C2 " pF	30			
C3 ' µF	.0015			
C4 " µF	.005			
C5 " µF	.02			
C6 " µF	.05			
C7 " pF	5			
C8 " µF	1			
C9 " µF	1			
C10 " µF/WV	30/10			
C11 " µF/WV	30/3			
C12 " µF	.005			
C13 " µF/WV	30/6			
C14 " µF/WV	30/3			
C15 " µF	.02			
D1 ZENER VDC	1.6			
D2 " VDC	N.R			

VALUES				
CHANNEL	OMNI	OTHERS		
ENERGY VDC	9	9	15	22.5
R1 RESISTOR K	5			
R2 " K	3.9			
R3 " K	33			
R4 " Ω	300			
R5 " Ω	100			
R6 " K	5			
R7 " K	56			
R8 " K	10			
R9 " Ω	470			
R10 " Ω	100			
R11 " K	3.3			
R12 " Ω	560			
R13 " Ω	100			
R14 " Ω	EXP			
R15 " Ω	N.R			
T1 AUDIO KHZ	455			
T2 " KHZ	455			

*20TH CENTURY TERRAN EARLY DEVELOPMENT

EAR RECEIVER
FOR NON-PUBLIC RECEPTION

FOR USE IN CONCENTRATING ON TRANS-
MISSIONS IN ACOUSTICALLY DISTRACTING
SITUATIONS, OR FOR SPECIFIC RECEPTION
OF NON-PUBLIC TRANSMISSIONS

OPERATION IS BY CLOSED LOOP ON ALL
STAR FLEET PRIME COMMUNICATIONS SUB-
SPACE CHANNELS

THE TRANSPARENT HALF-HARD PLASTIC
EAR-PIECE IS CUSTOM MOLDED TO A PRE-
CISE IMPRESSION OF THE USER'S EAR

SPECIFICATION:
    MODEL: SFAF/CC-MK05-0
    SIZE: 0
    LENGTH OVERALL (CM)_ _ _ _ _ _ _6.55
    WIDTH OVERALL (CM)_ _ _ _ _ _ _3.15
    MAXIMUM DIAMETER (CM)_ _ _ _ _2.6
    WEIGHT (GM)_ _ _ _ _ _ _ _ _ _ _57

Ⓐ MOLDED PLASTIC EAR-PIECE

Ⓑ EAR-PIECE RETENTION PLATE

Ⓒ EARPHONE HOUSING

Ⓓ RECEIVER HOUSING

Ⓔ ENERGY CELL HOUSING

Ⓕ HIGH GAIN ANTENNA GRID AND HEAT
    SINK

Ⓖ EAR-PIECE SWIVELS STIFFLY HERE

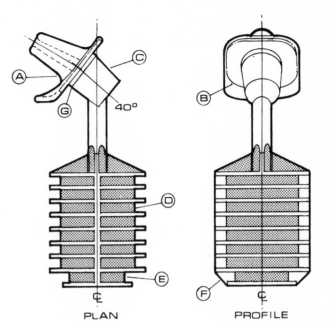

PLAN   PROFILE

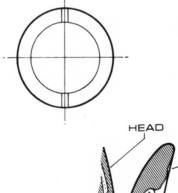

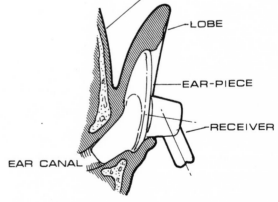

HORIZONTAL SECTION THROUGH LEFT
EAR AT MID-CANAL LEVEL

COLORS:
⬜ ANTIMONY №SF02UC
▨ BLACK   №SF32UC

0 1 2 3 4
CENTIMETERS

UNIVERSAL TRANSLATOR
U.F.P STANDARD

FOR COMMUNICATION BETWEEN UNITED
FEDERATION LANGUAGE FORMS AND WITH
UNKNOWN ALIEN LANGUAGE FORMS IN
THE TREATY EXPLORATION TERRITORY

SPECIFICATION:

    MODEL; SFAF/CC-MK-01

    TYPE: I

    LENGTH OVERALL (CM)_____28

    MAXIMUM DIAMETER (CM)_____4.8

    WEIGHT (GM)_____500

Ⓐ SPEECH CHARACTERISTICS SENSORS

Ⓑ OTHER PARTY SPEAKER/MICROPHONE

Ⓒ DECODING/ENCODING SECTION

Ⓓ COMPUTER FUNCTIONS DISPLAY PANEL

Ⓔ PRIMARY COMPUTER SECTION

Ⓕ OPERATOR'S SPEAKER/MICROPHONE

Ⓖ ACTIVATING SWITCH

Ⓗ DATA STORAGE BANKS SECTION

Ⓙ TRANSPARENT COVER

Ⓚ REAR COVER

Ⓛ HOUSING

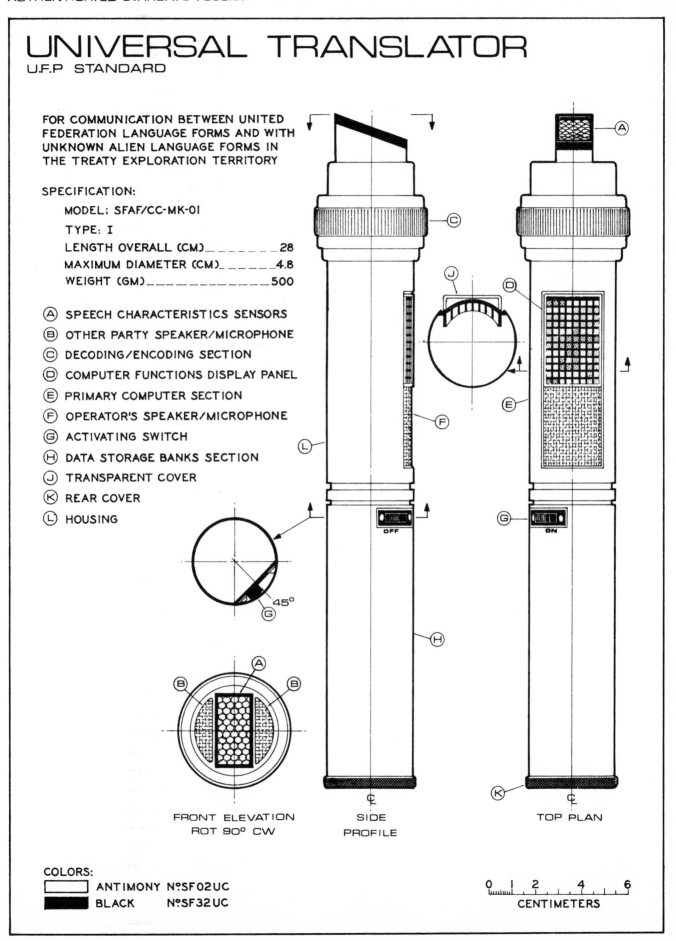

FRONT ELEVATION
ROT 90° CW

SIDE
PROFILE

TOP PLAN

COLORS:
    ANTIMONY N°SF02UC
    BLACK   N°SF32UC

0 1 2   4   6
CENTIMETERS

ENGINEERING
MAIN BRIDGE STATION - CLASS I STARSHIPS

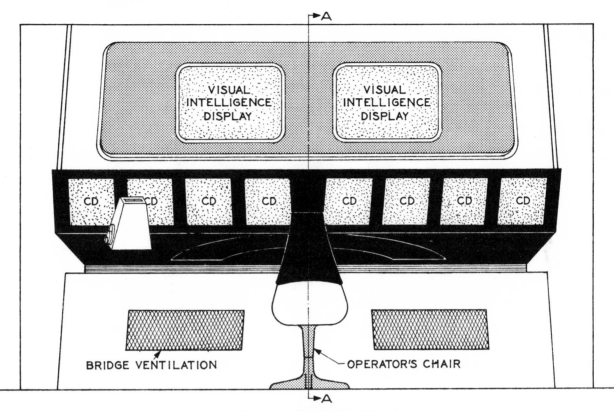

FRONT ELEVATION

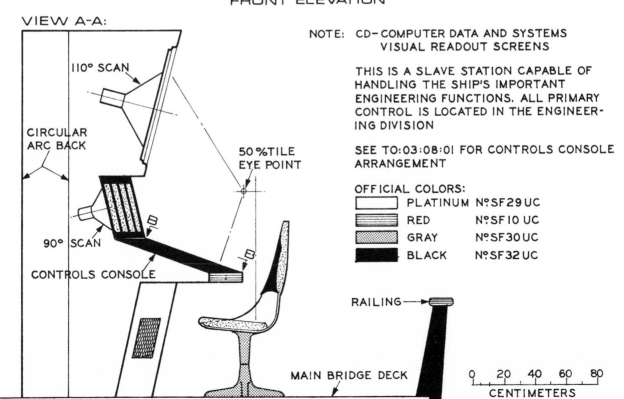

VIEW A-A:

NOTE: CD—COMPUTER DATA AND SYSTEMS
VISUAL READOUT SCREENS

THIS IS A SLAVE STATION CAPABLE OF
HANDLING THE SHIP'S IMPORTANT
ENGINEERING FUNCTIONS. ALL PRIMARY
CONTROL IS LOCATED IN THE ENGINEER-
ING DIVISION

SEE TO:03:08:01 FOR CONTROLS CONSOLE
ARRANGEMENT

OFFICIAL COLORS:

	PLATINUM	N°SF29UC
	RED	N°SF10UC
	GRAY	N°SF30UC
	BLACK	N°SF32UC

CONTROLS CONSOLE
VIEW B-B OF TO:03:08:00

REFER ELSEWHERE IN THIS SECTION
FOR DETAILED OPERATIONS PROCED-
URES, AND SYSTEMS FUNCTIONS
SPECIFICATIONS.

REFER ELSEWHERE IN THIS SECTION
FOR SYSTEM SCHEMATICS, WIRING
DIAGRAMS, AND STANDARD MAIN-
TENANCE PROCEDURES.

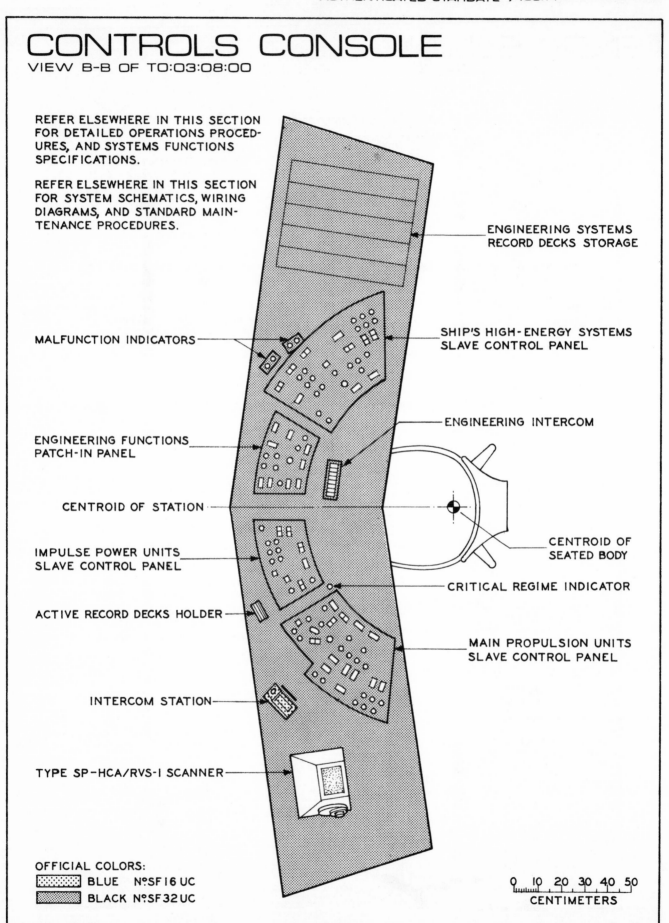

ENGINEERING SYSTEMS
RECORD DECKS STORAGE

MALFUNCTION INDICATORS

SHIP'S HIGH-ENERGY SYSTEMS
SLAVE CONTROL PANEL

ENGINEERING INTERCOM

ENGINEERING FUNCTIONS
PATCH-IN PANEL

CENTROID OF STATION

CENTROID OF
SEATED BODY

IMPULSE POWER UNITS
SLAVE CONTROL PANEL

CRITICAL REGIME INDICATOR

ACTIVE RECORD DECKS HOLDER

MAIN PROPULSION UNITS
SLAVE CONTROL PANEL

INTERCOM STATION

TYPE SP-HCA/RVS-I SCANNER

OFFICIAL COLORS:
BLUE   N°SF16 UC
BLACK N°SF32 UC

0 10 20 30 40 50
CENTIMETERS

ENGINEERING SECTION
PRIMARY HULL - CLASS I STARSHIPS

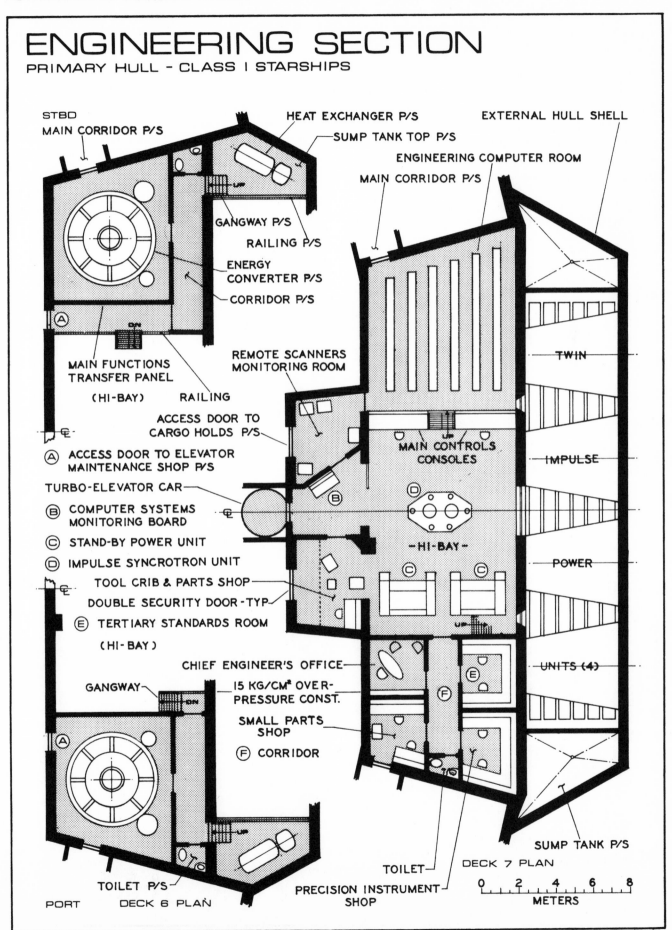

STBD
MAIN CORRIDOR P/S

HEAT EXCHANGER P/S

SUMP TANK TOP P/S

EXTERNAL HULL SHELL

ENGINEERING COMPUTER ROOM

MAIN CORRIDOR P/S

GANGWAY P/S

RAILING P/S

ENERGY
CONVERTER P/S

CORRIDOR P/S

TWIN

Ⓐ

MAIN FUNCTIONS
TRANSFER PANEL

(HI-BAY)   RAILING

REMOTE SCANNERS
MONITORING ROOM

MAIN CONTROLS
CONSOLES

ACCESS DOOR TO
CARGO HOLDS P/S

IMPULSE

Ⓐ ACCESS DOOR TO ELEVATOR
MAINTENANCE SHOP P/S

TURBO-ELEVATOR CAR

Ⓑ

Ⓓ

Ⓑ COMPUTER SYSTEMS
MONITORING BOARD

POWER

Ⓒ STAND-BY POWER UNIT

Ⓓ IMPULSE SYNCROTRON UNIT

Ⓒ   Ⓒ

—HI-BAY—

TOOL CRIB & PARTS SHOP

DOUBLE SECURITY DOOR-TYP

Ⓔ TERTIARY STANDARDS ROOM

(HI-BAY)

UNITS (4)

CHIEF ENGINEER'S OFFICE

Ⓔ

GANGWAY

15 KG/CM² OVER-
PRESSURE CONST.

Ⓕ

SMALL PARTS
SHOP

Ⓕ CORRIDOR

SUMP TANK P/S

DECK 7 PLAN

TOILET

TOILET P/S

PORT   DECK 6 PLAN

PRECISION INSTRUMENT
SHOP

0 2 4 6 8
METERS

IMPULSE POWER UNIT
CLASS I STARSHIPS - EXTERNAL ARRANGEMENT

- (A) TWIN UNIT HOUSING
- (B) FIELD FLUX DIP CONSTRICTION
- (C) MAGNATOMIC FLUX CIRCULATION TUBES (12)
- (D) FUEL HOPPER FEED CHUTE
- (E) FLUX RECIRCULATION TUBES TO HEAT EXCHANGERS (5)
- (F) FIRING CHAMBER (2)

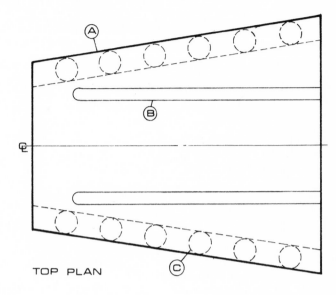

TOP PLAN

SPECIFICATIONS:

LENGTH OVERALL (M)_ _ _ _ _ _ 5.2
WIDTH OVERALL (M)_ _ _ _ _ _ _ 4.5
HEIGHT OVERALL (M)_ _ _ _ _ _ 2.8
WEIGHT - D.W.T (M.T)_ _ _ _ _ _ 2800
MODEL: IP186E/2-IR

OPERATION IS BASED ON SUBATOMIC
UNIFIED ENERGY IMPULSE POSTULATE

POWER IS REVERSIBLE BY PROPER CONTROL
OF THE EXTERNAL VENT SHIELDS

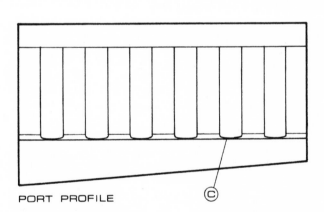

PORT PROFILE

ELEVATIONS

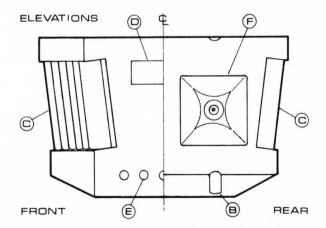

FRONT   REAR

STAR FLEET TECHNICAL ORDER

MAIN PROPULSION
CLASS I STARSHIPS - EXTERNAL ARRANGEMENT

Ⓐ SPACE ENERGY/MATTER SINK (ACQUISITION)

Ⓑ SPACE ENERGY FIELD SENSOR (3)

Ⓒ MAGNATOMIC FLUX CONSTRICTION – FIRST STAGE

Ⓓ INLET FLOW SENSOR

Ⓔ CONTROL REACTOR LOOP (PRIMARY POWER STAGE)

Ⓕ OUTLET FLOW SENSOR

Ⓖ POWER STAGE MAGNATOMIC FLUX CHILLER (3)

Ⓗ MAIN ENERGY STAGE MAGNATOMIC FLUX CHILLER (5)

Ⓙ MAIN PROPULSION HOUSING (NACELLE - AND DEFLECTOR SHIELD)

Ⓚ FINAL STAGE INTERCOOLERS P/S

Ⓛ FINAL STAGE MAGNATOMIC FLUX CHILLERS P/S

Ⓝ SPACE ENERGY/MATTER MATTRIX RESTORATION COWL

Ⓞ SPACE ENERGY/MATTER SOURCE (FIELD RESTORATION)

SUPPORT PYLON LOCATIONS:

Ⓟ MK-X DREADNOUGHT NO.'S 1 AND 3

Ⓡ MK-X DREADNOUGHT NO. 2

Ⓢ MK-IX HEAVY CRUISER NO.'S 1 AND 2

Ⓣ MK-VIII DESTROYER NO. 1
MK-VII SCOUT NO. 1

Ⓤ MK-VI TRANSPORT/TUG NO.'S 1 & 2

NOTE: UNIT Ⓥ IS ROTATED 90° TO BOTTOM ₵ ON MK-VIII AND MK-VII MODELS

SPECIFICATIONS:
LENGTH OVERALL: (M) ＿＿＿153.619
MAX. DIAMETER: (M) ＿＿＿＿＿17.3
WEIGHT –D.W.T: (M.T.) ＿＿＿＿31,000
MODEL: SW40/5-3KT

OPERATION IS BASED ON UNIFIED FIELD SPACE ENERGY/MATTER MATTRIX WARP POSTULATE

THE SYSTEM IS REVERSIBLE WITH MODERATE POWER CAPABILITY AND MINIMUM SPACE E/M MATTRIX DEGRADATION

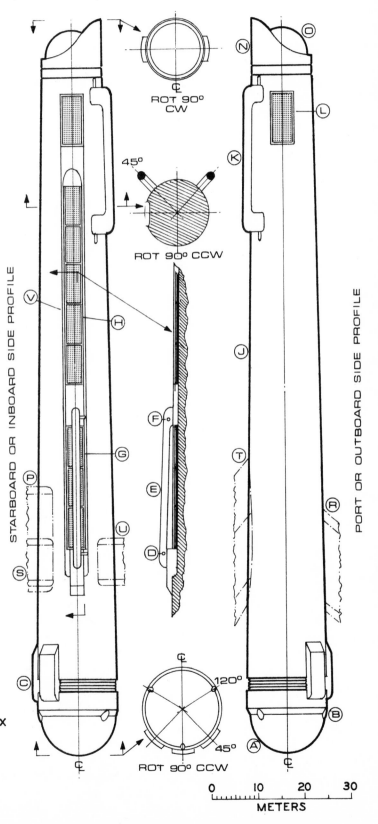

ROT 90° CW

ROT 90° CCW

45°

STARBOARD OR INBOARD SIDE PROFILE

PORT OR OUTBOARD SIDE PROFILE

120°

45°

ROT 90° CCW

0   10   20   30
METERS

TRANSPORTER
STANDARD 6 PERSON - PRIMARY HULL - CLASS I STARSHIPS

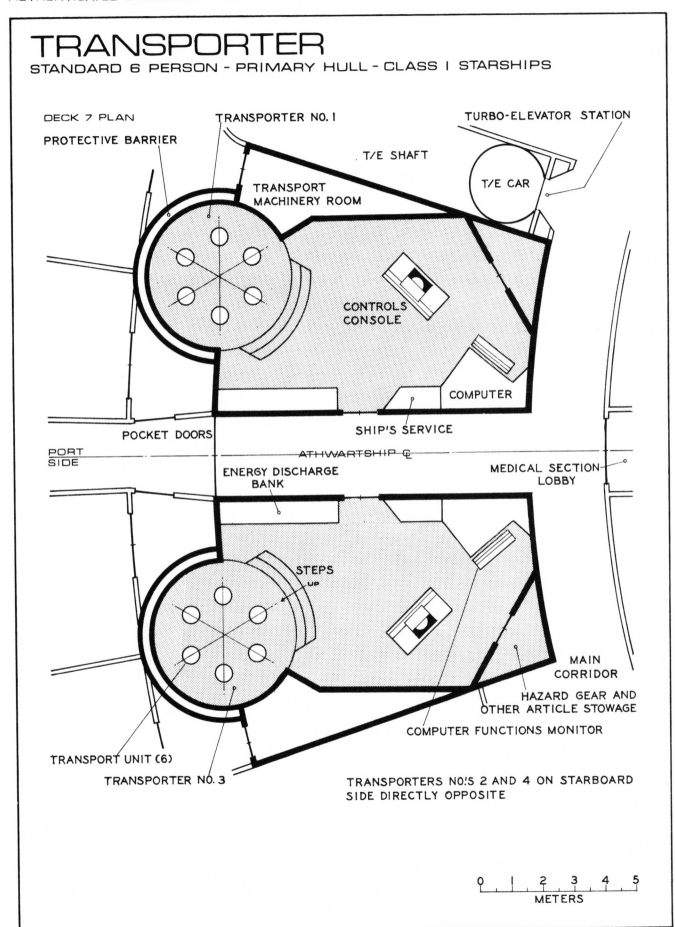

DECK 7 PLAN

PROTECTIVE BARRIER

TRANSPORTER NO. 1

TURBO-ELEVATOR STATION

T/E SHAFT

T/E CAR

TRANSPORT MACHINERY ROOM

CONTROLS CONSOLE

COMPUTER

POCKET DOORS

SHIP'S SERVICE

PORT SIDE

ATHWARTSHIP ℄

MEDICAL SECTION LOBBY

ENERGY DISCHARGE BANK

STEPS UP

MAIN CORRIDOR

HAZARD GEAR AND OTHER ARTICLE STOWAGE

COMPUTER FUNCTIONS MONITOR

TRANSPORT UNIT (6)

TRANSPORTER NO. 3

TRANSPORTERS NO!S 2 AND 4 ON STARBOARD SIDE DIRECTLY OPPOSITE

0 1 2 3 4 5
METERS

TRANSPORTER
EMERGENCY - PRIMARY HULL - CLASS I STARSHIPS

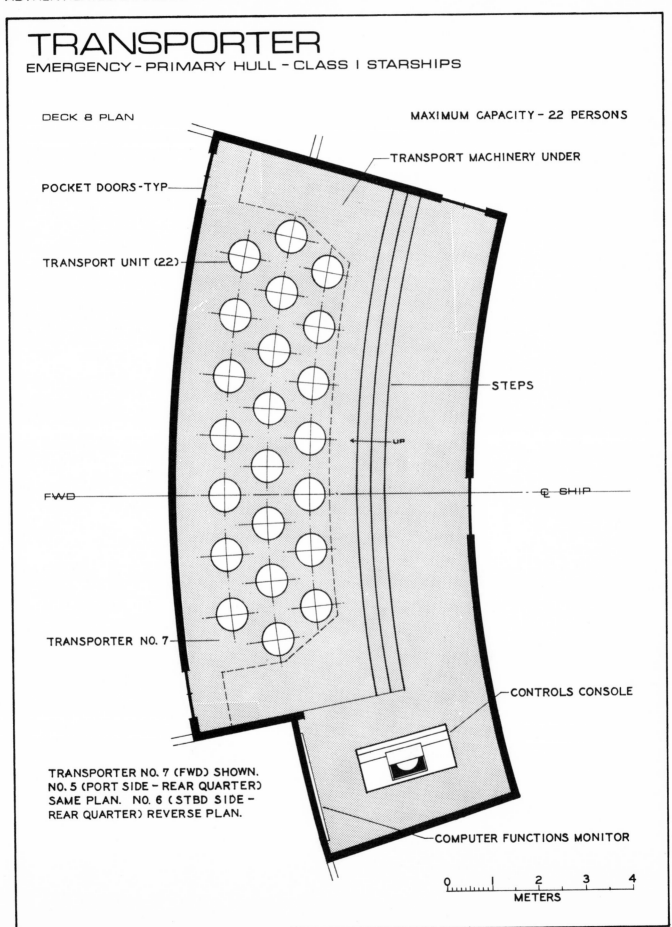

DECK 8 PLAN

MAXIMUM CAPACITY - 22 PERSONS

TRANSPORT MACHINERY UNDER

POCKET DOORS - TYP

TRANSPORT UNIT (22)

STEPS

UP

FWD

C SHIP

TRANSPORTER NO. 7

CONTROLS CONSOLE

TRANSPORTER NO. 7 (FWD) SHOWN.
NO. 5 (PORT SIDE - REAR QUARTER)
SAME PLAN. NO. 6 (STBD SIDE -
REAR QUARTER) REVERSE PLAN.

COMPUTER FUNCTIONS MONITOR

0   1   2   3   4
METERS

TRANSPORTER
CARGO - PRIMARY HULL - CLASS I STARSHIPS

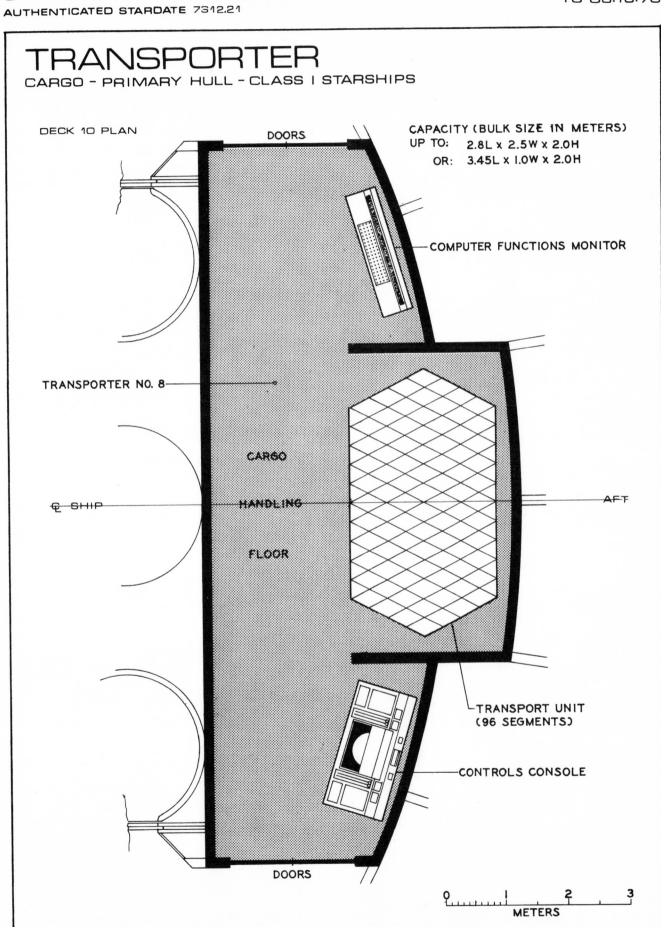

DECK 10 PLAN

DOORS

CAPACITY (BULK SIZE IN METERS)
UP TO: 2.8L x 2.5W x 2.0H
OR: 3.45L x 1.0W x 2.0H

COMPUTER FUNCTIONS MONITOR

TRANSPORTER NO. 8

CARGO

HANDLING

FLOOR

℄ SHIP

AFT

TRANSPORT UNIT
(96 SEGMENTS)

CONTROLS CONSOLE

DOORS

0   1   2   3
METERS

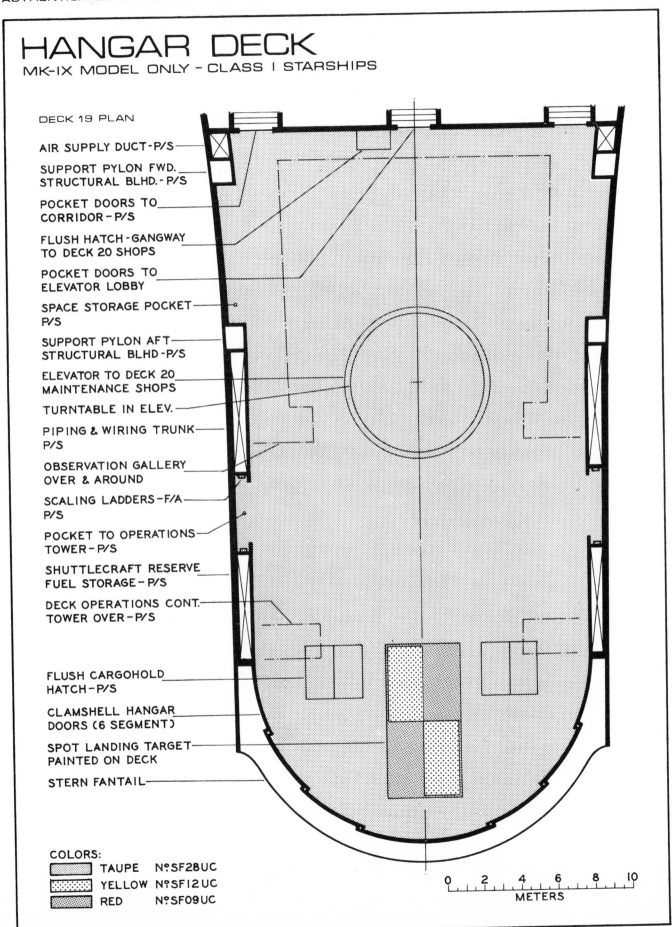

HANGAR DECK
MK-IX MODEL ONLY - CLASS I STARSHIPS

DECK 19 PLAN

AIR SUPPLY DUCT-P/S

SUPPORT PYLON FWD. STRUCTURAL BLHD.-P/S

POCKET DOORS TO CORRIDOR-P/S

FLUSH HATCH-GANGWAY TO DECK 20 SHOPS

POCKET DOORS TO ELEVATOR LOBBY

SPACE STORAGE POCKET P/S

SUPPORT PYLON AFT STRUCTURAL BLHD-P/S

ELEVATOR TO DECK 20 MAINTENANCE SHOPS

TURNTABLE IN ELEV.

PIPING & WIRING TRUNK P/S

OBSERVATION GALLERY OVER & AROUND

SCALING LADDERS-F/A P/S

POCKET TO OPERATIONS TOWER-P/S

SHUTTLECRAFT RESERVE FUEL STORAGE-P/S

DECK OPERATIONS CONT. TOWER OVER-P/S

FLUSH CARGOHOLD HATCH-P/S

CLAMSHELL HANGAR DOORS (6 SEGMENT)

SPOT LANDING TARGET PAINTED ON DECK

STERN FANTAIL

COLORS:

▨	TAUPE	N°SF28UC
▨	YELLOW	N°SF12UC
▨	RED	N°SF09UC

0 2 4 6 8 10
METERS

HANGAR DECK
PRINCIPAL ELEVATION - MK-IX MODEL ONLY

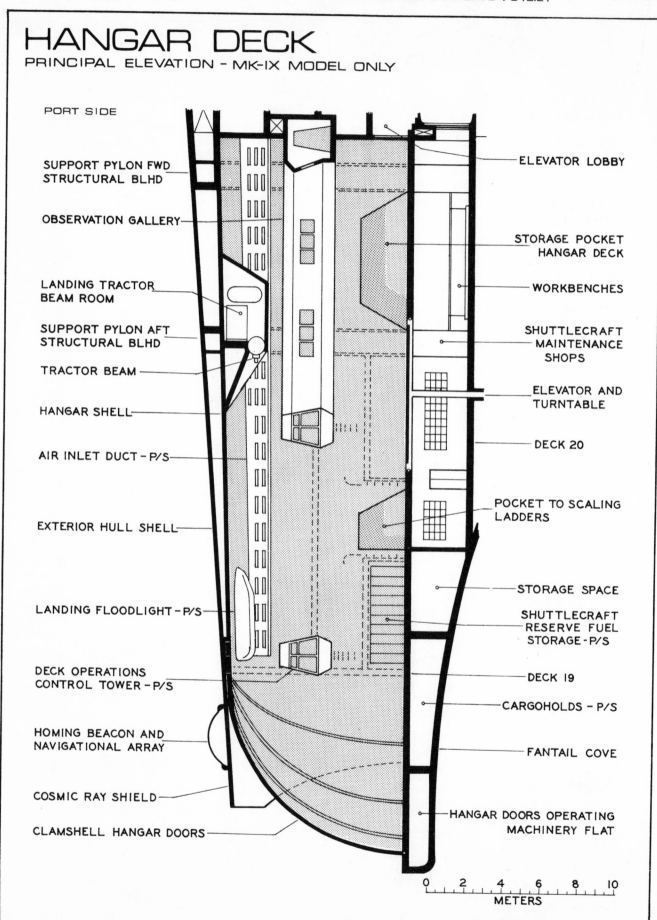

PORT SIDE

SUPPORT PYLON FWD STRUCTURAL BLHD

OBSERVATION GALLERY

LANDING TRACTOR BEAM ROOM

SUPPORT PYLON AFT STRUCTURAL BLHD

TRACTOR BEAM

HANGAR SHELL

AIR INLET DUCT – P/S

EXTERIOR HULL SHELL

LANDING FLOODLIGHT – P/S

DECK OPERATIONS CONTROL TOWER – P/S

HOMING BEACON AND NAVIGATIONAL ARRAY

COSMIC RAY SHIELD

CLAMSHELL HANGAR DOORS

ELEVATOR LOBBY

STORAGE POCKET HANGAR DECK

WORKBENCHES

SHUTTLECRAFT MAINTENANCE SHOPS

ELEVATOR AND TURNTABLE

DECK 20

POCKET TO SCALING LADDERS

STORAGE SPACE

SHUTTLECRAFT RESERVE FUEL STORAGE – P/S

DECK 19

CARGOHOLDS – P/S

FANTAIL COVE

HANGAR DOORS OPERATING MACHINERY FLAT

0 2 4 6 8 10
METERS

VULCAN LYRETTE
ORCHESTRAL MODEL MUSICAL INSTRUMENT

AN UNUSUALLY HARMONIOUS AND MELODIC ACCOMPANIMENT OR SOLO INSTRUMENT WHOSE ORIGIN IS LOST IN VULCAN ANTIQUITY. IT COMBINES THE TONAL QUALITIES OF A HARP, LUTE, SITAR, AND TO SOME EXTENT, VIOLIN.

THE MOST FAMOUS MODELS WERE MADE BY SARPK SOME 5 VULCAN CENTURIES AGO OF WHICH, SOME 300 ARE KNOWN TO STILL BE IN EXISTENCE. OTHER FAMOUS MODELS WERE MADE BY SAJEK OF VULCAN AND SEPAR OF TRILAN.

THE TONAL PATTERN IS MODAL DIA-TONIC RATHER THAN CHROMATIC AND REQUIRES A HIGH DEGREE OF SKILL TO PERFORM IN THIS REGISTRATION.

WHILE A SKILLED PERFORMER MANIPULATES THE STRINGS WITH THE FINGERS OF THE RIGHT HAND, A PLECTRUM MAY ALSO BE USED.

PITCH RANGE:
    LOWEST – 60 CPS
    HIGHEST – 3180 CPS

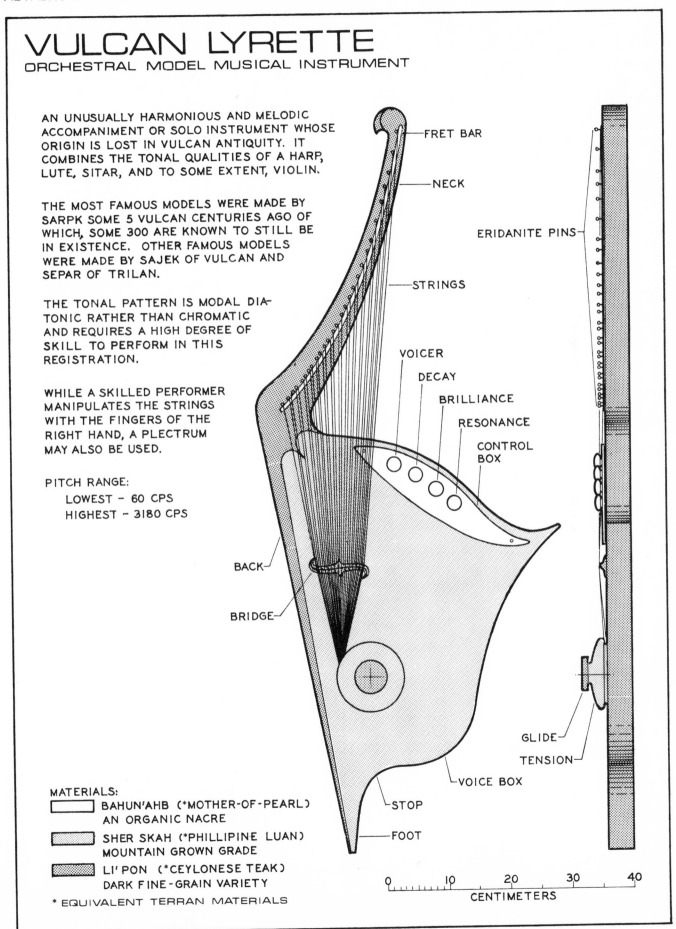

FRET BAR

NECK

ERIDANITE PINS

STRINGS

VOICER

DECAY

BRILLIANCE

RESONANCE

CONTROL BOX

BACK

BRIDGE

STOP

FOOT

VOICE BOX

GLIDE

TENSION

MATERIALS:
    BAHUN'AHB (*MOTHER-OF-PEARL) AN ORGANIC NACRE
    SHER SKAH (*PHILLIPINE LUAN) MOUNTAIN GROWN GRADE
    LI'PON (*CEYLONESE TEAK) DARK FINE-GRAIN VARIETY

* EQUIVALENT TERRAN MATERIALS

0   10   20   30   40
CENTIMETERS

TRIDIMENSIONAL CHESS
REGULATION TOURNAMENT BOARD

THIS IS THE MOST
COMPLEX FORM OF THE
ANCIENT GAME OF
CHESS YET DEVISED.
IT IS NORMALLY STUDIED
AND ATTEMPTED ONLY
BY PERSONS WITH
MASTER'S SKILLS IN
THE ORDINARY FORM
OF THE GAME.

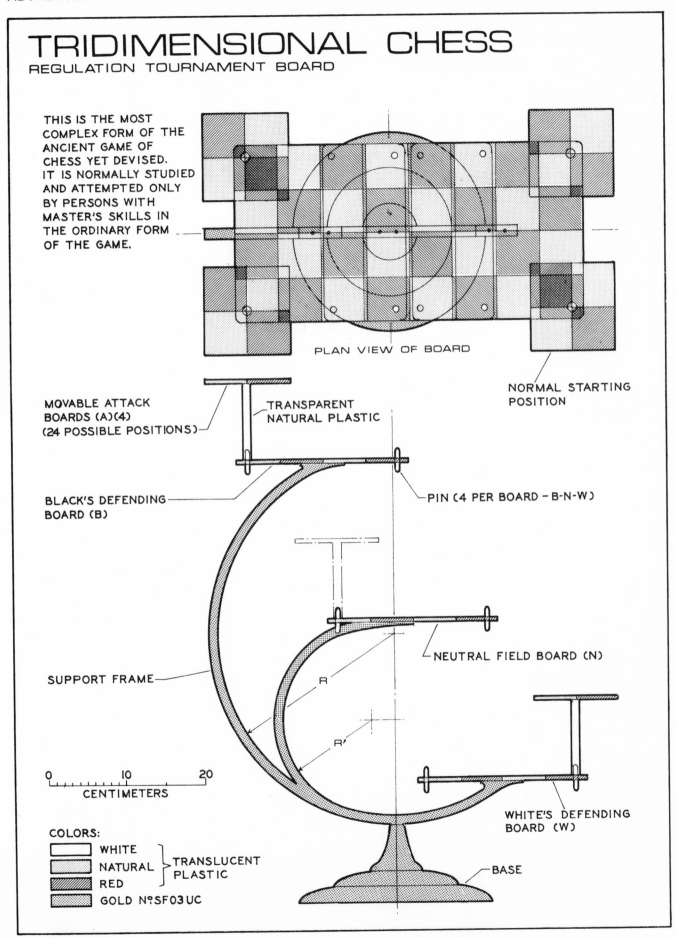

PLAN VIEW OF BOARD

NORMAL STARTING
POSITION

MOVABLE ATTACK
BOARDS (A)(4)
(24 POSSIBLE POSITIONS)

TRANSPARENT
NATURAL PLASTIC

BLACK'S DEFENDING
BOARD (B)

PIN (4 PER BOARD – B-N-W)

NEUTRAL FIELD BOARD (N)

SUPPORT FRAME

R

R'

WHITE'S DEFENDING
BOARD (W)

BASE

0   10   20
CENTIMETERS

COLORS:
☐ WHITE
☐ NATURAL   ⎫ TRANSLUCENT
▨ RED   ⎬ PLASTIC
▨ GOLD N°SF03UC

TRIDIMENSIONAL CHESS
REGULATION TOURNAMENT PLAYING PIECES

THE IDENTIFICATION OF EACH PIECE
GIVES ITS NAME – POINT VALUE – AND
QUANTITY. A STARTING SIDE, WHITE OR
BLACK, IS 16 PIECES AND 39 POINTS

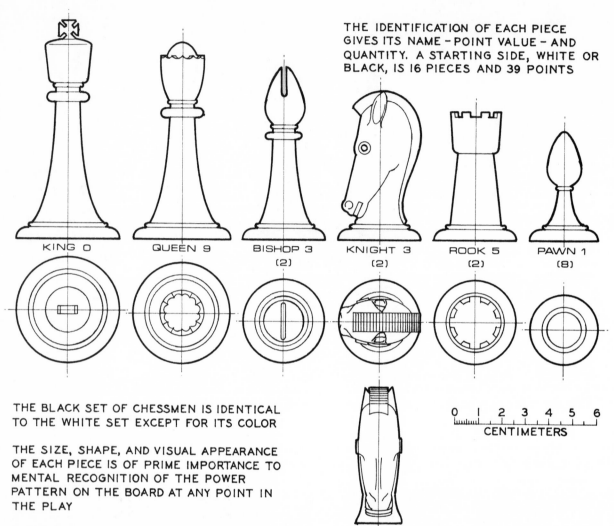

| KING 0 | QUEEN 9 | BISHOP 3 (2) | KNIGHT 3 (2) | ROOK 5 (2) | PAWN 1 (8) |

THE BLACK SET OF CHESSMEN IS IDENTICAL
TO THE WHITE SET EXCEPT FOR ITS COLOR

THE SIZE, SHAPE, AND VISUAL APPEARANCE
OF EACH PIECE IS OF PRIME IMPORTANCE TO
MENTAL RECOGNITION OF THE POWER
PATTERN ON THE BOARD AT ANY POINT IN
THE PLAY

REFER TO THE GENERAL BIBLIOGRAPHY
SECTION FOR TEXTS ON THE FUNDAMENT-
ALS OF TRIDIMENSIONAL CHESS

EACH PIECE MOVES EXACTLY THE SAME AS
IN CONVENTIONAL CHESS EXCEPT THAT
SUCH MOVES HAVE TRIDIMENSIONAL FREE-
DOM TO THE EXTENT OF AVAILABLE CON-
SECUTIVE SQUARES

16 OF THE 64 SQUARES ARE MOVABLE IN
4 GROUPS OF 4 SQUARES EACH. THEY MAY
BE MOVE TO ONE ADJACENT PIN POSITION
AT A TIME PROVIDED THEY ARE EITHER
VACANT OR OCCUPIED BY ONLY ONE OF
THE PLAYER'S PAWNS, AND SUCH ACTION
CONSTITUTES A MOVE IN REGULAR TURN.
AN OCCUPIED ATTACK BOARD CANNOT BE
MOVED TO AN INVERTED PIN POSITION

0 1 2 3 4 5 6
CENTIMETERS

STARTING ARRANGEMENT:

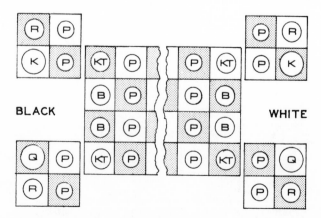

BLACK

WHITE

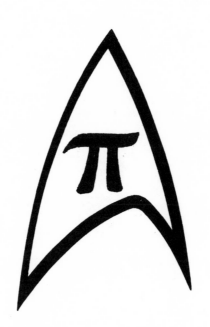

MISCELANEOUS SECTION

STAR FLEET COMMAND
STAR FLEET HEADQUARTERS
UNITED FEDERATION OF PLANETS

FRANZ JOSEPH
UNITED FEDERATION REPRESENTATIVE   STARDATE 7504

APPENDIX A

TO ALL CIVILIAN AUXILIARIES OF SFAF,
UNITED NATIONS/EARTH/SOL SYSTEM

THE TECHNICAL ORDERS COMPRISING THIS SECTION WERE NOT INCLUDED IN

THE UNORTHODOX TRANSMISSION OF STARDATE 3113. UNTIL SUCH TIME AS

THESE DATA CAN BE MADE AVAILABLE, WE SUGGEST YOU CONSIDER USING

THIS SECTION TO FILE MISCELANEOUS INFORMATION YOU HAVE COLLECTED

IN THE GENERAL SUBJECT AREAS OF THE TECHNICAL MANUAL

SUBJECT | STARDATE

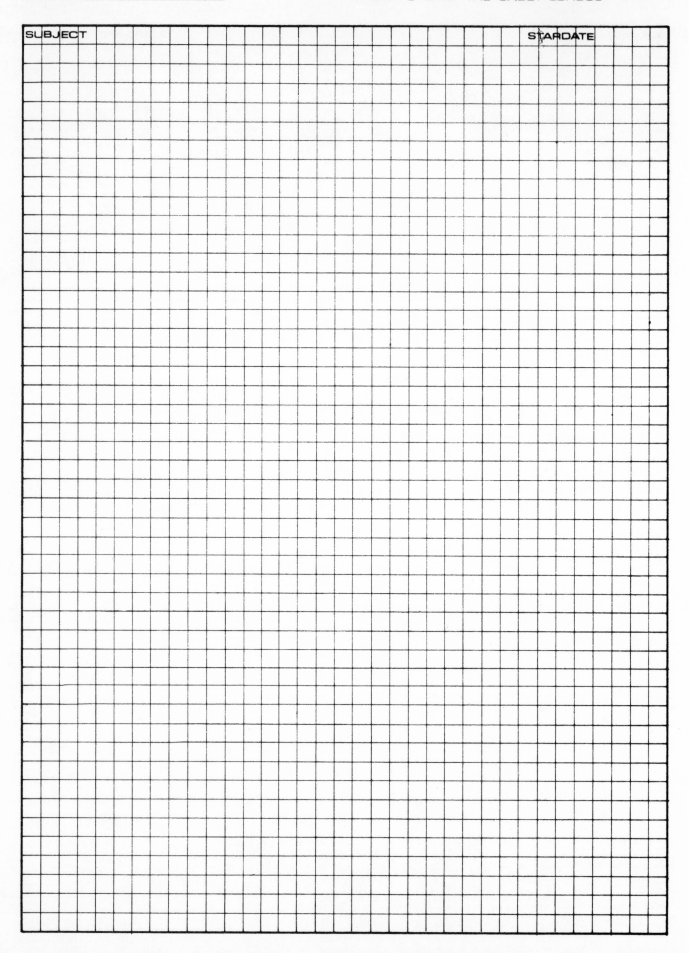

CADET_____

DIVISION_____

SUBJECT

STARDATE

SUBJECT

STARDATE

SUBJECT

STARDATE

SUBJECT

STARDATE

SUBJECT

STARDATE

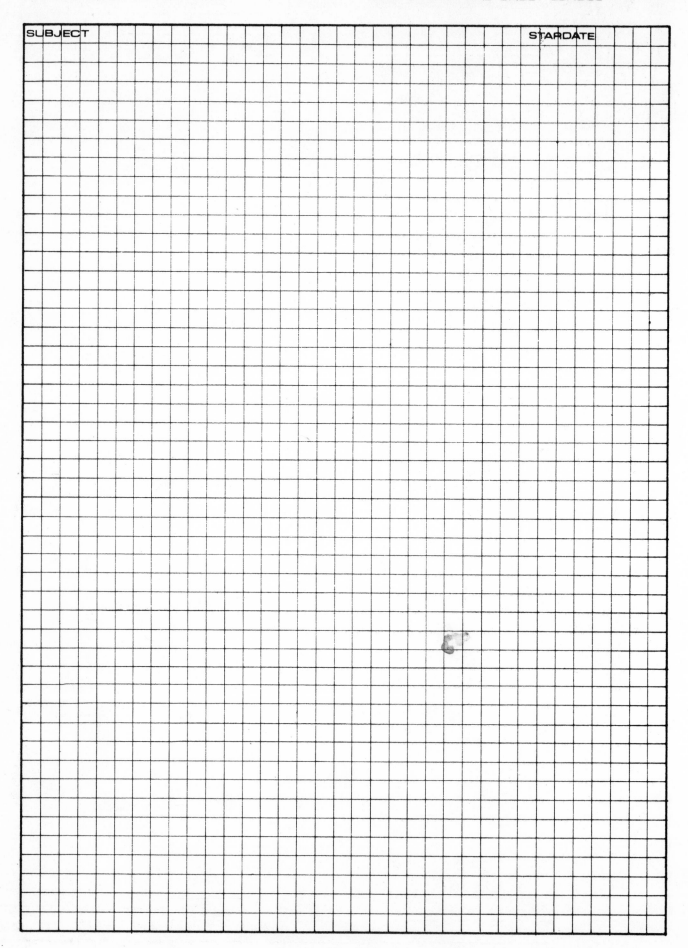